DISRUPTING QUEER INCLUSION

Sexuality Studies Series

This series focuses on original, provocative, scholarly research examining from a range of perspectives the complexity of human sexual practice, identity, community, and desire. Books in the series explore how sexuality interacts with other aspects of society, such as law, education, feminism, racial diversity, the family, policing, sport, government, religion, mass media, medicine, and employment. The series provides a broad public venue for nurturing debate, cultivating talent, and expanding knowledge of human sexual expression, past and present.

Other volumes in the series are:

Edited by OmiSoore H. Dryden
and Suzanne Lenon

DISRUPTING QUEER
INCLUSION

Canadian Homonationalisms and
the Politics of Belonging

UBCPress · Vancouver · Toronto

23 22 21 20 19 18 17   5 4 3

Printed in Canada on FSC-certified ancient-forest-free paper
(100% post-consumer recycled) that is processed chlorine- and acid-free.

Library and Archives Canada Cataloguing in Publication

Disrupting queer inclusion : Canadian homonationalisms and the politics of belonging / edited by OmiSoore H. Dryden and Suzanne Lenon.

(Sexuality studies series)
Includes bibliographical references and index.
Issued in print and electronic formats.

ISBN 978-0-7748-2943-4 (bound). – ISBN 978-0-7748-2944-1 (pbk.). –
ISBN 978-0-7748-2945-8 (pdf). – ISBN 978-0-7748-2946-5 (epub)

1. Sexual minorities – Canada. 2. Social integration – Political aspects – Canada. 3. Belonging (Social psychology) – Political aspects – Canada. 4. Queer theory – Canada. I. Dryden, OmiSoore H., 1965-, author, editor II. Lenon, Suzanne, 1966-, author, editor III. Awwad, Julian, 1976-. Queer regulation and the homonational rhetoric of Canadian exceptionalism. IV. Series: Sexuality studies series

HQ73.3.C3D58 2015   306.760971   C2015-903884-7
                                                                      C2015-903885-5

Canadä

UBC Press gratefully acknowledges the financial support for our publishing program of the Government of Canada (through the Canada Book Fund), the Canada Council for the Arts, and the British Columbia Arts Council.

This book has been published with the help of a grant from the Canadian Federation for the Humanities and Social Sciences, through the Awards to Scholarly Publications Program, using funds provided by the Social Sciences and Humanities Research Council of Canada.

Printed and bound in Canada by Friesens
Set in Myriad SemiCondensed and Minion by Artegraphica Design Co. Ltd.
Copy editor: Robert Lewis
Proofreader: Lana Okerlund
Indexer: Cameron Duder

UBC Press
The University of British Columbia
2029 West Mall
Vancouver, BC V6T 1Z2
www.ubcpress.ca

Contents

Foreword
The Homosexuals Have Arrived!

RINALDO WALCOTT

The essays in this book are more than an intervention. They require, without a strident call, that the grounds of homosexual arrival, or rights, be fundamentally rethought. The necessity of such action – that is, of rethinking homo-rights – is that rights bestowed by the nation throw up into stark sight the problem of incorporation at the expense of excision, regulation, and, in the most egregious cases, death. Let me be clear, homo-rights follow in a long tradition of national containment, wherein more peoples and their practices are brought into the national body who then come to perform more expertly the brutal forgetting of the post-Enlightenment, modernist organization of human life, which can otherwise go by the name "global colonialism." These insightful essays ask at every turn that other considerations, beyond the modernist normative ones, animate the conversation, that new considerations fuel the imaginary for those whose lives modernity seems to regard only with contempt. Indeed, the essays strike a particularly ethical call for ways of organizing life and belonging beyond capitalist modernity.

I have used the term "homosexual" here as a distinctive move to signal that the long *durée* of modernity now provides a set of parameters that suggests we now understand exactly what the homosexual is, and therefore can adjust or renovate its ideas of freedom and rights to accommodate the homosexual within its sphere. Indeed, this shift in practices as a means to reincorporate the homosexual into a specific body politic takes its mandate from an ongoing reformist tradition that is a part of the post-Enlightenment, modernist, colonial practices of containment that have provided this tradition with cover over the past five hundred years or more. However, in every instance of reform, what has remained stable and unbroken is white supremacist organization of all of human life. Therefore, it is not just any homosexual who is now accorded rights in Canada and beyond. Indeed, the "queer-homo" (to suggest such a phrase) remains outside such political imaginaries, by which I mean those nonheterosexual and heterosexual beings who refuse the normative modes of the modernist imaginary of and for state recognition of their sexual beings.

There can be no doubt that the project of homosexual arrival benefits the ongoing global colonial project, referred to in this book as "settler colonialism" and illustrated using the borders of Canada as one example of a phenomenon that is quickly becoming global. However, it might be useful to note that these dynamics, although nation-bound, are never simply just that. For example, Canada is deeply involved in exporting its homosexual rights agenda elsewhere, and even within its borders, its homosexual rights agenda differentiates across race, sexual practices, and place of "origin." Thus, even though it remains useful to read how these practices play out in a national context, it is always necessary to remember that the national – despite the various violences that it enacts in order to appear singular and contained – is never just singular. The national always leaks elsewhere.

Significantly, these essays pose and recall a moment of queer politics in which, because of their messiness, non-normative sexual desires, practices, and identifications can signify without attachment to a recognizable signified. This politics suggests an imaginary of queer that requires no fixed identity and thus no rights-bearing subjectivity – in other words, one that can lay claim to practices of life without a corresponding identity. To recall such articulations and utterances of queer is to throw state recognition and its rights regimes into chaos and to demand a world where the colonial project might be imagined to reach a potential conclusion. In contrast to such an outcome, these essays clearly demonstrate how homosexuals have been recruited for the sustenance of the late-colonial, capitalist, modernist nation-state. But it is my contention that notions of "queer" could offer other possibilities for new horizons and imaginaries. In particular, such imaginaries might be characterized as a politics of just *be*-ing.

Rights talk tends to reproduce the contemporary ongoing colonial "State" with its multiple violent inequalities. It does so by providing space for elites within (nation) states to self-express while arguably alienating the poor, the black, and those who engage in taboos of all kinds. In the case of sexual minorities, rights talk often works to produce and police sexuality based on singular terms that force sexual minorities into a "one size fits all" model. Rights talk

Rinaldo Walcott

and its attendant practices often produce benefits for those who are mobile in this newer version of globalization – for example, by enabling them to enjoy their privileges across different spaces such as queer cruises, metropolitan worldwide Pride events, queer festivals, and so on. In short, the benefits that come from rights talk in no way threaten the hegemony of state organization or force the state to change its fundamental disciplinary apparatus of citizenship. Instead, rights talk most often asks that homosexual citizenship mirror hetero-sexual citizenship. Heteronormativity and homonormativity then become two sides of the same coin, colluding in policing sexually desiring bodies, practices, and communities in a tacit "sexual contract" with the "State." What I have termed elsewhere a "homopoetics" of selfhood, or just *be*-ing, is not possible under these terms. The complexities of homopoetic selves and lives are and must be forcibly submerged, discredited, and deemed deviant by the state's subactors of homo- and heteronormativity.

Citizen practices and their state bestowal of rights call for knowable identi-ties – indeed, this predictability is central to the management of citizenship. However, pursuing sexual practices – which, as we all know, are multiple and varied – does not require a manageable identity. This understanding places sexual practices, behaviours, and desires in suspension by refusing to give them a proper name, even if "queer" sometimes stands in. Thus queer can now find its conceptual and political possibilities only in its originary refusal of all forms of the normative. In refusing the normative at each turn, queer conceptually and politically demands actions that create an opening, a set of acts that one undertakes never knowing what doing so might mean in advance. Queer can now be an opening to a future shaped by the centrality of desirous sex and sexu-ality to *be*-ing. In such desire, we seek political futures beyond the making of identity boundaries. Contemporary human (sexual) rights are based on a claim to identity – a knowable identity. The ethics of the situation demand a call for rights without identity claims. Sexual practices without attendant identities and a move that advances this claim can pose new and important questions for the remaking of the late-modern state. Refusing homosexual arrival, as these essays do, takes us part of the way toward achieving queer's potential contribution to our sexual politics and more in the twenty-first century.

Acknowledgments

Disrupting Queer Inclusion is rooted in our continuing commitment to and interest in the complicated realities of the lives of queer and trans people in the racialized diasporic region known as "Canada." This collection reflects our shared commitment to a continued disordering of the processes of racism, white settler colonialism, and neoliberalism. The contributors met us in this work. What they offered us as editors not only shaped our own thinking about homonationalisms but also disturbed our assumptions about our individual lives. We thank each of them for their patience, their hard work, and their important insights.

When we began this project, we believed in its necessity without actually knowing the trajectory of the journey upon which we were embarking. Along the way, many people, grants, technologies, and institutions supported us in this work. We greatly appreciate Darcy Cullen and her unwavering support, her patience with our many (and at times frequent) questions, and her clear and explicit directions. We are grateful to the University of Lethbridge for a research-dissemination grant that enabled the hiring of Cameron Duder, who created the book's index with perception and aplomb. We thank the Global Queer Research Group, Critical Studies in Sexuality, and the Liu Institute for Global Issues at the University of British Columbia for inviting us to speak about this project in its early stages. We thank Gada Mahrouse for providing valuable feedback on an earlier version of the Introduction. We thank Cassandra Lord for important and necessary conversations. We extend our gratitude to the anonymous reviewers whose thoughtful and detailed suggestions were immensely productive and invaluable in pushing us to more clearly explicate the complicated layers that make up this work. We also thank our partners Annelies van Oers and Gwen Bartleman for their continued patience with our endless texts and Skype calls and for gracefully accepting the forced injection of this book into their lives. We also want to acknowledge the role that Skype, Dropbox, and texting played as key technologies in facilitating the writing process across geographies and time zones.

Suzanne thanks Michelle Brandsma, Lisa Lambert, and Crystal Phillips for their stellar research assistance; her colleagues Carol Williams, Glenda Bonifacio, and Jo-Anne Fiske in the Department of Women and Gender Studies at the University of Lethbridge for fostering a supportive working environment; França Gucciardi, Kara Granzow, Gada Mahrouse, Em and Mark Pijl-Zieber, and Marcia Oliver for their loveliness and sustaining friendship; and her family for their unwavering support and for always being interested in her work. She thanks OmiSoore for her poetic style, friendship, and spirit of generosity throughout this project and for saying "yes!" all the time and in many ways that went beyond this book. Much love to Annelies for our journey together and for all the ways that you care for me.

OmiSoore thanks her mom, O. Veronica Dryden *(maferefun egungun!);* her brother, Wayne Dryden; her nephew, Nathan Dryden, and her aunt, Auntie! – I appreciate your love and support, which extend far beyond our blood ties. She thanks Suzanne for her generous spirit, clarity of thought, and direct approach. This book is the outcome of a great working relationship with a wonderful friend. And with deepest love and respect, OmiSoore thanks her wusband, Gwen, whose support has never wavered.

DISRUPTING QUEER INCLUSION

Introduction
Interventions, Iterations, and Interrogations That Disturb the (Homo)Nation

SUZANNE LENON AND OMISOORE H. DRYDEN

The question of just how not to do state work at a moment of empire is one
of the most crucial questions we must confront in living a transformative politic.

– M. Jacqui Alexander, *Pedagogies of Crossing*

And when I speak of change, I do not mean a simple switch of positions or a
temporary lessening of tensions, nor the ability to smile or feel good. I am speaking
of a basic and radical alteration in those assumptions underlining our lives.

– Audre Lorde, *Sister Outsider*

Two events of 2010 were notable for the disparate ways each spoke of and to
the nation, signalling a contested terrain of contemporary lesbian-gay-queer-
trans politics in Canada: the inauguration of Pride House and the formation
of Queers against Israeli Apartheid (QuAIA). The creation of Pride House as
part of the 2010 Winter Olympic Games, which were held in the Coast Salish
territory now called "Vancouver" and in the Squamish and Lil'wat territories
now called "Whistler," participated in the figuration of Canada as a "gay haven."
Imagining itself as a "safe" space and place where sexual minorities (both athletes
and their allies) from around the world were welcome, Pride House showcased
Canadian (sexual) exceptionalism on a world stage. This event rendered invisible the ongoing racializing and settling of the geography called "Canada" while

simultaneously participating in such nation-making practices. In this way, Pride House as a metaphor for sexual modernity traverses the discursive terrain of the phrase "queerly Canadian."[1] We understand "queerly Canadian," particularly the juxtaposition of "queerly" with "Canadian," as assembling both a subject position and a form of politics that seeks to "queer" Canada by narrowly challenging grounds of homophobic exclusions while knitting "queer" into the neoliberal multiculturally imagined fabric of Canadian national identity. "Queerly Canadian," then, is as much an effect of modernity's desires as it is productive of them. A few months later, in the spring of 2010, public debates vociferously erupted over the participation of QuAIA in Toronto Pride events, particularly the Dyke March and the main Pride Parade, because of the group's use of the phrase "Israeli Apartheid."[2] Pride Toronto's own limits on inclusion signalled an instance of rupture in the imagined unity of a "just gay," "queerly Canadian" sexual politics. In an attempt to contain, correct, and discipline this rupture, the City of Toronto threatened to withhold funding from Pride Toronto.

At first glance, Pride House and QuAIA appear to be distinguished by an uncomplicated political cleavage between the desire of the first for inclusion in a neoliberal, global, corporate sporting event and the insistence of the second on a transgressive, anti-racist, decolonial, transnational queer politic. Pride House, for example, was imagined and positioned as proudly Canadian and proudly gay, the natural outcome of a successful equality rights movement. In this telos, lesbians and gay men are liberated, shining exemplars of how "it gets better"[3]: they are free to be out, to marry, to serve in the military, to adopt and raise children. Pride House embraced the modernity of a Canada where lesbian and gay citizens stand as civilized global leaders and saviours, providing inspiration, guidance, direction, and refuge to "Other" (i.e., immigrant, foreign, Indigenous, and racialized) gays. QuAIA, on the other hand, was envisioned as an articulation of a radical queer activism that moves beyond the limits of liberal inclusion or political agendas based on equality rights. Advocating for Palestinian liberation, sovereignty, and decolonization, QuAIA's activist work interrogates how multiple (lesbian-gay-queer-trans) bodies are implicated in the colonization and settling of the nation. The opposition forged against QuAIA has included attempts to position the group's activism as misguided in its critiques of the Israeli state, as unnecessarily unruly, and as at fault in its rupture with Pride Toronto. In this way, QuAIA has become a catalyst for an unsettling of the (homo)nation.

Pride House and QuAIA are but two examples of the multifarious, multiscalar cacophony of a lesbian-gay-queer-trans politics in Canada that continues to engender spaces and places of pain, injury, and possibilities. Yet understanding

Suzanne Lenon and OmiSoore H. Dryden

these two moments in dichotomous terms – as representative of the "liberal gays" who carry and celebrate the mantle of Canadian nationalism versus the "radical queers" who challenge and criticize the colonial history and imperial becoming of the Canadian nation – conceals the complicated layers, socialities, and materialities in which both exist. This collection seeks to disorder, unsettle, and disturb such facile binaries of the liberal "good gay" and the radical "bad queer" by speaking to the complicated and often uneven relationships between exclusion and belonging, complicity and community. In doing so, it engages uncomfortable places and spaces of flux, fluidity, and instability while grappling with the tenuous nature of inclusion, (un)belonging, (dis)location, and home. Here, we take seriously the opening epigraph by Audre Lorde (1984, 127), who reminds us as co-editors and you as the reader of this book how deeply discomfiting yet potentially radical is the act of reflexivity in order to disturb and unsettle the "assumptions underlining our lives," including assumptions about sexual politics, nation, home, belonging, solidarity, and community.

One of this book's central arguments is that contemporary articulations of sexual citizenship are not only complicit with a conservative, neoliberal Canadian nation but also predicated on foundational Canadian national mythologies that inscribe whiteness as the embodiment of legitimate citizenship and belonging (Bannerji 2000; Thobani 2007, 75). Ranging from the tangible spaces of prisons, Pride marches, Pride House, fetish fairs, and feminist porn awards to the material effects emanating from spaces of legal regulation and governance such as marriage law, hate crime laws, citizenship guides, blood donation, and refugee claims, the chapters interrogate the conditions of, and entangled relationships between, exclusion and inclusion. In doing so, they grapple with a range of cultural and political processes occurring in contemporary lesbian-gay-queer-trans politics that interpellate a normatively raced, gendered, sexed, and classed Canadian (homo)sexual subjectivity to uphold the modernity of the white settler nation-state. It is the relational aspects of these processes with which this book is concerned. The conversations contained herein elucidate ways that deployments of dispossession and (un)belonging are the very conditions for inclusion to occur.

Often messy and sometimes incoherent, such processes include the incorporation of lesbian and gay identities into economic and legal registers, where equality becomes linked with individual freedom, access, opportunity, and choice, and where private property not only of objects owned but also of oneself becomes constitutive of self-worth (Alexander and Mohanty 1997, xxxiii; Hong 2006). This liberal inclusion of (some) lesbian-gay-queer-trans subjects is as much the consequence of homonormativity – a dominant form of queer sexual politics oriented toward privacy, consumption, and domesticity – as it is of a resurgence in nationalism, imperialism, and militarism (Bacchetta and Haritaworn 2011; Eng 2010). A concept made popular by Lisa Duggan (2002), homonormativity sustains dominant heteronormative assumptions of and about social life while fostering a queer sexual politics solidly anchored in the aspirations and dreams of what Lauren Berlant (2011) terms "the good life" fantasy – that is, normative kinship structures, property ownership, self-realization, and domesticity.

In her ground-breaking theoretical work, Jasbir Puar (2007) extends Duggan's analysis to foreground convergences and collusions between homosexuality and US nationalist projects – what she terms "homonationalism." Written in the aftermath of 9/11, Puar's book *Terrorist Assemblages: Homonationalism in Queer Times* has captured the focus of intellectual and political imaginaries for its erudite theorization of homonationalism as a process whereby the combined ascendancy of whiteness, imperialism, and secularism produces lesbian-gay-queer subjects[4] as "regulatory" over perversely queered populations, rendered monstrous, feminized, and abnormal (Puar 2007; Puar and Rai 2002). Homonationalism, according to Puar (2013b, 337), is "an assemblage of geopolitical and historical forces, neoliberal interests in capitalist accumulation both cultural and material, biopolitical state practices of population control, and affective investments in discourses of freedom, liberation, and rights." Centrally, it is an imperial biopolitics that exerts terrorizing control over othered racial and sexual populations marked for death. As a field of power, homonationalism apprehends how the "turn to life" for some lesbian-gay-queer subjects (i.e., their enfoldment within legal, cultural, and consumer arenas) is now possible *because of* the simultaneous curtailing of welfare provisions and immigrant rights, as well as the expansion of state powers to conduct surveillance and to (indefinitely) detain and deport. Thus how queerness and racialization interlock becomes a critical factor in determining whether and how the turn to life is experienced, if it is experienced at all (Puar 2007, xii-xiii; see also Haritaworn, Kuntsman, and Posocco 2014). As a critique of lesbian and gay liberal rights discourses, homonationalism attends to how such discourses produce narratives of progress and modernity that continue to accord some populations access to cultural and legal citizenship at the expense of the delimitation and expulsion of racialized others (Puar 2013b, 337). As Puar (2011, 139) observes, the question "how well do you treat your women?", serving since colonial times as a determining factor of "a nation's capacity for sovereignty, has now been appended by the barometer of 'how well do you treat your homosexuals?'" (139). Homonationalism, then, is both a facet of modernity as well

Suzanne Lenon and OmiSoore H. Dryden

as an analytic useful to historicize how and why status as a "gay-friendly" nation-state became desirable in the first place.

How queerness simultaneously folds into settler colonialism further illuminates the biopolitics of homonationalism, where the dreams for, ideals of, and successful incorporation into (sexual) citizenship through freedom from state-sanctioned persecutions are generative of affective and material aspirations of settler citizenship and belonging. Naming this field of power "settler homonationalism," Scott Morgensen (2010, 2011b) extends Puar's analytic by centring settler colonialism as a condition of queer theory, queer politics, and sexual modernity in the Americas. Settler homonationalism signals the biopolitics of settler colonialism and its accompanying logic of Indigenous elimination. Understanding settler colonialism as a complex social formation and as continuous over time – "a structure rather than an event" (Wolfe 2008, 105) – suggests that modern queer subjects and politics continue to naturalize settlement of the white supremacist (Canadian) nation-state through desires for and claims to sexual citizenship and belonging (what we are calling the "queerly Canadian"). Morgensen argues that such claims are deeply embedded in the notion of settler sovereignty and in the concomitant legal and political severing of Indigenous relationships to land, language, and community. It is important, however, to distinguish between types of relations of power that constitute queer settler subjects as well as to interrogate the category of "settler" more generally. This category has emerged out of differential yet interlocking racial-sexual histories and encounters, including genocide, slavery, and indentured labour. The insidious prevalence of white supremacy structures ongoing colonial relations with Indigenous and racialized peoples within Canada. Consequently, the subject categories of "settler" and "queer settler" are not equally inhabited and therefore are not commensurate in their interpretation.

Analytic and activist critical uses of homonationalism now extend to geo-political contexts outside the United States (the country in which Puar's original project arose) and also coincide with other transnational analyses. These include (but are not limited to) "gay imperialism"[5] (Haritaworn, Tauqir, and Erdem 2008), which foregrounds the figure of the white gay activist carrying "the white man's burden" of saving "gay Muslim victims"; "homopatriotism," in which queer fantasies of militarization and eroticizing warfare function as claims to national belonging (Kuntsman 2008, 114–17); "homonostalgia," a sentiment that has the performative effect of rendering homosexuality part of a nation's history, norms, and values in a way that makes racism and white supremacy seem innocent or even absent (i.e., a time when gay liberation could, allegedly, be taken for granted before it was under threat by Islam (Gloria

Wekker, cited in Bracke 2012, 245); and "pinkwashing," a term coined by activists to describe the process by which the Israeli state seeks to deflect attention away from the military occupation of Gaza and the settler occupation of the West Bank (see Puar and Mikdashi 2012; and Chapters 3 and 8 of this collection). These overlapping and transnational conceptual frames are not parallel to homonationalism; rather, Puar (2013b) asks us to consider the way that they are possible within and because of homonationalism as a field of power and as a structure of (neo)liberal modernity.

These transnational analyses seek to ascertain the constitutive conditions of race, gender, sexuality, and class in our historical present. They circulate in a number of arenas, including academic conferences such as "Homonationalism and Pinkwashing," organized by the City University of New York Graduate Centre in April 2013; the solidarity network in Germany for queer and trans people of colour, No Homonationalism, set up to form local and transnational coalitions in the struggle against gay racism, homonationalism, and gay imperialism[6]; the mobilization to oppose the East End Gay Pride in London, England[7]; the opposition of African activists to the neocolonialism of northern activists and their governments with respect to sexual politics in various African countries (e.g., see ActionAid et al. 2011; Aken'Ova et al. 2007; and Ekine 2010); and the emergence of queer anti-apartheid groups such as QuAIA and Pinkwashing Israel.

Disrupting Queer Inclusion seeks to apply, extend, think through, and rework homonationalism in a "Canadian" context as it is articulated through four phenomena: racialization structured by white supremacy; current and ongoing settler colonialism; neoliberalism, which works with white supremacist settler capitalism to constitute the contemporary Canadian nation-state; and the persistence of imperialist mythologies that continue to position Canada as a peacekeeper, a middle power, and a land of freedom. The chapters collectively present a snapshot of these variegated formations of homonationalisms at different temporal and spatial sites. As Puar (2007, 10) states, there is no cohesion among homonationalisms; they are, instead, "partial, fragmentary, uneven formations, implicated in the pendular momentum of inclusion and exclusion, some dissipating as quickly as they appear." Thus the intentional reference to "homonationalisms" in the plural attends to the multiplicities of analytics and geographies contained within this book.

Although this collection centres analytics of homonationalisms, we understand the book to be in respectful conversation with intellectual and activist histories and genealogies that engage with epistemological and theoretical relationships between nation, capital, empire, self-determination, colonialism,

Suzanne Lenon and OmiSoore H. Dryden

race, and sexuality.[8] This longstanding historical and contemporary theoretical work by Indigenous, racialized, working-class, and lesbian feminist thinkers guides this endeavour to disturb the increasingly frequent practices and processes of homonationalisms in Canada, even though not all authors in this collection take up these intellectual histories. As both a field and an analytics of power, homonationalism is understood here not as a teleology of improvement of this body of theoretical work; rather, these intellectual and activist genealogies are seen as continuing to produce knowledge and to direct theoretical interrogations toward thinking about and extending the analytics of homonationalisms, including in this book.

Theorizations of racialization, diaspora, settler colonialism, and empire have long been integral to intellectual and activist genealogies of women's, gender, and feminist studies, even when such work appears under the sign of token inclusion or disappears from the institutional memory and canonical formulations of women's studies knowledges (Alexander and Mohanty 1997, xvi; Brandzel 2011). But such work continues to be at the margins and to be rarely understood as the "proper object" of institutionalized sexuality studies (Butler 1994; Wiegman 2012). Instead, such discussions are often framed as extraneous to the authentic, "real" question of the insider-outsider status of "sexual minorities," where the privileged positioning of injury (re)articulates and further solidifies a heterosexual-homosexual binary (e.g., see FitzGerald and Rayter 2012; and Knegt 2011). This perpetuates a form of homo-innocence that positions gay and lesbian bodies as outside of systems of coercive power and within the confines of a minority-status victimhood that ultimately forecloses any interrogations into its "naturalization."

Disrupting Queer Inclusion provides a complicated reading of the realities of gender, sex, sexuality, and sexual citizenship in the at once settler colonial, racialized, and diasporic region known as "Canada." It is a project motivated by the concern with how bodies and subjectivities are produced by, and taken up in, relational projects of inclusion. The conversations contained within this collection expand the analytic terrain and scholarly field of sexuality studies in Canada. The contributors offer a study of racialized sexuality and racialized queerness that takes to heart the intellectual and political question posed by M. Jacqui Alexander (2006b) in the opening epigraph: the implications of the sometimes too ready convergences between intellectual and activist endeavours at a moment of ongoing empire and colonization.

Persistent and enduring myths surrounding the founding of Canada, what Canada is today, and who Canadians are advance seemingly unceasing narratives of Canadian benevolence and exceptionalism that exist within a bilingual, multicultural racelessness (Haque 2012; see also Backhouse 1999b; Brand 1994; and Thobani 2007). Sherene Razack (2004a), for example, reveals the civilizing and imperial racial violences that profoundly shape modern "peacekeeping" enacted in the name of nation. Canada's imagining of itself as a middle power and peacekeeper affords its national subjects an intimate and innocent sense of self, history, and place. Mythologies, Razack (ibid., 9) argues, "help the nation to forget its bloody past and present" – they effectively erase, or "unwrite," the violence of the histories of Canadian nation making. The Conservative government's 2013 "Speech from the Throne" perpetuated this unwriting and disavowal of conquest, genocide, and slavery as foundational to the building of the nation. Prime Minister Harper spoke of the settlers who founded the country, stating, "They dared to seize the moment that history offered. Pioneers ... reached a vast continent. They forged an independent country where none would have otherwise existed" (Government of Canada 2013). This fantasy of Canada as peacefully settled, not violently colonized, was given renewed life. In yet another example, the celebratory representations of Canada as a safe haven for African and African American refugees fleeing the institution of slavery in the United States during the nineteenth century obscures the realities of slavery and the treatment of the enslaved in Canada (see Bakan 2008; Cooper 2006; and Nelson 2004). A vision of Canada predicated on the hopeful fictions of the Underground Railroad provides the conditions for the Canadian nation-state, as well as its citizens themselves, to deny racism's temporal continuities (see McKittrick 2007).

The Underground Railroad has become a truncated victory that is now used in what are *thought of* as analogous sites of citizenship inclusion, such as the Civil Marriage Trail. On the Valentine's Day weekend in 2004, same-sex couples from the State of New York travelled to Toronto to marry. The premise of this Civil Marriage Trail event was the mythology of the Underground Railroad and Canada as a safe haven and land of freedom. A more recent example is the advocacy group Rainbow Railroad. Describing itself as working "in the spirit of and with homage to the Underground Railroad," the Rainbow Railroad (n.d.) is committed to helping LGBT people from around the world (outside of North America) to find a *safe haven* in Canada from "state enabled violence, murder or persecution."

Predicating the name and focus of the organization upon the imagined racialized benevolence of the Underground Railroad, notably by including a picture in its publicity that features railroad tracks with rainbow-coloured rail ties, situates this activist endeavour within the field of Canadian homonationalisms, where racial, imperial and colonial agendas foster conditions of

Suzanne Lenon and OmiSoore H. Dryden

inclusion, safety, and sanctuary that are precarious, unstable, and conjectural. The deployment of racial analogies, in which discrimination against same-sex couples is *now* like oppression faced by African Americans *then,* evokes an "earlier" politics of race as the precedent for a "later" gay rights struggle. Such an analogy enables the privilege of forgetting race, with the result that there is little or no accountability to historical and contemporary anti-racist struggles (Grillo and Wildman 1991). In her work on whiteness and the literary imagination, Toni Morrison (1992, 52) offers a compelling way to consider what the Underground Railroad and its Africanist presence *do* in their moments of invocation: they are the vehicle by which one "knows itself as not enslaved, but free; not repulsive, but desirable; not helpless, but licensed and powerful; not history-less, but historical; not damned, but innocent; not a blind accident of evolution, but a progressive fulfillment of destiny."

This book speaks back to such narratives of Canadian benevolence and exceptionalism while actively working to resist the urge to look elsewhere (i.e., "over there," or outside of the nation, as the Rainbow Railroad does) for horrors of homophobia and to frame Canada as a safe haven where gays are accepted. One such example of this urge was the international outrage directed toward Russia in 2013 for enacting laws "to prevent homosexual propaganda," which, in turn, prohibited the registration of Sochi Pride House as part of the 2014 Winter Olympic Games (Associated Press 2013).[9] One response to this outcome was a call to strip Sochi of the games and return them to Vancouver, the host of the previous Winter Olympics (see Change.org 2013). The push to have the 2014 Winter Olympic Games returned to Canada invoked a patriotic image that "loyally repeats the nation" (Haritaworn 2008) as a land of (queer) freedom, "the True North, strong and free." In such contexts, loyal repetitions of the nation are enriched and sustained through benevolent yet provisional gestures of the nation-state toward (some of) its sexual Others. Canadian sexual exceptionalism has become normatively manifest through the inclusion of lesbians and gay men in the military (1992); the inclusion of sexual orientation in the equality provision (section 15) of the Canadian Charter of Rights and Freedoms (1995); the recognition of common law relationships among lesbian and gay couples (1999); the legalization of same-sex marriage (2003–05); and the conditional inclusion of "gay blood" in the national blood supply (2013).[10]

Yet as the book's chapters demonstrate, the idea of Canada as a safe haven is decidedly questionable, relying as it does both on the erasure of violences and on benevolent colonial practices. The book's chapters expose the interlocking relations of racialization, settler colonialism, neoliberalism, and imperialism to traverse and give shape to the field of power that forges homonationalisms in the Canadian context. The opening chapter by Julian Awwad, "Queer Regulation and the Homonational Rhetoric of Canadian Exceptionalism," elucidates significant shifts within the Canadian political landscape with the election of a majority Conservative government under the leadership of Stephen Harper in 2011. Awwad examines the complexities of the Conservative government's relationship to queer citizens, shifting the focus away from the perception that the Conservative agenda is "anti-gay" in order to highlight public discursive gestures that *do* take queerness into account. Focusing on government efforts to tighten and reform Canada's immigration and refugee system, Awwad illustrates how the lexicon of sexual rights and Canadian sexual exceptionalism, in adjudicating the viability of queer refugee claims, corresponds with Canada's coming-out about its newfound imperial purpose under a Conservative government. This "queer state of imperial becoming," he contends, is made possible by the subsuming of queerness in order to govern it. His chapter argues that the performative rhetoric of Canadian nationhood and exceptionalism provides the basis for recuperating (white and nonwhite) queer sexuality as a colour-blind modality of neoliberal governance by producing exceptional queer subject-citizens and by asserting Canada's exceptional status in the world.

In Chapter 2, "Unveiling Fetishnationalism: Bidding for Citizenship in Queer Times," Amar Wahab explores how queer sexual-erotic others are assembled through the field of homonationalism in spite of their radical political claims to denaturalize normative conceptions of sexuality and erotic life. Writing about fetish counterpublic politics, Wahab contends that although the fetish subject understands itself as transgressive and dissident, neoliberal logics of Western sociality and political life condition its dissident citizenship in ways that feed into the generative force of homonationalism. In an analysis of online debates regarding the rebranding of Toronto's Fetish Fair to make it more "family friendly," Wahab considers how the deployment of gendered Islamophobia becomes the foil against which the fetish subject's bid for citizenship is articulated. It is through the projection of the veiled Muslim woman as a "terrorist" in the online rebranding blogs that the collusion between fetish counterpublic politics and dominant Canadian Islamophobia emerges, staging what Wahab terms "fetishnationalism." Here, glimpses of the "fetish patriot" emerge through routes of settler citizenship, whose nationalized radicalism is also deeply enmeshed in Canadian imperialism both at home and abroad. So, although the rebranding of Toronto's Fetish Fair may signal a homonationalist project in the urban context, Wahab's chapter looks at how the presumed transgressiveness of queer counterpublic politics themselves enlivens and elaborates homonationalism.

Chapter 3, "Pink Games on Stolen Land: Pride House and (Un)Queer Reterritorializations," offers a critical examination of the 2010 Winter Olympic Games held in the Coast Salish territory now called "Vancouver" and in the Squamish and Lil'wat territories now called "Whistler". Here, Sonny Dhoot focuses on the creation of Pride House as both a queer and colonial making of homonational space. Dhoot employs the concept of "pinkwashing" to explore the operations of biopolitics and necropolitics at the heart of Canadian settler society in order to foreground queer complicities in settler colonialism that helped to make Pride House appear as a project of emancipation and inclusion, what he terms "homocolonialism." The chapter begins with a discussion of Indigenous opposition to hosting the 2010 Winter Olympics on unceded Coast Salish, Squamish, and Lil'wat lands. As Dhoot argues, the colonial violence required to host the games took many forms, including imprisonment of Indigenous activists, continued land theft, as well as ecological and cultural destruction of Indigenous territories. Dhoot then turns to the themes of belonging, settlement, and neoliberal collaborations to make visible the ways that pinkwashing occurred via Pride House, whose figuration as a "safe haven" simultaneously displaced Indigenous claims to sovereignty and self-determination. As he contends, the pinkwashing that made Pride House possible (and successful) will always be useful for the settler colonial project, as it lies at the heart of what must be concealed and denied, namely Canada's colonial present.

In Chapter 4, "Disruptive Desires: Reframing Sexual Space at the Feminist Porn Awards," Naomi de Szegheo-Lang explores the Feminist Porn Awards (FPA) as a potential site of resistance to, and unsettling of, (homo)normative conceptions of sexual citizenship. She argues that through their focus on pleasure, desire, and boundary-expanding representations, the FPA reimagine sexual citizenship in ways that blur the lines between public and private spheres that so often demarcate respectable sexuality and sexual desire(s). De Szegheo-Lang suggests that one of the FPA's most valuable contributions has been their demand for public presence in a way that both disidentifies with mainstream pornography and consciously remakes it. By creating space for critical dialogue and representation, the FPA reframe possibilities for sexual citizenship by unsettling normative constructions of desire, intimacy, and national (un)belonging. In her discussion of desire's role in feminist porn production, de Szegheo-Lang draws connections between sexual depiction, queer (re)formulations, and homonationalist state-sponsored space so as to explore what is at stake in shifting porn's terms of engagement. As she contends, both the FPA and the communities they support are a means of challenging the sexual policing of bodies that is so deeply embedded in colonial systems and national histories. As such, the FPA have implications that reach beyond the porn industry; they are connected to the disruption of all borders: gendered, raced, classed, colonial, and national.

In Chapter 5, "Monogamy, Marriage, and the Making of Nation," Suzanne Lenon critically discusses the 2011 BC Supreme Court *Reference* decision that upheld the criminalization of polygamy in Canada. She contends that this decision articulates a homonational critique of polygamy by enfolding lesbian and gay subjects, via same-sex marriage, into its idealization of monogamous marriage as exemplary of Western sexual modernity. Conceptualizing marriage law as a palimpsest – that is, as something whose historical investments in the logics of white nation making are never fully erased but rather persist into the contemporary moment – Lenon illuminates sets of historical relationships that joined across time to enable the *Polygamy Reference*'s homonationalist claims to be made in the first place, namely settler colonialism, racialization, and empire. She discusses how the court's critique of polygamous marriage as antithetical to Western civilization required a disavowal of settler colonialism that naturalized the Canadian nation-state as a liberal democracy unmoored from its colonial past and present. She also draws attention to the racial, and implicitly imperial, narrative of the *Reference* decision, arguing that it is haunted by the fear of the cultural-racial Other as Muslim. Its homonationalist critique of polygamy, she contends, not only ensconces monogamy as the normative kinship structure but also sutures monogamy to white (homo)nation making.

In Chapter 6, "Homonationalism at the Border and in the Streets: Organizing against Exclusion and Incorporation," Kathryn Trevenen and Alexa DeGagne examine homonationalist formations at two different sites of racialized state power: immigration control and policing. In the first instance, Trevenen and DeGagne compare the responses of two groups, Egale Canada and No One Is Illegal (NOII), to the proposed exclusions of lesbians and gay men from the revised Canadian citizenship guide *Discover Canada: The Rights and Responsibilities of Citizenship*. The authors argue that Egale Canada protested such exclusions through a discursive field of nationalism and a "single issue" sexual rights politics, whereas NOII's response connected the Conservative government's marginalization of queers in *Discover Canada* with its repressive crackdown on activists, its "tough on crime" agenda, and its focus on safeguarding national borders from "illegitimate" refugees. Moving to an analysis of "homonationalism in the streets," Trevenen and DeGagne examine the responses of two different lesbian-gay-queer groups in Edmonton to the police handling of a violent assault and briefly discuss debates about a police presence at the Ottawa Dyke March. The authors suggest that disrupting homonational politics of inclusion in all three cases – a government publication, the responses to a violent attack, and the challenges of organizing the Dyke March – highlights how different populations are queered and racialized as they circulate through the Canadian imaginary, depending on their national standing and "value."

In Chapter 7, "'A Queer Too Far': Blackness, 'Gay Blood,' and Transgressive Possibilities," OmiSoore H. Dryden explores the varying analytics of racialized sexuality, specifically the queerness of blackness, through an exploration of "gay blood" and blood donation. Narratives of blackness have been employed in the construction of a "gay" Canadian subject and homonationalist blood. Employing a black queer diasporic analytic to interrogate the homonationalist construction of blood, Dryden traces how national blood narratives, such as blood protection laws, blood quantum, and miscegenation, provide a genealogy for current blood donation practices. As the knowledge produced through the donor questionnaire confirms that black subjects are already both queer and "queer too far" subjects whose blood and bodies are already out of place in "gayness" and in Canada, this chapter seeks to explore potential possibilities for imagining transgressive futures.

Chapter 8, "National Security and Homonationalism: The QuAIA Wars and the Making of the Neoliberal Queer," discusses the controversy generated by the presence of Queers against Israeli Apartheid (QuAIA) in Toronto Pride events. Here, Patrizia Gentile and Gary Kinsman situate this terrain of struggle as dramatizing the historical shift, within Canadian nation-state formation, of queers from enemies of the state to defenders of Canadian national security. Their chapter traces how conditions of neoliberalism and Islamophobia have informed this shift. For Gentile and Kinsman, Canadian homonationalism is structured both by settler colonialism and by the Orientalism of empire, and these conditions of nationalism become significant in the important and critical discussions of QuAIA as an example of "rebellion" against this emergent homonation. Although they suggest that the work and effects of QuAIA may recapture forms of activism and liberationist organizing reminiscent of earlier activist histories, Gentile and Kinsman also point toward the need for a stronger and more integrated class analysis and capitalist intervention.

In the closing chapter, "Don't Be a Stranger Now: Queer Exclusions, Decarceration, and HIV/AIDS," Marty Fink situates prisons and incarceration at the heart of a reimagined queer politics, expanding the notion of what and who constitutes queer community. Drawing from artistic materials designed by incarcerated trans and queer inmates and circulated by Montreal's Prisoner Correspondence Project, Fink looks to cultural production as a site of intervention against carceral and national exclusion. Such cultural materials reimagine queer sexuality apart from homonationalist punitive measures and situate those locked inside prisons *as* members of queer communities. As national belonging is often imaged through who is omitted, Fink reminds us that cultural production becomes an important site of intervention both in the nation and in queer agendas. Creating art connects incarcerated queer and trans people with larger queer and trans communities, enabling those inside prison to disrupt the tides of their disappearance by "keeping in touch." Moving toward a vision of utopic queer futures inspired by José Esteban Muñoz (2009), Fink recentres incarcerated queer and trans people as valuable members whose broader struggles of resistance are necessary for a reimagined queer-sexual politics beyond liberal inclusion.

As this introduction makes clear, this book is unapologetically and overtly political in its interrogation of the various interlocking relations of power that enable practices of homonationalisms. If there is a "queer" impulse underlying this book, we understand it as one that harkens to an older meaning of the word: to make odd, strange, peculiar.[11] We have intentionally not organized the book under various thematics, as we believe that doing so might have caused a "break" in the conversations while also forcing and limiting conversations in a particular way. Rather, we see the chapters forming a collective whole, speaking back and forth to each other and across each other in order to "queer" – disturb, unsettle, make strange – Canadian sexuality studies. These chapters provide direction to facilitate such disruptions through not yet imagined enriching sites and approaches. Woven into this undertaking is inspiration drawn from the writing of José Esteban Muñoz (2009, 185, 1), who envisions queerness as a mode of desiring, a longing, and a performative that propels us to vacate the here and now for a then and there, to collectively enact and imagine other ways of being in the world, insisting on the potentiality for or concrete possibility of another world. We present these scholarly interventions not to argue for inclusion, or being "let in," but to insist on the continual interrogation of the associated complicities, collusions, and *costs* of inclusion in order to unsettle it as a signifier for liberation and justice – that is, to disturb and unsettle the idea(l) and dreams of "inclusion" itself.

Notes

1 This is the title of a recent book on sexuality studies in Canada (see FitzGerald and Rayter 2012).

2 On its website, QuAIA states, "Queer Palestinians continue to face the challenge of living under occupation and apartheid, subject to Israeli state violence and control, regardless of liberal laws within Israel that allow gays to serve in the military, or recognize same sex

marriage and adoption of Israeli citizens. QuAIA works to fight homophobia, transphobia and gender expression where they exist" (QuAIA n.d.). After seven years of Palestine solidarity work in LGBTQ communities, Queers Against Israeli Apartheid officially retired at the end of February 2015.

3 Founded in 2010 by Dan Savage and Terry Miller, the "It Gets Better" campaign is an Internet-based project whose goal is to prevent suicide among LGBT youth by having adults (gay and straight) convey a video message to these teens that however "bad" things are, life will "get better" (see http://www.itgetsbetter.org). However, as Jasbir Puar (2010a) critiques, this campaign is notable for its erasure of systems of racialization, colonialism, class, and ableism that construct the neoliberal "just gay" subject for whom life will get better.

4 For discussions on how trans subjects and trans politics can also function as regulatory, see the work of Dean Spade (2011, 2012) and Lane Mandlis (2011).

5 Haritaworn, Tauqir, and Erdem's "Gay Imperialism: Gender and Sexuality Discourse in the 'War on Terror'" appears as a chapter in the book *Out of Place: Interrogating Silences in Queerness/Raciality* (Kuntsman and Miyake 2008). This chapter offers a trenchant analysis of the ways that racism and Islamophobia are the basis on which white gays and feminists are incorporated into the political and social mainstream. The authors insist that because of this context "all feminists, gays, lesbians, queers, transpeople and other actors of gender and sexual politics take a clear position on the role offered to them in the imperialist project" (Haritaworn, Tauqir, and Erdem 2008, 89). They discuss the invisibility, silencing, and marginalization of queers of colour in the British gay and lesbian mainstream, and they examine the figures of the "white gay savior" and the "gay Muslim victim" that circulate in European gay politics and activism. In this analysis, they are highly critical of prominent British gay rights activist Peter Tatchell. In September 2009 Raw Nerve Books, the small, independent, feminist publisher of *Out of Place,* issued a controversial public apology to Peter Tatchell based on some of the content of the chapter by Haritaworn, Tauqir, and Erdem (Raw Nerve Books 2009). In November 2009 Raw Nerve Books released a further statement apologizing for the chapter's "inaccuracies" and "errors" and said that it would not republish the book or make it available for reordering. It remains out of print. As Douglas, Jivraj, and Lamble (2011, 108) remark, "The authors and editors of *Out of Place* have become effectively subject to the same form of silencing they critique."

6 As an activist and online network, No Homonationalism (2010) connects queer and trans people of colour "to express solidarity and share about each other's work in various places and connect multiple struggles against violence in all its forms – from the intimate and interpersonal to the everyday, normalized violence of the market and the systematic target-ing of racialized people inside Europe and in the countries of occupation and war by the prison and military industrial complex." This network of local and transnational queer and trans activists and academics was instrumental in facilitating Judith Butler's refusal of the Civil Courage Award (Zivilcouragepreis) presented to her by the Christopher Street Day (CSD) Parade in Berlin, Germany, in June 2010. After meeting with local groups and being apprised of the ways that CSD Pride had espoused anti-Muslim and anti-immigrant senti-ments, Butler (2010) said in her speech, "I must distance myself from this complicity with racism, including anti-Muslim racism." She offered the prize instead to Gays and Lesbians from Turkey (GLADT); to LesMigraS, an anti-violence and anti-discrimination support group for migrant women and black lesbians; to SUSPECT, a queer group for building the anti-violence movement; and to ReachOut, a counselling centre for victims of right-wing

violence. Although Butler's act of refusal is a significant one, as SUSPECT writes, it is important to situate it as a result of the collective labour and the local and transnational histories of organizing. For more on this, see SUSPECT (2010).

7 The East End Gay Pride March was organized in response to homophobic stickers that had been put up around London's East End. It was subsequently cancelled when the Safra Project, run by a group working on issues affecting queer Muslims, revealed that the march's organizers had close ties with the far-right, anti-immigrant English Defense League. Safra also contested this Pride march on the grounds that it would fuel Islamophobia. Instead, it asked for everyone "to voice their opposition to overt and covert racism and Islamophobia especially in the name of gay rights. All forms of prejudice must be understood in their overlapping ways and to ignore this lived reality, particularly that of Queer Muslims, is to avoid engaging with underlying issues of social, economic and political injustice and disadvantage" (Safra Project 2011).

8 A partial list of some significant and important genealogies includes M. Jacqui Alexander and Chandra Talpade Mohanty's *Feminist Genealogies, Colonial Legacies, Democratic Futures* (1997), Gloria Anzaldúa's *Borderlands/La Frontera: The New Mestiza* (1987), Maria Campbell's *Halfbreed* (1973), Cathy Cohen's "Punks, Bull-daggers, and Welfare Queens: The Radical Potential of Queer Politics?" (1997), the Combahee River Collective's "Statement" (1977), Angela Davis's *Women, Race and Class* (1983), Enakshi Dua and Angela Robertson's *Scratching the Surface: Canadian Anti-Racist Feminist Thought* (1999), Marie Anna Jamies Guerrero's "Civil Rights versus Sovereignty: Native American Women in Life and Land Struggles" (1997), Audre Lorde's *Zami: A New Spelling of My Name* (1982) and *Sister Outsider: Essays and Speeches* (1984), Lee Maracle's *I Am Woman* (1988), Patricia Monture-Angus's *Thunder in My Soul: A Mohawk Woman Speaks* (1995), Cherrie Moraga and Gloria Anzaldúa's *This Bridge Called My Back* (1981), Adrienne Rich's *On Lies, Secrets, and Silence: Selected Prose, 1966-1978* (1986) and "Notes towards a Politics of Location" (2003), and Andrea Smith's *Conquest: Sexual Violence and American Indian Genocide* (2005).

9 On 29 October 2013 Pride House International (PHI), a coalition of LGBT sport and human rights groups, launched efforts to partner with national houses at the 2014 Sochi Winter Olympic and Paralympic Games. The objective was "to overcome the legal obstacles from Russian authorities to the creation of a Pride House at the Games." PHI asked its supporters to contact their National Olympic Committee and request that it host Pride House events (see Pride House International n.d.).

10 With respect to state gestures towards trans inclusion, Canadian parliament is now in its fourth attempt to pass legislation with respect to gender identity. Bill C-279 when passed will protect transgender people in Canada in both the Canadian Human Rights Act and the Criminal Code by making it illegal to discriminate against transgender people or to promote hatred based upon gender identity.

11 See "queer" in the *Oxford English Dictionary* at http://www.oed.com/search?search Type=dictionary&q=queer&_searchBtn=Search.

Queer Regulation and the Homonational Rhetoric of Canadian Exceptionalism

JULIAN AWWAD

Mapping the Ethos of the Nation

These are queer times for Canada. With their majority government win in 2011, the Conservatives have arrived. This election signalled new political trends and altered the political landscape. During the Conservative Party Convention that followed their election win, party leaders mapped out the ethos of the nation. According to Prime Minister Stephen Harper, strength is a "vital necessity," and moral ambiguity and moral equivalence are "dangerous illusions," so the party aims to prepare Canada "to shoulder a bigger load, in a world that will require it of us" (Payton 2011). The then Citizenship, Immigration, and Multiculturalism Minister Jason Kenney asserted that Conservative values are Canadian values, claiming that the party, speaking on behalf of Canadians, "does not mistake relativism for tolerance" and is "not afraid to call a barbaric cultural practice what it is" (ibid.). Where queer rights are concerned, this vision of the new Canada has served as the foundation of a homonational rhetoric that has been constitutive of a new queer public.

Criticism of the prime minister and the Conservative Party for pursuing a right-wing agenda and policies that jeopardize Canada's democratic traditions is ubiquitous. Where it concerns queer communities, criticism abounds on myriad issues. As early as June 2006, the Conservatives proposed to amend the Criminal Code by raising the age of sexual consent from fourteen to sixteen in an attempt to curb sexual predators (CBC 2006). In November 2009 an updated version of the citizenship and immigration guide, *Discover Canada: The Rights and Responsibilities of Citizenship*, eliminated references to homosexuality, including decriminalization and gay marriage, before adding a single reference in a revised version that acknowledges gay rights (CBC 2011). In May 2010 the Conservatives withdrew government subsidies from their tourism-stimulus package for Toronto's lucrative Pride Parade (CBC 2010b), a fate its counterpart in Montreal, Divers/Cité, similarly experienced (CBC 2009).

To describe these policies as repressive does not capture the complexity of the Conservative government's relationship to its queer citizens. As Christian Nadeau (2011, 82) observes, explicitly advocating homophobia would be a politically costly endeavour for the Conservatives, who instead "alternate between a repressive attitude towards 'sexual deviants' and a kind of paternalism regarding what a good society should be" (ibid., 78–79). In addition to the cursory amendment to the citizenship and immigration guide, other initiatives and political postures indicate the delicate balance that the Conservatives are attempting to strike in the management of queerness in Canada. The Conservative government's decision to investigate same-sex divorce options and Prime Minister Harper's reiteration that his government has no intention of reopening the same-sex marriage debate (McGregor 2012) exemplify this delicate balance.

Framed by this concatenation of events, this chapter provides a contextual examination of how the Conservative rhetoric of Canadian nationhood, at the intersection of sexuality, race, and citizenship, subsumes queerness in order to govern it. The instability of "queer" as an analytical concept animates a consideration of how queer publics are produced based on homonational appeals. The aim is to shift the focus away from the perception that the Conservative agenda is "anti-gay" in order to highlight discursive gestures in Canadian public discourse that do take queerness into account. As David Eng (2010, xi) observes, the term "queer" has been unmoored from its original references to a political movement and to a critique of normative and exclusionary practices and "has come to demarcate more narrowly pragmatic gay and lesbian identity and identity politics, the economic interests of neoliberalism and whiteness, and liberal political norms of inclusion." By focusing on the refugee context as a case example, and following Eithne Luibhéid (2005, 72–73), the chapter also aims to demonstrate how sexuality serves as a key site for remoralizing and refashioning the responsible autonomy and civic virtue of the queer citizen under the leadership of a Conservative government. The chapter argues that, through this homonational rhetoric, Canadian exceptionalism provides the basis for recuperating racialized (white and nonwhite) queer sexuality as a

Julian Awwad

colour-blind modality of neoliberal governance by producing exceptional queer subject-citizens and asserting Canada's exceptional status in the world.

Queerly Conservative

If the message at the Conservative Party Convention, with its call to action, is understood to be inclusive of all Canadians, then it implies a rehabilitative invitation for queer citizens to identify with a normative form of sexual citizenship. In this sense, the figure of queerness in Conservative discourse derives from a rhetorical impulse to constitute particular subjects and identities. The newly constituted (Conservative) queer subject, in turn, ought to be motivated by imperial aspirations and moral certitude and eschew relativism in the name of tolerance. The blogosphere exemplifies figures of this new form of queerness. In his blog, *Political Thoughts from a Gay Conservative,* Chris Reid, former Conservative Party candidate for Toronto Centre, describes himself as pro-life and a supporter of limited government, individual liberty, and strong national defence, whereas another gay Conservative blog, *Gay and Right,* endeavours to "expose the threat of cultural relativism, post-modernism, and radical Islam" and states its support for "the right of the State of Israel to live in peace and security."

Indeed, such political positioning introduces novel queer prospects. If the term "queer" as an analytical category has been theorized both as a noun that signifies *non*-normative subjects or identities and as a verb that signifies the enactment of a skeptical attitude and *non*-normative political stance (Leckey and Brooks 2010, 2), then Conservative discourse engages in a "queering of queer" as it constructs the figure of the queer citizen-subject. In Conservative public address, the figure of "queerness" is performative: through ideological recuperation of the disruptive non-normative queer subject in political action, it functions to displace opposition to essentialism and normative definitions. In other words, "queer" and "Conservative" are no longer paradoxical or antithetical propositions. Conservative discourse can equally establish political stances representing normative queer subjects.

Arguably, this possibility is engendered by "queerness" itself. As Eve Sedgwick (1993, 8, emphasis in original) remarks, the term "queer" can refer to "the open mesh of possibilities, gaps, overlaps, dissonances and resonances, lapses and excesses of meaning when the constituent elements of anyone's gender, of anyone's sexuality aren't made (or *can't be* made) to signify monolithically." That it can, furthermore, be seen as "a zone of possibilities in which the embodiment of the subject might be experienced otherwise" (Edelman 1994, 114) suggests that the "gay conservative" as a discursively constructed identity is queerly possible.

The "gay conservative," as a queer identity, should not and does not contradict the spirit of queerness as it has been theorized, for assuming otherwise fails to account for the dissonances and lapses, the definitional openness and indeterminacy, within this very theorization. And it is indeed upon dissonances, gaps, lapses, and fractures that non-normativity is based in queer theorizations and upon which the spirit of theorization thrives. Although it is the case that "queer" has not been treated simply as synonymous with "gay," the former continues to include and subsume the latter within its rubric. Sedgwick (1993, 8, emphasis in original) underscores this point when she observes that "queer" can simply denote "same-sex sexual object choice, lesbian or gay, whether or not it is organized around multiple criss-crossings of definitional lines." She adds that "given the historical and contemporary force of the prohibitions against *every* same-sex sexual expression, for anyone to disavow those meanings, or to displace them from the term's definitional centre, would be to dematerialize any possibility of queerness itself."

It is in the tension between resistance to reification and fixity and the possibility of stabilization that queerness attaches to its citizen-subjects. As Judith Halberstam (1997, 260) claims, "'queer' is in danger of stabilizing into an identity rather than remaining a radical critique of identity." Moreover, she points out that queer theory is problematic because it fails to specify the type of sexualities with which scholars ought to be preoccupied in their scholarly examinations. It is simultaneously the elusiveness of the term and its potential for stabilization in specific discursive contexts that allows Conservative discourse to recuperate it within its agenda. In other words, the rhetorical impulse in accounting for queerness in Conservative discourse derives from the figure of "queer" itself because it resists definition and categorization as it attaches to the queer citizen-subject whom it constructs.

Queer Subjects, Queer Publics

By articulating an inclusive notion of the "Canadian people" and constituting particular queer publics, Conservative rhetoric relies on a locutionary position that is based in identification as ideological interpellation. It constitutes a "people," a rhetorical fiction that does not exist prior to rhetorical action yet in which we are invited to participate. This is the "ideological 'trick' of such a [constitutive] rhetoric," as Maurice Charland (1987, 137) refers to it, which

Julian Awwad

"presents that which is most rhetorical, the existence of a [people], or of a subject, as extrarhetorical." It is what legitimizes the "people" in concrete terms. The "Canadian people," whom the Conservatives address, is a notion that implicitly subsumes "queers," invoking the spectre of non-normativities at the moment of their normalization in order to manage and regulate their queerness.

An understanding of this new queer public is tied to an understanding of "the people," or in this case, the "Canadian people" that Conservative rhetoric – and indeed most political rhetoric – invokes. As Stuart Hall observes, "politicians always think they know what people feel. It's a fallacy, because there is no such thing as 'the people.' It is a discursive device for summoning the people that you want. You're constructing the people, you're not reflecting the people" (Z. Williams 2012). Hall's statement builds upon earlier scholarship in rhetorical theory that emphasizes how social identities and collectivities are invited to participate in a proposed vision by becoming "the people" described in rhetorical address (see McGee 1975). Based on the notion of "the people" as rhetorical fiction, Charland (1987, 134) proposed that rhetoric is constitutive insofar as it involves a process of interpellation in which it "always already" presumes the constitution of subjects, a process that positions individuals "towards social, political, and economic action in the material world" (ibid., 141) within a "textualized structure of motives [that] inserts them into the world of practice" (ibid., 142).

What kind of queer subject is consequently called into being, which is to say, interpellated or "constituted," and what type of rhetoric constitutes it? To what political ends is the queer person motivated to act? Lisa Duggan (2002, 179) has remarked on the "new liberal sexual politics," the trademark of a new type of queer conservative politics in the United States, or what she terms the "new homonormativity." She explains that "it is a politics that does not contest dominant heteronormative assumptions and institutions but upholds and sustains them while promising the possibility of a demobilized gay constituency and a privatized, depoliticized, gay culture anchored in domesticity and consumption." As Jasbir Puar (2007, 39) remarks, the assumption that the state is only supportive and productive of heteronormativity and repressive and denying of homosexuality is complicated by the diversity of sexual practices that not only contradict or resist heteronormativity but also mimic and parallel it.

This is how homonormative constituencies in Canada come to identify with a new nationalist ideology. It is "homonationalism," Puar's (2007, 38) shorthand for "homonormative nationalism," that Conservative rhetoric invokes in constituting new queer subjects, who form a public in the making. Homonationalism subscribes to what Eng (2010, 3) terms a "queer liberalism" that forms the basis for the liberal inclusion of particular queer citizen-subjects petitioning for rights and recognition. In this light, the queer citizen-subject is recuperated into dominant neoliberal state structures and institutions in a manner that suggests queerness does not necessarily signify a disruption of national modes of belonging (Leckey and Brooks 2010, 6).

Indeed, the relationship between nationalism and queerness is ambivalent. As Jon Binnie (2004, 21) points out, considerations of "the extent to which some nationalisms may be perceived as positive towards some sexual dissidents" entail recognition of "the active agency that many queers play within nationalist politics." Furthermore, although liberal underpinnings of the self-possessed speaking subject invested in individual agency can "labor to insistently recentre the normative queer subject as an exclusively transgressive one," queerness can also be a biopolitical project "that both parallels and intersects with that of multiculturalism, the ascendency of whiteness, and may collude with or collapse into liberationist paradigms" (Puar 2007, 22). What this means is that queer citizenship, as a constant process of becoming, cannot be strictly reduced to either a politics of assimilation or a politics of transgression, a dichotomization that, according to Brenda Cossman (2007, 160), "misses the messiness, ambivalence and multiplicity of the inclusions and exclusions of citizenship" (see also Wahab, this collection). This is congruent with Eng's (2010, xi) observation that deployments of the term "queer" no longer render it paradoxical or antithetical to the term "rights," which follows from the unmooring of the term "queer" and the consolidating effect of queer liberalism. Therefore, shifting focus onto the discursive function of neoliberal governmentality highlights how queerness is a process and a self-fashioned endeavour implicated in a rights discourse that emphasizes free markets and individualism, as well as its attendant posture of Western moral superiority.

Queer Rights, Queer Exceptions

The focus on individual merit, particularly as a function of neoliberal governmentality, underpins the discourse of Conservative immigration policies. Not only does homonational rhetoric, as constitutive rhetoric, call a queer public into being, but it equally calls its antagonists into being. In February 2011 Minister Jason Kenney delivered a speech in which he accused judges of indulging spurious refugee cases and announced changes to the immigration and refugee system. Citing a poll in which respondents from countries with problematic human rights records were at the top of the list of those who wished to immigrate to Canada, he asserted that "Canada is not able to welcome every

Julian Awwad

person who says that they'd like to immigrate here" (Kenney 2011). In addition to an enthymematical assumption that all these respondents would *actually* move to Canada, thereby overwhelming his department with the processing of immigration applications, Kenney maintained that this was also about ensuring that the integrity of the immigration system was not compromised while maintaining the confidence and respect required of law-abiding immigrants (ibid.). It was also about maintaining public support for "generous levels of immigration" by sustaining faith in the government to control and secure the nation's borders against those people who would try to enter the country by any (illegal) means (ibid.).

By referring to exemplars of dubious refugee claims, Minister Kenney advanced his argument of the illegitimacy of claims by dismissing poverty as a legitimate ground and characterizing claimants as fraudulent, criminal, and/or sexist. The significance of his depictions for this analysis lies less in the narrative fidelity of the stories, or the extent to which they ring true to his audience (see Fisher 1984), than in the way they reveal how this depiction subscribes to and cultivates new modalities of homonormative governmentality based in public moral argument. The racialized (queer) citizen-subject is co-opted into the constitution of the law-abiding citizen, exemplifying how a queering of the racialized refugee becomes part of the biopolitical project to which Puar (2007, 22) refers – a project implicating multiculturalism and the ascendency of whiteness and exacerbating internal divisions within racialized, immigrant communities. As Eng (2010, 45) argues, "Queer liberalism is not necessarily about excluding bourgeois racial subjects from its aegis. To the contrary, it is about failing to recognize the racial genealogy of exploitation and domination that underwrites the very inclusion of queers and queers of color in this abstract liberal polity."

To be a law-abiding citizen, according to Minister Kenney, queer individuals must engage in an immigration system that is colour-blind, presumably based on individual merit. A refugee claimant must conform to "fair and reasonable criteria for admission," which include "an objectively demonstrated proficiency of English or French, a prearranged job offer, or an offer of admittance to a recognized university" (Kenney 2011). Because "these criteria are closely linked with Canada's success" (ibid.), it is only immigrants with (means to) an education and capital to contribute to Canada's economic prosperity, including affluent foreign students and highly skilled professionals, who end up having a chance at permanently crossing the border into Canada. This is in line with the Conservative government's initiatives to open a special immigration stream for entrepreneurs who would be connected to private-sector groups (Payton 2012).

Such initiatives followed on the heels of changes to immigration policy. They include the Balanced Refugee Reform Act, which was introduced into law in June 2010, and proposed changes under Bill C-31, which Minister Kenney introduced to filter out "bogus refugees," effectively granting the minister more power (Elliott and Payton 2012). Changes and proposed changes include a decrease in waiting times for a hearing at the Immigration and Refugee Board (IRB) from eighteen months to ninety days (McKiernan 2011), unilateral determination of "irregular arrivals" and their automatic detention for up to one year, unilateral determination of "safe countries" without consultations with human rights experts, and denial of appeal options for rejected claimants applying from "safe countries" (Elliott and Payton 2012). Under such time and other constraints, it has become even more challenging for claimants to prove their case and get appropriate representation (McKiernan 2011).

For queer refugee claimants in particular, these changes have adversely impacted their claims, especially where sexuality is the basis for distinguishing "bogus" from legitimate refugees. As Eithne Luibhéid (2002, x, emphasis in original) observes, such endeavours are intimately tied to an immigration system that is "charged with *trying* to know" the legitimacy of refugee claims. In constructing this knowledge, as Eng (2010, 4) contends,

> Queer liberalism does not resist, but abets, the forgetting of race and the denial
> of racial difference ... The logic of queer liberalism works to oppose a politics
> of intersectionality, resisting any acknowledgment of the ways in which sexu-
> ality and race are constituted in relation to one another, each often serving to
> articulate, subsume, and frame the other's legibility in the social domain.

Because a successful claim requires evidence that a queer refugee is a member of a social group and that there is a well-founded fear of persecution, a decrease in wait times effectively means increasing constraints on the ability to gather sufficient evidence to support the claim.

This new challenge exacerbates an even more significant and older one: convincing members of the IRB of a claimant's sexual orientation in fulfilling the first requirement. Members of the board often rely on "folk knowledge" or "judicial common sense on sexuality" in making their decisions, and this reliance on "their own culturally bounded knowledge ... [of] non-normative and culturally 'strange' sexuality ... may be more myopic and fearful – with profound effects" (Miller 2005, 138). Evidence of homosexuality often involves the collapsing of gender identity and sexual orientation (LaViolette 2007; Millbank 2002), and despite legal measures undertaken to separate the two, adjudicators

Julian Awwad

continue to conflate gender identity and sexual orientation in making determinations (LaViolette 2007).

Although queer narratives ought to inspire empathy, it often seems unachievable. As Richard Delgado (cited in Millbank 2002, 156) remarks, narratives must be ostensibly noncoercive: "They invite the reader to suspend judgment, listen for their point or message, and then decide what measure of truth they contain. They are insinuative, not frontal; they offer a respite from the linear, coercive discourse that characterizes much legal writing." Instead, refugee claimants are forced to (re)present themselves in reductive ways in order to render their claims intelligible to adjudicators. It is a form of "captivity narrative," which implicates a sort of "coercive mimeticism" through "which the ethnic person is expected to come to resemble what is recognizably ethnic" (Chow 2002, 107). As Rey Chow (ibid.) defines it, this mimeticism is "a process (identitarian, existential, cultural, or textual) in which those who are marginal to mainstream Western culture are expected ... to resemble and replicate the very banal preconceptions that have been appended to them, a process in which they are expected to objectify themselves in accordance with the already seen and thus to authenticate the familiar imaginings of them as ethnics."

Coercive mimeticism is equally a legal process implicated in the intelligibility of narratives. Whether claimants deliberately frame their narratives in a form of "coercive mimeticism" or adjudicators seemingly make sense of them only through projections, such "dangerous shortcuts," or "simplifications powered by the search for winning stories" (Jacqueline Bhabha, cited in Miller 2005, 165), ignore the diversity of sexualities intersecting with racial histories and the manner in which refugee claimants embody multiple identities. And a winning story means one that is intelligible to adjudicators; even if a claimant's rendition is believable, it does not mean that it will be intelligible. Jenni Millbank (2002, 157) describes unintelligible queer narratives as "a kind of mysterious blank – like the maps of the early colonial eras, with the edges of continents like Australia disappearing into nothingness where the map makers had not yet travelled." She adds that "it is this enforced blank of lesbian and gay experience that is then written upon, as the decision-makers impose a series of preconceived notions of self." Because adjudicators are unable to "hear" the narratives of queer refugees, their "experience is erased or rewritten in the decision making process ... form[ing] an unreadable blank, onto which decision-makers project their own sense of reality, of self and other, of acceptable conduct, of public and private" (ibid., 145).

"Proving" that a refugee claimant is homosexual effectively means subscribing to a particular epistemology that understands same-sex practice in identitarian terms. The "immutable queer" requirement fixes gay identity as a category. If sexuality is associated with an identity that requires proof, then it must equally be a category that elides. As Eithne Luibhéid (2002, ix) notes, "Lesbian and gay exclusion is less the history of a minor group than of self-constituting actions by the powerful who then erase the traces of their own production while stigmatizing and policing others." In the context of refugee migration, it is "less about the problem of detecting a hidden sexual or racial trait than about our collective refusal to see difference in the face of it ... [a refusal] characterized by a persistent disavowal of race in the name of freedom and progress" (Eng 2010, 2).

It is no cause for wonder that, in addition to overall inconsistent approval ratings (Sheppard 2012), bisexual refugee claimants, for example, encounter particular difficulties, as Sean Rehaag argues, precisely because sexual orientation is understood as an innate and immutable personal characteristic (Rehaag 2008) and adjudicators are unlikely to perceive bisexuality, unlike homosexuality, as a sexual identity (Rehaag 2010). Because the law has the tendency "to prefer fixed identities, identities that map neatly and recognizably onto conduct" (Miller 2005, 138), as far as the law is concerned, sexual conduct *requires* an identity.

Moreover, in establishing winning narratives, the relationship between recognizing "authentic" queers and producing intelligible narratives of persecution reveals the nefarious machinations of queer refugee regulation. The arbitrariness in deciding refugee cases based on determination of the risk of persecution lies in confused and subjective interpretation of what a "well-founded fear" entails (Miller 2005, 147–48). Lesbian sexuality, for example, "is constructed as rightfully private and often therefore not requiring protection, as future persecution is unlikely or past persecution is characterised as 'merely personal'" (Millbank 2002, 145, 158–63; on the contested nature of persecution, see also Miller 2005, 147–48). Nevertheless, legal questions are shifting from issues of sexual orientation and well-founded fear of persecution to distinguishing between persecution and discrimination, regional differences in treating sexual minorities, and the availability of state protections (LaViolette 2010).

It is upon this shifting legal terrain that exceptionalism emerges and that queer narratives of persecution, as intelligible ones, function as a modality of exceptionalism. The dominant view of the "immutable queer" as connected to persecution alerts us to its relationship to the sexual exceptionalism that underlies Canadian homonationalism. Canadian exceptionalism is established in a double sense: that of being excepted *for* and that of being excepted *from* admission into Canadian society. Because embracing homosexuality in identitarian terms offers no guarantees, the management and regulation of sexuality presume immutable characteristics that are nevertheless evasive, potentially yielding arbitrary results. According to Jessica Chapin (quoted in Binnie 2004, 96), the legal motivation to establish certainty and proof through legal recognition and knowledge construction about queers is implicated in both xenophobia and homophobia: "Xenophobia and homophobia converge in a search for secure knowledge, a reactionary effort to regain an epistemological footing by targeting and expelling such indecidable and therefore threatening figures as 'illegal aliens' and 'queers.'" Although the law constitutes queer identity through the *stigmatizing* function of legal mechanisms such as sodomy statutes, it is ironic how refugee-case determinations contribute to the constitution of a global notion of "the homosexual" by producing a popularly recognizable gay identity through the legal *rewards* afforded successful claimants (Miller 2005, 138).

These paradoxes emerge as the fault lines of the constitutive rhetoric of homonationalism. They suggest that Conservative regulation of queerness is less about normalizing (at least some) forms of otherwise non-normative sexuality than about how its recuperation of queerness entails particular forms of queer management as norm. Characterizing asylum as a process that has more to do with inclusion than with exclusion (Miller 2005, 161), or emphasizing the former at the expense of the latter, misses how inclusion implicitly informs exclusion, how their dynamic interplay endows or denies value to particular sexual practices. In other words, considering what is excluded, as a supplement to identifying what is included, exposes the function of queer inclusions as a norm of governance. This function of exception not only negatively marks what or who is to be excluded and denied protection but positively "include[s] selected populations and spaces as targets of 'calculative choices and value-orientation' associated with neoliberal reform" (Ong 2006, 5).

Queer Transnationalism

Exceptionalism equally serves to promote Canada's exceptional status in the world. Similar to the US context, the regulation of queer refugees is implicated in immigration processes that shape the production of exclusionary forms of nationalism, which extend beyond national borders and the specific visions of Canada and its citizens (Luibhéid 2002, xi; see also Eng 2010, 8–9). If queer stigmatization informs a national sense of self, it follows that legal reward is intimately tied to violation abroad. As Alice Miller (2005, 139) notes, "In examining asylum cases involving (homo)sexuality, we are attending to how and where sexuality-oriented violations claims emerge, and how [heterosexual and homosexual] identities are built in relation to the acceptable narration of both violation and responses to violation." The transformation from abject persecuted subject to empowered queer rights holder "produces a moment of transnational judgment, when the decision-makers of one nation decide not only on the credibility of the individual asylum claimant, but on the errors or strengths of the protection of rights in the country from which the claimant flees" (ibid., 143). This "violent gift" (Kristen Walker, quoted in ibid., 144) bears upon Canada's moral superiority as determined by rules of intelligibility that rewrite queer experiences of persecution as "authentic" or not. The focus on evaluating legitimate experiences of persecution furthermore implicates moral superiority in forming the basis for distinguishing Canada from other countries, most problematically in the absence of adequate documented evidence in support of claimants' applications (see ibid., 148).

Although a conception of "gay identity" recognized by Canadian adjudicators may not impose itself upon the rest of the world, it does inform a global discourse about this identity. As Miller (2005, 161) points out, "At a minimum, the recognition of particular kinds of gay identities within a national legal context is ... deployed as part of a complicated, international conversation about gayness and gay rights." Whereas homophobia is displaced onto countries of the global South, the homophobia of countries of the global North is masked through rhetorical appeals to gay rights as human rights with tenors of moral superiority. For example, Minister Kenney has singled out the persecution of gays and lesbians in Iran, yet in a typical neoliberal appeal, he places the onus on private gay and lesbian organizations to sponsor more refugees and bring them to Canada (CBC 2010a). Despite the prevalence of such sponsorships, some organizations do not have the resources or the means to provide this type of support as an ongoing service (ibid.). And where gay capital is involved, Puar (2002a, 102) observes the irony, in the context of gay tourism, when "the United States and British states advocate protection for cruise ships in the Caribbean while granting no such rights when the cruisegoers return home." As Miller (2005, 164) similarly indicates in the refugee-determination process, "Adjudicators in receiving countries proclaim the failures of the state of origin without having to reflect on how the actions of the receiving state might be connected to those very abuses (or on how such representations might reproduce colonial relations of power)." What the currency of the notion of the "global gay" reveals, then, is what Binnie (2004, 68) calls a "new racism" that "masks the extent to which so-called 'progress' on matters of sexual diversity has been achieved in the west." This "new racism" overlooks how gay rights activism informed by queer liberalism consigns racial discrimination to the past and

Julian Awwad

how sexual and racial discrimination are coextensive in the implementation of immigration policies at home (Eng 2010, 17).

Arguably, what undergirds international human rights is a local, queer recuperation of sexual rights at home. Underpinning this complicity is the discourse of the "global gay," or what Joseph Massad (2002, 362) has termed the "Gay International," a complex of "missionary tasks, the discourse that produces them, and the organizations that represent them." For Massad, the transformation of same-sex practitioners into subjects who identify as homosexual is an outcome of the discourse that human rights organizations adopt and of the work that they employ in countries of the global South. Others have noted this collapsing of gay rights into human rights as constituting a form of "moral" or "norm" entrepreneurship whereby advocates employ refugee cases "to re-frame the place of the national in the international, as in the local application of an international right, or as in a national commentary on another nation's practice" (Miller 2005, 162). What this form of entrepreneurship reinforces is "the self-congratulatory posture inherent in the geopolitics of asylum: the northern nations that receive asylum seekers are constituted as good and just, while the nations that send are constituted as failures. The North receives worthy *victims* and presumably represses only unworthy *behaviors*" (ibid., 146–47, emphasis in original). It may well be that "the assertion of queer liberalism on the global stage may be less about gay and lesbian rights, recognitions, and privileges than about codifying across the planet a Euro-American liberal humanist tradition of freedom and democracy" (Eng 2010, 48), one in which Canada, no less, wants to participate.

Establishing clear guidelines for determining refugee protection based on sexual orientation is problematic not simply because it assumes that such an identity can or should be fixed without doubt but also because it *can* be doubted or misrecognized, wilfully or not, after state violations in the country of origin have been experienced by same-sex practitioners, who now *have* to identify as homosexual, wilfully or not, in the pursuit of winning narratives. And here is where complicit violations of "benevolent" countries like Canada begin to emerge. Whereas sexual orientation requires "proof" as an identity category, it ironically remains questionable until an adjudicator recognizes the claim. The life and death nature of these decisions overlooks the impact of nonrecognition or misrecognition, one that is ultimately tied to the decision maker's understanding of persecution in strategically designated "safe" or "unsafe" countries. Especially in instances of publicized, unsuccessful cases, claimants run the risk of serving as sacrificial tokens in the service of Canada's exceptional status in the world. When the claimant relies on the epistemology of homosexual identity as "proof" or as a strategic legal argument, an unsuccessful claim includes self-admission, which further serves as grounds for persecution in the home country upon deportation. Unsuccessful claimants become the sacrificial subjects who subsequently experience "barbaric cultural practices" and violations of human rights *because* they have identified themselves as "gay" or "homosexual." As Canadians react to horrific human rights abuses in other countries, our complicity in the violation through our own legal regimes is overlooked.

Coda: Pinkwashing, Blue Strokes, and Shades of Purple Queer

The performative rhetoric of Canadian nationhood requires taking queerness into account. If the Conservative rhetoric of homonationalism adopts the lexicon of sexual rights as a gesture of national recognition and inclusion, then this inclusion presumes *exclusion* of those who do not merit the extension of rehabilitative citizenship. This is ultimately tied to a transnational discourse on queer sexuality that is brought "into the national consciousness of who is here, or who *should* be here, [and] can be seen as part of a broader engagement with multi-layered legal principles, national prejudices, and struggles for public space involving not only asylum seekers but their advocates, including NGO champions" (Miller 2005, 144–45, emphasis in original). The emergence of national homosexuality operates based on sexual exceptionalism: it "is contingent upon the segregation and disqualification of racial and sexual others from the national imaginary" (Puar 2007, 2). By figuring the Canadian context in terms of Puar's (ibid.) analytical framework, Canadian homonationalism, like its American counterpart, corresponds to the coming-out of Canadian exceptional imperial designs: Canadian homonationalism corresponds to the new-found imperial purpose to which Canada, under a Conservative government, is aspiring. It is a homonationalism that emplaces Canada from within "imperial formations" that are understood as "states of becoming" in constant formation, "polities of dislocation, processes of dispersion, appropriation, and displacement ... [that] are dependent both on moving categories and populations ... [and] on material and discursive postponements and deferrals" (Stoler and McGranahan 2007, 8).

Nowhere does this queer state of imperial becoming better manifest itself than in the immigration and refugee context. This is a context where, based on the foregoing, queerness as an unstable, moving category is endowed with stability by an imperial formation that includes "a broader set of [economic, social, ideological, and cultural] practices structured in dominance" (Stoler and McGranahan 2007, 8). Bids for inclusion in the national imaginary, such as gay

Julian Awwad

marriage and serving in the military, in addition to refugee claims, suggest that the nation-state does matter for queer subjects as a safeguard for rights (see Binnie 2004, 28–29). Homonationalism and queer liberalism, as modalities of neoliberal governance, furthermore propose that queer subjects can be transformed into compatriot-citizens. Homosexuality is not defined *against* nationalism but through and with it, presenting the prospect of rehabilitating exceptional queer citizens.

As other chapters in this collection discuss, the relationship between exceptional queers and exceptional nation-states is not restricted to the context of immigration alone. Indeed it indicates that regulatory norms operate across multiple sites. In 2010 a controversy broke out when the group Queers against Israeli Apartheid (QuAIA) was initially banned from marching in the Toronto Pride Parade because of its use of the phrase "Israeli apartheid" (see Gentile and Kinsman, this collection). When the ban was overturned, the group was allowed to march without incident. Despite a report in 2011 that found use of the term did not contravene the city's anti-discrimination policy, the then Mayor Rob Ford vowed to withhold funding from the parade. This incident coincided with the Israeli government's attempts to improve Israel's global image as a modern and relevant country by including the gay community in its "Brand Israel" marketing campaign, a participatory initiative in the Euro-American liberal-humanist tradition of freedom and democracy that was perhaps not a paradoxical undertaking despite charges against Israel's violations of the human rights of its gay citizens. As Sonny Dhoot examines in his chapter about the 2010 Winter Olympic Games, activists have termed this strategy "pinkwashing," which Schulman (2011) defines as a strategy "to conceal and deflect the continuing violations of Palestinians' human rights through an image of modernity signified by Israeli gay life."

Prompted by Rob Ford's intransigence, QuAIA elected to hold its Pride events outside the parade, which, according to the group's spokesperson, Elle Flanders, was meant to grant the mayor a choice between funding the parade and exposing his homophobia (QuAIA 2011). This tactic might have played into the exclusionary logic of homonationalism and queer liberalism as a sign of deviant queerness that does not merit the rights associated with the civic virtues prescribed by neoliberal governmentality and is thus self-sacrificed for the sake of the queer community at large. Pressured to assimilate into an overly defined sexual identity and shaken by a colour-blind backlash against the group's involvement in the parade, Suhail Abualsameed, a figure involved in the queer community, claims that members of this community will "welcome you as one of them, but the moment you bring in your politics and solidarity is involved, they don't want to hear it" (Safieddine 2011). Certainly, as Michael Warner (1993, vii) observes, "Sexual desires themselves can imply other wants, ideals, and conditions."

Whatever liberatory projects or movements queerness informs, it cannot be, as Robert Leckey and Kim Brooks (2010, 3) point out, "unalloyed emancipation." It is dependent upon the rhetorical context in which it is invoked, the locutionary position of speaking. As the late Edward Said (1986, 140) writes, "We can read ourselves against another people's pattern, but since it is not ours ... we emerge as its effects, its errata, its counternarratives. Whenever we try to narrate ourselves, we appear as dislocations in their discourse." Yet, if these dislocations offer stability for exceptional narratives, standing in for who and what is excluded, then queer sexuality is always already a dissonant locutionary position that offers immutably queer possibilities for political transformation since the "blue" strokes cast upon "pink" states can only yield shades of purple queer.

2

Unveiling Fetishnationalism
Bidding for Citizenship in Queer Times

AMAR WAHAB

Building on and extending Lisa Duggan's (2002) concept of homonormativity, Jasbir Puar's (2007, 38) concept of homonationalism focuses on the complex ways that homonormativity crucially informs and is informed by national-normative demands inside and outside Western nation-states. Seeking rights-based equality through formal reforms, gays and lesbians in the West have inadvertently helped to consolidate the Western neoliberal nation-state. Both concepts urge us to recognize mainstream gay and lesbian appeals to hetero-normative institutions for inclusion and equality as blurring the binaristic distinction between dominant heterosexual citizens and sexual others. This folding of some non-normative others into heteronormative formations has yielded yet another separation of hetero- *and* homonormative subjects from supposedly anti-normative queer others. Consequently, the term "queer" has been deployed as part of a counterpublic politics[1] that radically resists both heteronormativity and mainstream gay and lesbian politics. Although the elu-siveness of this term continues to condition the possibilities of this radical political project, this chapter questions and complicates the presumed exclusiv-ity between queerness and homonationalism.

In *Terrorist Assemblages,* Puar (2007, 77) claims that "there is nothing inher-ently or intrinsically antination or antinationalist about queerness, despite a critical distancing from gay and lesbian identities ... Queerness is also under duress to naturalize itself in relation to citizenship, patriotism, and national-ism."[2] Furthermore, Scott Morgensen (2011b, 27), in theorizing settler homona-tionalism, claims that "queer radicalisms and liberalisms arise interdependently within white-supremacist settler colonialism." These claims imply a need for vigilance about the ways that queer counterpublic discourses might inadvertently contribute to the proliferation of homonationalism, especially through their dissident politics. If, as Puar (2007, 69) states, "queerness has already been assimilated into the homonational," we must inquire into the conditions through which this interpellation is produced to critically reassess the situating of queerly dissident subjects in opposition to national-normative formations.

In this critical reassessment of queer dissidence, I am interested in understanding how queer sexual-erotic others are assembled through the discourse of homonationalism despite their radical political claims to denaturalize national-normative conceptions of sexuality and erotic life. Is the call for dissident citizenship by queer others so clearly demarcated from homonationalist assemblages, or is dissidence conditioned by the neoliberal logics of Western sociality and political life? In posing this question, I am also concerned about what constitutes the rational threshold of dissidence and the ways that national calculations of proper dissidence also feed into the generative force of homonationalism. As similarly discussed by Julian Awwad in Chapter 1, these calculations concern political gestures that are assessed as tolerable by the nation-state because they do not radically contest the founding principles of liberal democracy, thus enabling the Western nation-state to make claims about its capacity for exceptional tolerance. Although the nation-state selectively prioritizes those counterpublics on the margins that tentatively deserve tolerance, it also demarcates certain others as being immutably incompatible with Western-national codes of liberal democracy. Bidding for priority along this scale of tolerance, some queer counterpublics rely on this national calculation to distance themselves from those other others who are constructed as "too dissident to be queer" since they are imagined as "too irrational to be properly dissident." In this regard, we might also recognize a discursive parallel to homonationalism – queernationalism – whereby queerly dissident subjects make claims about their citizenship-worthiness by displacing anxieties about national terror onto other subjects whose dissidence is informed by intersections of gender, sexuality, and race.

In this chapter I explore how online debates about the rebranding of Toronto's Fetish Fair have activated this binary along the lines of race, sexuality, and gender in an undertaking that effectively translates into a bid for queer citizenship – a bid that requires the reproduction and circulation of state-national discourses of gendered Islamophobia to construct the queer exception as worthy of national tolerance. In my reading of the rebranding debates online,

I question the juxtaposition of the queer subject (the fetish subject in this particular case) who advocates for recognition as the properly dissident subject vis-à-vis the figure of the veiled Muslim woman (who is figured in the online debates), imagined in the West as "terrorist" and therefore outside the limits of proper dissidence. This juxtaposition is crucial to understanding the salience of race and gender in the making of queernationalism and its strategic appeal to Western nation-states at a historical moment in which the supposed "achievement" of formal gender equality and sexual liberation mark the West as exceptionally tolerant.[3] I first provide a background of the recent rebranding of Toronto's Fetish Fair to highlight the complex discourses that circulate within the category of "fetish." In the next section I examine online responses to the rebranding (from online newspaper articles and resulting blog posts) to highlight the tensions between homonormativity and what might be termed "fetishnormativity." In the final section of this chapter, I examine online blog posts that bring the figure of the veiled Muslim woman into central focus within the rebranding debates. In this section I signal the deployment of gendered Islamophobia by fetish subjects as a crucial tactic in the bid for queer/fetish citizenship. Although this particular case raises more questions than can be addressed in this chapter, it provides a glimpse into how queer counterpublic politics, marked as properly radical and transgressive, might elaborate homonationalist assemblages through Islamophobia.

Rebranding Fetish

In 2011 the seventh annual Church Street Fetish Fair in Toronto's Church-Wellesley gay village was officially rebranded the "Church Street Village Fair." The rebranding decision came after the Church-Wellesley Village Business Improvement Area (CWVBIA) – an organizing committee comprising entrepreneurs from the Church-Wellesley village – decided to market the event as "family friendly." The CWVBIA represents part of the City of Toronto's Business Improvement Area (BIA) mechanism for encouraging economic development across the mosaic of neighbourhoods in multicultural Toronto. Whereas in previous years the Fetish Fair was one of the few exclusively sex-positive and erotic-positive public venues, the CWVBIA's rebranding decision aimed to sanitize and respectabilize the event, driven primarily by the BIA's entrepreneurial mandate. It was felt that the original fair was too off-putting to the general public and too limited in its appeal to a niche market of fetish enthusiasts and practitioners. Rebranding would selectively censor the less palatable aspects of the fair to widen its appeal to heteronormative consumers. The rebranding entailed relocation and quarantine of staple fetish events and performances outside the physical boundaries of the CWVBIA's official fair zone, replacing fetish demos, especially those related to leather and BDSM,[4] with extended patios, a mechanical bull ride, a Ferris wheel for children, and games like gay men's twister.

In the previous year (2010), the main village newspaper, *Xtra!*, reported on demonstrations of fire breathing, fire whips, piercing, flogging, and so on that represented a diverse spectrum of sexual and erotic liberatory performances and practices. This celebration of "the perverse" tentatively marked the fetish politic as radically progressive and resistant to what one *Fab Magazine* journalist described as "squeamish city officials" (Rowsome 2010) raising moral panics about the fair. Especially set against the increasing momentum of homonormativity within the gay community (e.g., private condominium development for gay couples and the closure of gay public bathhouses), the pre-2011 Fetish Fair might be read as a queer counterpublic that resisted the privatization and regulation of intimacy, sex, and eroticism. Interestingly, although the Fetish Fair and its sexual-erotic positivity represented a critical response to the historical regulation of sex publics in the Canadian context, it was promoted as "being for all people in our community to come out and express themselves" (ibid.). This claim echoed the neoliberal rhetoric of inclusivity and tolerance and was premised on the public confessional of "coming out" so central to mainstream gay and lesbian politics.

Online discussions reflected this tension between the fair's homonormative rebranding and fetish counterpublic contestation. The removal of BDSM and leather-based fetish performances and demonstrations as a result of rebranding produced voices of resistance and criticism from the fetish community online. From blog posts with headlines such as "Inclusiveness Excludes" (Dave 2011), "Rebranding Fail" (Ryan 2011), and "BIA Shoves Triangle Pegs into Square Holes" (Johnny Ransom 2011), it was clear that pro-fetish advocates viewed the rebranding as a deliberate attempt by a sex- and fetishphobic CWVBIA to sanitize, corporatize, and heteronormalize the event. Fetish advocates responded critically to what they perceived as a homonormative policing of the fetish counterpublic sphere (by the CWVBIA) in an attempt to destigmatize and re-normalize[5] the fair. These counterarguments aimed to unsettle and reverse dominant demands for the repudiation of sexuality and erotics in public. Although the 2011 fair was poorly patronized, members of Toronto's Leather Pride[6] (evicted from the official CWVBIA zone) staged a march through the Church Street Village Fair to contest the rebranding. *Xtra!* reporter Andrea

Amar Wahab

Houston (2011) described the "march through" as a "mob of sexual outlaws wearing leather and fetish gear ... to ensure that the festival stays kinky." One of the "flash mob" organizers, Victoria Windsor, commented, "We just made history. I'm pretty sure that was the first Toronto Leather Pride parade ever. And it was just us kinky folks saying, HI! HI! HI! HI! We're here! We're queer! We're kinky! We're not protesting. We're smiling and waving. We just took the sexual blinders off a long time ago. We brought fetish back to the Village." Houston's reference to the "mob of sexual outlaws" and Windsor's comment projected the fetish subject as an outlaw whose transgressiveness was radically progressive yet out of time with the more conservative homonormative turn in village-national politics. Beyond nostalgia for an idealized past of sexual liberation and indeterminate erotic expression (Langdridge 2006), the fetish outlaw emerges in this counterpublic response as properly transgressive – that is, as the subject who, although out of time with the neoliberal conservatism of the moment, has already assumed its role in the nation's progressivist narrative. In the next two sections, I question the givenness of this dualistic distinction between hetero- and homonormativity and queer/fetish to suggest that it works to deflect a critical attention to the ways that fetish counterpublic politics generates parallel normativities that enliven and extend homonationalist assemblages.

Normalizing Fetish

Similar to pornography as analyzed by Naomi de Szegheo-Lang in this collection, state legal-medical-psychiatric discourses have historically pathologized, stigmatized, and regulated BDSM and various sexual-erotic practices in public to procure national-normative notions of good (i.e., hetero) sexual citizenship. Activists and scholars such as Patrick Califia (1988), Dangerous Bedfellows (1990), Berlant and Warner (1998), and Gayle Rubin (2011) have been part of a wave of voices contesting the policing of public sex and eroticism, arguing that sex publics and their "unruly" (Stychin 2001) subjects potentially subvert national-normative conceptions of gender, sexuality, and eroticism. This counterdiscourse has met with opposing reactions not only from state-national discourses but also from liberal-feminist arguments linking BDSM to nonconsensual conduct and patriarchal violence (see Dworkin and MacKinnon 1988; and Pateman 1988). The rebranding of Toronto's Fetish Fair as a homonormative project represents yet another layer in this war on sexual-fetish publics, serving to mark the boundaries between what Carl Stychin (2001) views as a categorical distinction between "good gay" and "bad queer." Furthermore, this assimilation of some sexual others (i.e., Stychin's "good gay") into hetero-normativity produces a further distinction between respectable hetero- *and* homonormative citizens and dissident sexual-fetish outlaws. Although national-normative conceptions of good sexual citizenship are conditioned by demands for privacy and domesticity, de-eroticization, and the depoliticization of sex (see Cossman 2002; and again, de Szegheo-Lang, this collection), the fetish domain productively perverts these conditions as a sort of "edge play" (Newmahr 2011, 150). Consequently, events like the Fetish Fair constitute a sexual-erotic counterpublic politics that aims to question and revise the conditions of possibility for what Darren Langdridge (2006, 374) terms "the sadomasochistic citizen" or what David Bell (1995, 143) refers to as the "citizen-pervert."

As mentioned above, the appeal by fetish dissidents for recognition has produced neoliberal counter-responses from the state, liberal feminists, and the mainstream gay and lesbian community, especially constructing the do-main of BDSM as violent, nonconsensual, and patriarchal and therefore as incompatible with liberal-humanist conceptions of citizenship. Although fetish (and especially BDSM) discourses are produced as the unruly outside of hetero- and homonormative projects, I would like to rethink this discourse of in-compatibility instead as a co-construction by *both* fetish counterpublic advocates and their antagonists. In doing so, I would like to inquire about whether sup-posedly subversive fetish counterpublics, by playing at the edges of neoliberal logics, inadvertently elaborate modes of normalcy *through* transgression.

A central problematic around fetish transgression concerns its definitional inconsistency and its refusal to authorize a contained fetish subject. Although it is an umbrella term for a plural domain of non-normative sex- and erotic-positive discourses and subjects linked through various modes of affiliation, practices, and performances, the meaning of "fetish" is ambiguous and cannot be reduced to any singular reconfiguration of national-normative logics about sexuality, gender, desire, eroticism, and pleasure. According to Newmahr (2010, 329), the multiple pursuits of "kink" provide "for members a safe space and strong sense of belonging and identity, a place to learn and express highly spe-cialized skills and competence, and generates a deep and meaningful identifica-tion." It is this plurality and affirmation of difference in the fetish domain that supposedly bolster its exceptional capacity for tolerance. Yet, within this loose subcultural domain, there are asymmetrical power relations that distinguish between some fetishes as exceptionally transgressive and others as transgressive within reasonable limits. BDSM and leather-sex communities are especially marked as exceptionally problematic since they "may produce a sexual citizen that is simply too sexual, too erotic, and therefore too transgressive for full citizenship" (Langdridge 2006, 380).[7] Fetish counterpublic appeals for recognition and inclusion must therefore selectively calibrate which subcultures either enhance or threaten the viability of its appeals. In this regard, BDSM and leather-sex communities are constructed as liabilities that complicate and deter the viable contracting between counterpublic and state.

The definitional complications of fetish subjecthood are structured through its distinction from liberal-humanist conceptions of the citizen-subject. In addition to its plurality of subcultures, discourses, and subjects, fetish counterpublic politics is more or less framed as a refusal of a fixed, stable identity, instead viewing fetish subjectivity as a fluid and creative matrix of (dis)identifications through various modes of self-manipulation/self-transformation. Although these technologies of dynamic and reflexive self-cultivation aim to transgress the neoliberal limits of autonomous selfhood in a sexphobic and erotophobic public sphere, they effectively do not offer a stable, coherent identity or position from which to make claims on the nation-state and in turn to be recognized by the state as subjects worthy of equal rights (i.e., as governable subject entities). Although this might be read as a mark of incompatibility between the fetish and normative domains, is it possible to locate the subject who autonomously self-cultivates as an effect of deeply embedded neoliberal-humanist logics? If so, the emphasis on the self-cultivating autonomous subject through an elaborated ethic of self-care (see Weiss 2011) bears a curious resemblance to and possible compatibility with neoliberal logics of citizenship. In this sense, transgression and radical counterpublic politics can be read not only as anti-national-normative but also as potentially hyperbolizing liberalism through the fetish subject as a viable modernist secular subject.[8] In other words, although the fetish subject is constructed as transgressive and dissident, its liberal terms of operation inadvertently condition it as an abstract citizen-worthy subject whose status might anchor its bid for citizenship.

The conditions that make possible this appeal are rooted in liberal conceptions of choice and free-willed agency, the rational calculation of risk, the presumed autonomy of the fetish subject, and the capacity for tolerance (sexual and erotic in this case). For example, the BDSM mantra of "safe, sane, consensual" presumes the subject to be a rational-choice agent who possesses the right to self-cultivate and the capacity to deliberate consent. Fetish sociality and politics are therefore premised on the contracting between ethically guided, free-willed individuals who rationally transgress normative logics about gender, sexuality, and eroticism. This is interesting given that anti-BDSM discourses have historically conflated BDSM subcultures with nonconsensual conduct. Newmahr (2010, 319) argues that the condition of safe and consensual conduct within BDSM "distinguishes SM participants from criminals and the mentally ill, and SM from assault." In addition, the claim that fetish practices allow subjects to engage in a continuous process of subjectification and desubjectification[9] presumes a liberal conception of the fetish subject as transcendental – that is, as self-elaborating through its transgression. The production of an abstract fetish-citizen subject operating through secular-humanist guidelines of sociality encourages us to question the sharp distinction between the assimilated (good) gay subject and the transgressive (bad) fetish subject since both subjects emerge from and operate within a humanist framework as free-willed individual agents who "come out" in accordance with neoliberally calculated principles of consent, reciprocity, and individual autonomy. In this regard, both hetero- and homonormativity *and* fetish counterpublic politics coalesce around liberal requisitions for organizing sociality and political life – producing what I have termed "fetishnormativity." This is not to suggest that the fetish subject is a completely assimilated subject but to underscore the contentiousness of the fetish-citizenship bid in light of the ambiguities raised above. In fact, Langdridge (2006, 373) has observed that various BDSM subcultures or "voices from the margins" are suspended between what he terms "the moment of transgression" and "the moment of citizenship," thus locating BDSM within a discursive struggle. This contest shifts the dominant hetero- and homonationalist conception of fetish away from threatening, terrorizing dissidence and toward a progressive, disciplined transgression that is coterminous with the liberal nation. Consequently, anti-rebranding and pro-fetish discourse articulates its transgressiveness through a normative mode, or in the words of Puar (2007, 47), as a "domesticatable queerness that mimics and recenters liberal subjecthood." If the viability of the fetish-citizenship bid is premised on viewing the progressive dissident as the "domesticatable queer," who, might we ask, is the subject who represents an irresponsible, irrational, and excessive transgression, making it possible for the "citizen-pervert" to come out and into the nation?

Nationalizing Fetish

A curious development in the online rebranding blogs is a thread of blog posts (what might be termed a queer/fetish panic) that focused on the veiled Muslim woman as the authentic figure of terror, representing an "out-of-control, untetherable queerness" (Puar 2007, 47). Why does this racialized, gendered figure come into focus in this moment of contestation, and how is she made to function in the discursive production of the fetish-citizenship bid? If the dissident fetish

Amar Wahab

subject, in claiming to counter normative power-knowledge formations, "comes out" as a progressive dissident, how might we evaluate the veiled Muslim subject who refuses the disciplinary call to public visibility (i.e., to materially and symbolically unveil)? In this blog thread, we glimpse another binaristic strategy that separates the liberal fetish subject who is enmeshed in the whiteness of the Canadian nation and represents a "domesticatable queerness" from the racialized, gendered other who is enmeshed in her queerphobic Islamic culture and therefore represents the "undomesticatable" subject. In this section, I argue that in this summoning and redeployment of Canadian discourses of gendered Islamophobia, the veiled Muslim woman is interpellated as the foil against which the fetish subject's bid for citizenship is consolidated. Moreover, it is through the projection of the veiled Muslim woman as "terrorist" that we see the collusion between fetish counterpublic politics and dominant Canadian Islamophobia, effectively staging what we might term "fetishnationalism."

Scholars such as Jasbir Puar and Jinthana Haritaworn have shown how seemingly radical and conservative political formations have coalesced through Islamophobia[10] to position queer as antithetical to essentially other racialized subjects who are constructed as incompatible with liberal progressive ideals of gender equality and sexual liberation. According to Sirma Bilge (2010, 9), "Contemporary debates over citizenship and immigrant integration are increasingly characterised by the prescriptive normativity of gender equality and sexual freedoms, articulating women's rights and gay rights to the nation to draw civilisational boundaries between Western modernity, framed as liberal and secular, and non-Western countries, supposed to be illiberal and prone to religious fanaticism." According to Bilge the figure of the veiled Muslim woman in the Western imperial context is viewed either as a victim of false consciousness subordinated by her "ultra-patriarchal" (Jiwani 2009, 735), repressive Islamic religion and culture or as an active threat to Western modernity because of her refusal to unveil under Western eyes. Fixed as a victim of Islamic ultra-patriarchy, the veiled Muslim woman is viewed as incapable of properly deliberating choice, consent, and agency and therefore as being radically distinct from the fetish subject. As the terrorist figure who refuses the invitation of Western patriarchy *and* liberal feminism to unveil, she supposedly represents a misdirected agency that endangers Western democracy and its secular-humanist conceptions.[11] The figure of the veiled Muslim woman therefore represents self-alienation or terrorizing noncompliance vis-à-vis the liberal self-transformative and therefore "domesticatable" fetish subject (see also Gentile and Kinsman, this collection).

This binary logic is structured through the dominant national-normative discourse of Canadian multiculturalism – a discourse that positions Canada as having an exceptional capacity for deliberating tolerance. However, this deliberation operates under the condition that racialized, gendered others "come out" and "come into" Canadian citizenship through their compliance with the compulsory call to gender and sexual equality. These prescriptions, based on secular-humanist conceptions of settler citizenship, not only condition the integration of difference into the nation-state but also mark other-national subjects who refuse Western conceptions of gender and sexual equality as anachronistic and threatening. Within this Canadian imperialist logic, the refusal of Muslim women to unveil *in the West* is translated through what is often termed the "pitfalls of multiculturalism" discourse into a rejection of the compulsory invitation to gender and sexual equality. As a discourse of national punishment, the "pitfalls of multiculturalism" logic constructs the veiled Muslim woman as improperly "multiculturated" and therefore undeserving of Canadian tolerance. The terror she is made to represent within the nation-state is a sober reminder that even exceptional tolerance must be vigilantly calculated.

The rebranding blog thread I analyze below layers onto this national calculus whereby the refusal to unveil is now further translated into an attack on sexual-erotic queer others (including the fetish subject) as the victims of Muslim-imposed homophobic, queerphobic, sexphobic, and erotophobic terror.[12] In this queernationalist scene, multiculturalism is once again reproduced as a failed project whereby supposedly homo- and queerphobic communities of colour represent a vile "culturalized" intolerance of queerness through the rigid demands of their culture for heteronormativity, domesticity, and kinship – what Puar (2007, xxv) refers to as "multicultural heteronormativity." In this queer inflection of the state's counterterrorist discourse of "terror by culture," the veiled Muslim woman as the improperly multiculturated other is constructed as incompatible with and undeserving of tolerance in a queernational future. By recasting the queer subject as the victim of spoiled multiculturalism and Islamic terror, the queer/fetish panic in the rebranding blogs constructs the grounds for nationalizing fetish. It does so by constructing the "citizen-pervert" as *rationally* refusing "untetherable" transgressions (and therefore compatible with the nation), in opposition to the veiled Muslim woman's seemingly irrational rejection of the compulsory invitations of state-disciplinary multiculturalism. That this panic is premised on the self-construction of the fetish subject as a "rational-choice-oriented dissident" (Bilge 2010, 21) who is positioned against the irrational noncompliance of the incompatible dissident is the very condition of fetishnationalist appeal. Moreover, the queer/fetish panic provides a historic opportunity for the Canadian nation-state to ideologically displace sexphobia and queerphobia outside the West (through the supposedly queerphobic terrorist within the West) – what might be termed "queerimperialism" – thus producing the West as exceptionally tolerant (of sexual and erotic perversity) in opposition to the Islamic rest as naturally intolerant.

In the fetish-panic blog thread (in the *Xtra!* newspaper online), although pro-fetish advocates contested what they perceived to be the effects of municipal-corporate homonormative regulation of the fetish counterpublic, this anxiety was displaced onto Muslim others within Canada, particularly the figure of the veiled Muslim woman. In this way, fetish advocates constructed themselves as liberal victims of multicultural, especially Muslim, terror in appealing for state recognition and protection. One blog post by "faerie-dust-up" (2011) reflects this fetish panic, which operates through the fetish subject's distinct status as the victim of spoiled multiculturalism at the hands of queerphobic, racialized, gendered others who demand too much tolerance:

FETISH FAIR PROTEST

There are women in Niqabs walking on Church Street to pick up their children at the school on Alexander St [within the Church-Wellesley village]. There are amore [*sic*] and more women in Niqabs all over downtown Toronto. As they move in, will we be moved out, or restricted in our Gay/LGBT Village for our Un-Islamic behaviour – like in London and Amsterdam? The BIA wants a Fetish Fair for everyone and all ages. Will the Muslims wearing Niqabs (Masks) and their children and anti-Gay ideologies be there as well? Let's have a Fetish Fair protest with our own style of Fetishes to revitalize our Village and show those who don't like our ways that they don't have to come here. The stores may want to tone down having been threatened by the city, but individual citizens do not have to. Let us Gay/LGBT people, be who we are, at all times in our own home Village. Running around the street in weird or provocative costumes is and has always been our LGBT birthright and it is free. Canada is supposed to be a land of freedom. Let your inner child come out at the Fetish Fair. Just be who you are! (If you wear socks you're not nude:) Here is what will come if we give in and start being "proper."

If the above blog post (like many others that are too long to reproduce here) offers a narrative of fetish victimage, other posts are aimed at mounting a virtual counterattack through which the veiled Muslim woman can be punished and disciplined for the excessive transgressiveness she represents. Entitled "Bend over, Little Bitch!" a post by blogger Nadine (2011) stages a virtual BDSM fantasy scene that simulates a BDSM-disciplining of the veiled Muslim woman, perhaps illuminating BDSM as a viable national-imperial counterterrorist technology:

BEND OVER, LITTLE BITCH!

I would be totally into belting some bitch in a burqa. She'd love it too, the dirty little Shia whore! Sorry to hear about the pending orchidectomy of the Fetish fair. Now it sounds like a scaled down version of Taste of the Danforth, minus the meat and Greek boys. Yawn.

The reference to "the pending orchidectomy" sheds critical light on the problem of homopatriarchy within the Fetish Fair, but it problematically simulates what Puar (2007, 72) terms an "imperialist topping" by discursively positioning the veiled Muslim woman as a submissive subject. Although it is tempting to read this scene solely as a simulated punishment of the veiled Muslim woman for her refusal to comply with nationalist requisitions, it virtually interpellates the veiled Muslim woman into the BDSM scene as a free-willed submissive subject (i.e., as a subject who consents to her own submission). It is through this self-transformative artifice that she "comes out and into" the nation as a Western *and* queer subject. This is the very practice of self-disciplining through which the compulsory call to Canadian state multiculturalism aims to produce consensually docile subjects. The command uttered by the BDSM subject ("Bend over ...!") reiterates the national-imperial command of sociality through submission and, in doing so, shows the BDSM subject to be self-fantasizing as queer patriot by performing a kind of disciplinary labour that both hetero- and homonationalism have been unable to fully achieve. This simulates a counter to the anti-BDSM arguments of state and liberal-feminist discourses by demonstrating the capability of the BDSM domain to rationally calculate and coerce the consent of exceptionally transgressive others. In doing so, BDSM-disciplining, as a historically contentious and marginalized subcultural formation, simulates the restoration of multiculturalism's disciplinary force through fetishnationalist possibilities.

Although we might read blogger Nadine's queer Orientalist fantasy as an eroticization of nonconsensual relations (i.e., as proper conduct when dealing with the Orientalized subject), her reference to the "dirty little Shia whore" activates Orientalist signatures historically written onto the veiled Muslim body. Puar (2005, 19) claims that "underneath the veils of repression sizzles an indecency waiting to be unleashed," suggesting that Orientalist discourses construct veiled Muslim women as possessing a natural and primordial perversity – one that is closeted by the veil and stringently repressed by an ultra-patriarchal Islam. The blogger's refusal to see both subjects as sharing a "commonality of perversion" (Puar 2007, 71) in Western discourse is confounded by her insistent distinction between the self-transformative perversity of the BDSM subject and the fixed repressed perversity of the veiled Muslim woman. Consequently, Nadine's blog performs an unveiling and outing of the natural perversity of the (especially Shia) Muslim woman – whereby she is revealed to herself under Western-fetish eyes as "consensually handing over autonomy to the Dom/me" (Bardzell 2010, 4). Through this simulated fantasy, the "citizen-pervert" performs national service by reinforcing the compulsory invitation to Western sociality and public life, thus demonstrating the viability of fetish-nationalism in discourses of national security. Furthermore, this contest between marginal settler subjects elaborates homonationalism through already existing settler colonial discourses whereby fetish subjects emerge as proper settler subjects capable of settling racialized others through their compliance. As a result, through "normative routes of settler citizenship" (Morgensen 2011b, 27), *both* subjects emerge (although unevenly) into a "civilizational modernity" that consolidates the Canadian settler nation-state.

Conclusion

Although the queer dissidence of Toronto's Fetish Fair signals a critique of hardening homonationalist projects in the urban context, this chapter questions this singular reading by looking at whether the presumed transgressiveness of counterpublic politics simultaneously enlivens and elaborates homonationalism – what I see as the making of fetishnormativity and fetishnationalism in this case. My reading of the pro-fetish argument as always already tethered to the nation through its reiteration of liberal conditions of normalcy points to a calculated management of the fetish domain that enables the nation-state to expand on and govern the domain of the normal. Consequently, fetishnormativity operates as a form of contracting between fetish subjects and the state, whereby the dissidence of the former is constructed as progressive and therefore "domesticatable" at the same time as it presents an opportunity for the state to demonstrate its capacity for tolerance through the recognition and inclusion of queer others.

Furthermore, in this bid for fetish citizenship, the progressive dissident summons and deploys state-nationalist Islamophobic discourses that target the veiled Muslim woman (in the West) as representing a type of transgression that is "undomesticatable" and therefore unworthy of state tolerance. In this discursive and virtual recalculation, we glimpse the emergence of the fetish patriot, whose "nationalized radicalism" is deeply enmeshed in Canada's imperialist "war on terror" at home and abroad. In this move, the fetish counterpublic joins "the good war" – against the patriarchy, homo- and queerphobia, sexphobia, and erotophobia that are supposedly Islam – and, in doing so, enables Western nation-states to imagine themselves as exceptionally tolerant through a queer-national simulation of the nation's future.

Notes

1 M. Warner (2005, 56–63) defines a counterpublic as a particular public existing "in tension with a larger public," although it "enables a horizon of opinion and exchange; its exchanges remain distinct from authority and can have a critical relation to power."
2 Denike (2010a) provides a good summary of these "homonormative collusions."
3 See Bilge (2010) for a discussion of the Western discourse of gender exceptionalism.
4 The acronym BDSM is an umbrella category for bondage and discipline, dominance and submission, and sadism and masochism. See Weiss (2011) and Newmahr (2011) for elaborate discussions of the complexities of defining BDSM.
5 According to Cossman (2002, 487) "normalization, in renouncing sex, renounces S/M subjects, sex worker subjects, public sex subjects, transgendered subjects – all those dissident subjects who remain saturated in sex, who affirm the abject, the dignity of the indignity of sex. Normalization operates to both desexualize politics and depoliticize sex."
6 The Toronto Leather Pride activities are hosted by the not-for-profit organization Heart of the Flag Federation.
7 Langdridge (2006) highlights how the British state has historically denied SM subjects' claims to legitimate citizenship in his discussion of the *Spanner* case.
8 This idea is influenced by Bilge's (2010) discussion of liberal humanism.
9 See Weiss (2011) for a more substantive discussion of these self-cultivating processes within the context of BDSM.
10 For Haritaworn, Tauqir, and Erdem (2008, 72), Islamophobic racism has become a vehicle for incorporation of "white gays and feminists into the political mainstream" in the context of western Europe.
11 See Bilge (2010, 14) for a critical discussion of the incongruity between agency (rational) and religious submission (irrational).
12 Puar (2007, 43) claims that gay-queer bashing is now considered a terrorist crime within national discourses. This collapses gays and queers into the nation, all united as "victims of terrorism."

Amar Wahab

3

Pink Games on Stolen Land
Pride House and (Un)Queer
Reterritorializations

SONNY DHOOT

Pinkwashing is a relatively new concept used to describe a strategy states utilize to rebrand themselves as tolerant and civilized in order to conceal a failure in human rights elsewhere. "Pinkwashing," in relation to gay rights, was coined first by activists to describe the mobilization of gay rights by the Israeli state in order to deflect attention away from the military occupation of Gaza and the settler occupation of the West Bank (Puar 2011). Through pinkwashing, Israel's most cosmopolitan city, Tel Aviv, is demarcated as a new global gay hot spot while the surrounding Arab and Palestinian populations are marked as homophobic. Such a figuration draws attention away from Israel's human rights abuses against Palestinian people (Puar 2010b). The positioning of Tel Aviv as the "best gay city"[1] in the world does not address, nor is it concerned with, the rampant homophobia in conservative and Orthodox areas of Israel where homosexuality is not tolerated and gendered dress codes are publicly posted. Jasbir Puar argues that, as it relates to homonationalism, Israeli pinkwashing draws on the inclusion of Israeli gays in (biopolitical) life in order to exclude Palestinian people and territory from life, thus relegating them to (necropolitical) death, mediated through Israel's defence of gay rights.

Contributions from queer of colour critique have interrogated the ways that queer activisms and practices fixated on liberal rights and inclusion in the law have now become yardsticks for measuring modernity and progress, a move that distinguishes the global South as "premodern" (Haritaworn, Tauqir, and Erdem 2008). In a bid to appear "gay-friendly" and as human rights defenders, certain Western states assert themselves as enlightened leaders through their inclusive gay rights laws, thereby allowing them to repudiate other states for their anti-homosexual laws. Pinkwashing is one such technology. By linking gay rights with modernity, pinkwashing also requires queer populations willing to engage in practices of homonationalism. This strategy allows for the inclusion of a historically marginalized group within the nation-state and consumer market, couching it in a discourse of progression.

In this chapter, I argue that Canada has begun to engage in practices consistent with the concept of pinkwashing.[2] My site of analysis is the 2010 Winter Olympic Games and the creation of Pride House as both a queer and colonial making of homonational space. Pride House was a space designated for lesbian, gay, bisexual, and transgender (LGBT) people to "hang out" and watch the games. It was initiated by a "queer steering committee" headed by the CEO of GayWhistler, Dean Nelson, in collaboration with the Vancouver Organizing Committee (VANOC). As taken up in Canadian gay media, Pride House stood as "another way of showcasing the inclusiveness that is being touted as part of the 2010 Games" (Hainsworth 2009). Although he did not directly reference Pride House, Prime Minister Stephen Harper referred to the games as a "success" that "showcase[d] the very best Canada has to offer in terms of ingenuity, friendliness, culture and diversity" (Government of Canada 2010).

I examine queer complicities in settler colonialism that helped to make these games appear as a project of emancipation and inclusion, allowing the Canadian nation-state to appear progressive. Such colonial violence took multiple forms, including imprisonment of Indigenous activists, continued land theft, and irreversible ecological and cultural destruction of Indigenous territories. These forms of violence are not new but are part of the state's ongoing project to eliminate Indigenous nations (Razack 2011). Given the extent of the colonial violence required to host the games in the first place, my chapter disturbs and disrupts the homonationalism at the heart of Pride House.

I apply the concept of pinkwashing to the Canadian context in order to explore the conjoined operations of biopolitics and necropolitics in a "progressive" settler society. Uncritically reading the inclusion of queer people as a signifier of progress fails to ask why (now) LGBT rights have become so important. As well, such assumptions of inclusion and progress figure queers as outside oppression. An analysis of Canadian pinkwashing opens up space to consider the figuration of Canada as a "gay haven" that simultaneously displaces Indigenous claims for sovereignty and self-determination. A discussion of the rise in LGBT rights without cognizance and contextualization of Canadian history erases the points of conjuncture where LGBT rights interlock with Canadian settler colonialism.

Sonny Dhoot

I use the term "queer" in this discussion as a descriptor for gender or sexual identities that disrupt or do not fit into heterosexual notions of identity. Although queer is hardly a white-only identity, it is part of a racially white-centred and white-dominated politics (Barnard 2008). Although there exists a politicized standpoint for queer people of colour, as "QPOC," that can potentially recentre anti-racism and the lived experiences and identities of queer people of colour within normatively white, mainstream queer politics, this alone does not centre queer Indigenous people, nor does it necessarily disrupt the settler colonial project. Thus throughout this chapter the terms "queer" and "queerness" refer to a predominantly white-centred praxis focused primarily on gay and lesbian subjectivity, which can and does "include" nonwhite and trans[3] bodies. Queer participation in the nation through nation-building projects such as Pride House takes place not only because queer identities have been welcomed into the national fold but also because non-Indigenous queers are residents of the white settler society.

This chapter now turns to a focus on settler colonialism, peeling away its layers to examine various points where Indigenous rights collide with homo-national claims.

(Re)Colonizing Unceded Land

Pride House was the name given to two explicitly LGBT spaces created for the Olympics by queers in collaboration with VANOC. VANOC was composed of a combination of International Olympic Committee (IOC) figures and Canadian political leaders. Beyond the affirmation of LGBT space within the Olympics by VANOC, one of the Pride House sponsors was the International Lesbian and Gay Association (ILGA), the largest international human rights organization for lesbian, gay, bisexual, trans, and intersex (LGBTI) people. The ILGA's sponsorship of Pride House positioned and affirmed Canada as an international beacon of human rights, thereby reproducing Canadian national mythology.

Pride House had two locations, one in the Coast Salish territory called "Vancouver" and the other in the Squamish and Lil'wat territory called "Whistler." Leading up to the games, a number of Indigenous communities and individuals, primarily the Secwepemc and St'at'imc First Nations along with Squamish elder Harriet Nahanee, protested the destruction of Indigenous territories taking place to accommodate the Olympics. In 2003 a delegation from the Secwepemc community travelled to the IOC's head office in Switzerland to oppose Canada's hosting of the Olympics on the grounds that Canada had not respected

Indigenous rights or communities. They argued that the reterritorialization undertaken by VANOC would continue to cause severe cultural and ecological destruction of Indigenous communities. The IOC either refused or ignored the request for support, as it provided no assistance to those Indigenous communities whose rights were being eroded and it demonstrated no concern for Indigenous peoples who would face further cultural and territorial loss due to the Olympics.

Within the Squamish community and territory itself, the Indian Act band-council leaders supported the games. Elder Harriet Nahanee, however, opposed the expansion of the SkyTrain and other developments that would encroach on Indigenous territory. Nahanee led the Eagleridge Bluffs blockade to prevent Olympic development, as it would lead to further destruction of ecology and traditional lands. Because of her protests, she was arrested and jailed for two weeks; the week following her release from jail, Nahanee was hospitalized for pneumonia-like symptoms, and she died two weeks later. Whether Nahanee's death was related to her jail sentence remains contested. Family members and fellow activists have thus called for an inquiry into her death.[4] Following these events, as a sign of solidarity with the dissenting West Coast Indigenous peoples, Six Nations of the Grand River (Haudenosaunee) forced the 2010 games to reroute the running of the Olympic Flame, disallowing the torch to run through its territory.

Several community and national organizations also protested the 2010 games, including anti-poverty coalitions, various anarchist groups and individuals, the Native Youth Movement, and No One is Illegal (NOII). NOII was a key organizer of the anti-Olympics movement. The organization itself is a highly vocal grassroots movement opposed to the Canadian state's erosion of Indigenous rights. Most of these groups and individuals acted in solidarity with Indigenous peoples, as evidenced through the predominant slogan "No Games on Stolen Native Land." One of the key anti-Olympics actions undertaken was the Welcoming Committee's march on 12 February to protest the opening of the 2010 Winter Olympic Games. Indigenous elders led the Welcoming Committee with two key supporting groups: NOII and "black bloc anarchists." NOII was involved primarily because of its consistent support of Indigenous rights as well as its key role in anti-Olympics organizing. Black bloc anarchists were invited to march because of their use of *diversity of tactics*. The elders asked that once the march arrived at the police line intended to stop the marchers, the black bloc be moved to the front so that its members could break the police line and allow the march to continue (Walia 2010).

Sonny Dhoot

Despite this widespread and organized Indigenous opposition to the games, VANOC continued to engage in colonizing practices against Indigenous peoples. Although four First Nations were chosen by VANOC to act as partners and "hosts" of the games, their inclusion was minimal and at best symbolic (Bourgeois 2009; O'Bonsawin 2010). Robyn Bourgeois (2009, 43) situates the participation of the host First Nations not as an inclusion of Indigenous peoples but as "nothing more or less than insurance that First Nation communities will not disrupt the games." Furthermore, none of the First Nations, including the host nations, were invited by VANOC to discuss any ongoing land or sovereignty disputes (Boykoff 2011; O'Bonsawin 2010).

Pinkwashing and Homocolonialism: Settling, Belonging, and Neoliberal Collaborations

It is within this framework of Canadian-Olympic colonization that Pride House must be understood. Located on two different sites, Pride House operated in multiple ways as a site of belonging and a site of settlement, both of which are projects of what Scott Morgensen (2011b, 2) calls "settler homonationalism," which was then used for Canadian pinkwashing. Morgensen elaborates on homonationalism with a deeper reading of US settler colonial history, arguing that particular queer claims to sexual identification within settler states have helped to figure Indigenous peoples "outside of life" and marked for death. I map these two operations of Pride House as practices of settler homonationalism through the following self-description of the Pride House in Vancouver, located at Qmunity (British Columbia's queer resource centre):

> This is the operational hub of PRIDE house Vancouver, with special events happening at various venues around town. Friendly *PRIDE house ambassadors will be able to fill you in on all that is fabulously queer in Vancouver*. We will also have on hand *immigration and refugee experts with a wealth of knowledge and resources for you*. There will be free wi-fi and a public access computer for visitors' convenience as well as a TV playing non-stop sports excitement. (Pride House 2009a, emphasis added)

What I emphasize in this description are two operations through which pinkwashing and homonationalism occur: *belonging* and *settlement*. Queer belonging and settling are possible only through colonial territorializations, in which many queer populations engaged through their partnership with the state in creating Pride House. The notion that Pride House Vancouver can "fill you in on all that is fabulously queer in Vancouver" while "immigration and refugee experts" are on hand to assist queers (re)affirms a settler logic because it positions unceded and contested Coast Salish territory as a potential site for settling and it shapes queer belonging.[5] Clearly, this belonging is not a joining of a Coast Salish community; belonging is meant to follow the state's ongoing denial of Indigenous inhabitants' claims and in turn remake the space into something "fabulously queer." Thus Pride House requires not only a reterritorialization but also a *de*territorialization of Indigenous space and place (Deleuze and Guattari 2004, 279). The historical colonial process entails the deterritorializing of Indigenous lands and bodies and their reterritorializing into "Crown lands" and "Indians" under the law. Moreover, the colonial process of deterritorialization further reterritorializes the bodies of settlers into (Canadian) citizens and reterritorializes Crown lands into the property of settlers; in the case of settler homonationalism, Indigenous territories are territorialized into LGBT space.

Considering the complexities of Canadian settler colonialism, I want to briefly map the colonial context that underpins and continues to shape and reshape the geopolitical, necropolitical, and biopolitical realm of Canada (Morgensen 2011b; Razack 2011; Thobani 2007). This colonial reality has been constructed through multiple sites, including the Indian Act, reserves, residential schools, treaties (broken or held), forced resource extraction, land theft, missing and murdered women, removal of children, and burgeoning prison populations. Colonialism is a process that has produced a "colonized population" that has not only been hidden away on reserves but also assimilated. Colonization is a process that produces two groups – the colonizers/settlers and the colonized/Indigenous – in a psychological and material relationship (Fanon 1967). Elaborating on this conception, Sherene Razack (2011, 114) states,

> Colonisation is not understood as something that also produced white settlers and their entitlement to the land, and the most that settlers can be guilty of is not understanding the historical situation into which they haplessly wandered. What this leaves out, of course, is settler violence and its source in a white supremacist colonial project that is ongoing.

Colonialism, here, is a past historical process that not only created a disadvantaged group but also produced two groups, with one entitled to the (land of the) other. It is also important to note that along with colonized Indigenous populations and white settlers, most queer people of colour can take up similar settler positions even if they hold them differently. They are nonetheless defined relationally to Indigenous peoples (Lawrence and Dua 2005), particularly as defined under the law (Razack 2011).

To replace Indigenous communities with Pride House is to perform the *logic of elimination* (Wolfe 2006). Patrick Wolfe conceives the concept of logic of elimination as the implementation of (settler) colonial systems and laws that eliminate Indigenous cultures, economies, communities, and laws, including membership structures. The intention is to eliminate Indigenous peoples, not necessarily via direct genocidal killings but through the removal of what Indigenous peoples require to perform their ways of life as particular peoples. They are then essentially unable to perform their culture or indigeneity. If there is no way to perform indigeneity, there will be nothing to consider Indigenous, people or otherwise.

In what follows, I explicate ways that queer practices of settlement, queer desires for belonging, and queer neoliberal collaborations are embodied in and through Pride House.

Settling

Narratives that construct the land as "being" Canadian, such as that articulated by Pride House, construct a sense of entitlement that allows non-Indigenous queers to think of spaces within Canada as being available for their rightful use: a homonational colonial logic (i.e., homocolonialism) that may also be shared by many queer people of colour. In this framing, it becomes unfathomable for non-Indigenous populations, queer and nonqueer, to consider the presence of "other" inhabitants of the land from whom they must seek permission – who are still alive and present and who continue to participate in land reclamation.

Australian scholar Damien Riggs (2006) notes that queers often (mis)recognize their relationship with Indigenous peoples as being neutral or view themselves as an injured group unconnected to Indigenous peoples. Analyzing the gay-injury frame that clouds critical discussions of LGBT rights, Riggs argues that white queers hold a *possessive investment* in the notion of the nation as white property. This is not because queers hold white supremacist beliefs but rather because many queer rights claims (particularly those that attach themselves to gay and lesbian subjectivities) rest upon existing liberal rights frames premised on notions of singular identities, which themselves are deeply embedded in the notion of white sovereignties and the denial of Indigenous peoples' claims to collective rights.

In the case of Pride House, LGBT space is produced within and from Indigenous territories, a colonial practice of erasure, eviction, and elimination, for the purposes of providing a venue where participants can "hang out" and watch sporting competitions. This produces a homocolonial-based logic of elimination, whereby LGBT space is (re)figured as no longer exclusively subversive to state control and heterosexism. In the case of Pride House, the homonational right to settle on Coast Salish territory was protected and made possible by military and police violence. Violence was exercised in the breakup of the Eagleridge Bluffs blockade, the attempted blocking of the Welcome Committee, and the arrests of multiple Indigenous activists. This relies on and reinforces the state's necropolitical relations with Indigenous populations (i.e., its right to *let live or make die*) and reinforces the biopolitical induction of queer populations into the nation (Morgensen 2011b; Puar 2007). I am not arguing that queers, or queerness itself, necessarily follow the logic of elimination but rather that liberal rights models, to which most contemporary homonationalist claims adhere, follow this logic of elimination.

Recalling Puar's (2012) attention to the fact that Israeli queer inclusion is not available to Palestinian queers, I add that Two-Spirit individuals within the Canadian context are largely excluded from partaking in homonational space. Many Two-Spirit people, including those who were part of the anti-Olympics movement, were likely to be unwilling to partake in an event that continued to appropriate their communities' lands and cultures.[6] As explained by Indigenous scholar Deborah Miranda (2010, 276, emphasis added), Two-Spirit people "serve the recovery of their Indigenous communities via the spiritual and cultural arts of poetry, fiction, visual arts, basket weaving, tribal leaderships, and *environmental activism*." Miranda (ibid., 277) goes on to explain that Two-Spirit is a matter not of "identifying as both [Indigenous] and gay" but of fulfilling responsibilities to the "social and cultural needs of contemporary Indigenous communities in relation to such issues as suicide rates, alcoholism, homelessness, and AIDS." Thus Two-Spirit peoples, although often assumed by the mainstream LGBT movement to be naturally part of their sexual and gender struggle, are indeed directly tied to their Indigenous communities and lands (Driskill 2010), which the 2010 Winter Olympic Games sought to violently deterritorialize and reterritorialize. Regardless of queer actors' intentions, Pride House helped to shut down discussion of continued land theft through a figuration of the IOC and Canada as supporters of LGBT rights.

Belonging
Settler colonial contexts such as Canada frame discourses regarding space within liberal notions of "equal access," wherein space is understood as something that

Sonny Dhoot

belongs to the state and to which all citizens have equal access (Kendall, Tuffin, and Frewin 2005). Space is figured as something that cannot be privileged or reserved for a specific group, as such a bestowal of status would be unequal and discriminatory. Often, when Indigenous claims to space, particularly those concerning traditional practices, challenge non-Indigenous claims, a liberal narrative that everyone should have access to space is offered. This notion of equal access produces Indigenous rights as racist on the ground that they favour a particular "race." Not only does this rhetoric collapse "indigeneity" into "race," but it also displaces the social, cultural, and political relations of Indigenous peoples with traditional lands through an "equal footing" view (LaDuke 1994), wherein the members of no race should be privileged in their access to space and resources. In 2006 Prime Minister Harper referred to a set of Indigenous fishing rights as producing "racially divided fisheries," and other political commentators claimed that the access to fishing was "race-based" (Milke 2006). These claims are evidently liberalist in nature, as liberalist conceptualizations are based on a rationality that all citizens are equal and should have equal access to space within the nation-state (Kendall, Tuffin, and Frewin 2005). Evidently, such liberalist logic informs homonational claims to space; in the case of settler colonialism, queers bypass a discussion of complicity and colonialism by relying on a liberalist foundation that appears both natural and neutral.

Although the logic of settler states is genocidal, there is a much more insidious politics occurring within Canadian settler colonialism. Morgensen (2011b, 42) argues that queer appropriation of Indigenous intellectual histories regarding nonheteronormative identities absents Indigenous peoples but "does not erase them so much as produce knowledge about them as necessarily disappeared." Although Morgensen's analysis indirectly refers to the common trope of the "disappearing Indian," one heavily entrenched within US politics, it is much more complex within the Canadian multicultural imaginary. I agree with existing literature that locates genocidal intentions within settler colonialism as always in play; however, Indigenous peoples' resistance to settler colonialism has forcibly made them visible, an effect most obvious in Canada. This insidiousness is evident with regards to state interests in promoting the visibility of Indigenous peoples. The representation of Indigenous peoples in largely benign ways at the Olympics – insofar as they did not contest the settler colonial state – may appear to contradict the settler colonial narrative of representing Indigenous peoples as disappeared; however, I maintain that such representations within multicultural discourses conceal settler colonialism and underlying genocidal goals.

Such representations are part of a larger trope used by the Canadian state at the Olympics and beyond primarily in its performances of official multiculturalism, where Indigenous peoples are made visible but in strategic ways that do not contest the settler colonial narrative. This also falls in line with the Canadian nation's fantasizing of itself as a tolerant and diverse society that celebrates its cultural mixture and lives in harmony with *its* Indigenous population, often colloquially performed through a contrast to the United States, which proposes assimilation over multiculturalism. In keeping with settler colonialism, these representations of Indigenous peoples have been usurped in order not to disrupt the settler narrative of disappearance, which therefore remains concealed. In addition, state multiculturalism and the Olympics collapse "indigeneity" into "culture" (as cultural difference) and allow colonial violence, both historical and ongoing, to be erased and replaced with practices inclusive of Indigenous cultures (Thobani 2007). Thus given the way that multicultural representations work, we might conclude that multiculturalism performs in agreement with the logic of elimination.

Such multicultural inclusions of Indigenous cultures were evident at the 2010 Winter Olympic Games, whose opening ceremony was led by Indigenous performers from Coast Salish First Nations and for which four First Nations were chosen as "hosts." This Canadian imaginary, however, is not out of line with the logic of elimination, nor is the apparent multicultural "celebration" of Indigenous peoples, as their presence here (primarily, the Indian Act band-council leaders) supported rather than resisted the state's claim to sovereignty over Indigenous peoples. Many queers actively engaged in the settler project as recognized members of the nation: settlers territorializing Indigenous lands into (homo)national space. Thus homonational space such as Pride House denotes not only a queer (re)making of the space that once belonged to Indigenous peoples but also a pronouncement of Canadian sovereignty over that space: homocolonialism.

LGBT rights are often simplistically read through a teleological tradition whereby an upholding of such rights, publicly sanctioned by VANOC, is understood as progressive. However, such a singular rights-based framework assumes that LGBT rights necessitate a celebratory response. One effect is that this places LGBT rights in a trajectory where they can be read only as progressive. Such a reading ignores the extent to which queer rights discourses latch onto other forms of oppressions not to alleviate them but to rely on and reproduce them in order to advance homonational claims. This facilitates pink-washing, whereby LGBT rights conceal human rights abuses by the state against other groups. Although pinkwashing as a strategy used by settler states to conceal their denial of rights to other groups is a fundamental component of this analysis, this consideration alone does not recognize the extent to which non-Indigenous queers themselves actively participate in *their* settler states. I am speaking of queer complicities that are evident both in the acceptance of rights given out by the state and in the adamant claims by many queers themselves to these rights. Such adamant claims of entitlement to the space of Pride House were evident in every queer and gay magazine article that I read on this event and in all the news coverage that I viewed (a basic online search provides dozens of pages that take up this narrative).

The inclusion of openly queer people in the Olympics, displayed in public discourses solely through white gay subjects such as torchbearer Steve Parent-Korbie and Olympians Mark Tewksbury and Marion Lay, was paradoxically performed in a space apart and thus out of sight of the "heterosexual mainstream" (Alexander 2006a), which was presumably not as welcoming of queer people into the nation as it was made to appear. In response to an online *Xtra!* article about Pride House, one commenter sarcastically wrote, "Let's segregate ourselves while screaming for acceptance. Nice."[7] It is no wonder that many had not even heard of Pride House, least of all from the mainstream Canadian news channels that televised the 2010 Winter Olympic Games, which for the most part appear to have not even reported on Pride House. Much of the discussion regarding Pride House took place on gay-media news sites and, more importantly, in the international community. Pinkwashing has less to do with the state taking up LGBT rights than it does with the state creating the perception that it is taking up LGBT rights (i.e., "queer visibility").

Neoliberal Collaborations

Returning to Riggs's (2006) analysis, although I agree that many queers often misunderstand their relation to Indigenous peoples, I argue that homonational legal figurations in Canada help to facilitate pretexts for the dispossession and elimination of Indigenous peoples. Queer legal claims based in homonationalism add legitimacy to liberal framings of rights, where rights are understood as something possessed by individuals rather than collective groups. Within the liberal rights framework, Indigenous peoples may put forth rights claims only as individual persons. Such practices are evident in the reparation payments for residential school survivors, where compensation is given in the form of money, which is paid to individual survivors with no community payments. Furthermore, the discussions of reparation payments have never made room for the prospect of reparations through the returning of stolen lands. For Indigenous communities, these rights frameworks have often resulted in "justice" in the form of financial payments (to replace appropriated lands) or royalties for resource extractions that damage cultural and ecological systems. Such rights models also hold the potential to reduce Indigenous lands and communities to private properties rather than collectively held territory.

Liberal rights unsurprisingly flow into neoliberal models, where rights are consolidated through their relations to free markets. For queers, this has often taken the form of a right to their own markets, which has produced queer niche markets (Alexander 2006a). Pride House Whistler focused more on a commercial celebration compared to Pride House Vancouver, which focused on LGBT-resource information. Pride House Whistler was made possible through a colonial process undoubtedly similar to Pride House Vancouver. However, PRIDE House Whistler was in partnership with Pan Pacific Hotels and Resorts, which represents queer participation in an ever-expanding (globalizing) economy of hotels (Alexander 2006a; Puar 2002b). Pride House Whistler was located in Whistler Village. Dean Nelson, CEO of GayWhistler stated,

> We are so excited to be able to work with Pan Pacific Hotels and Resorts, a hotel chain that embraces similar values we hold dear; the value to be authentic, the value to embrace diversity and the value to be inclusive. Together, we will create a welcoming space for our gay and lesbian community and their allies to go to during the Olympics. (Pride House 2009b)

Within the Winter Olympics' settler colonial expansion onto Indigenous peoples' territory, Pride House took place through a neoliberal economy of hotels. As Sedef Arat-Koç, Aparna Sundar, and Bryan Evans (2007) explain, hotels in countries such as Canada rely primarily on exploitable labour of a racialized and migrant workforce whose members work dead-end and hazardous positions. These exploitive practices are directly tied to "neo-liberal restructuring and the logic of global hyper competition" (ibid., 17). This phenomenon is particularly evident with Pride House Whistler, where queer tourists (predominately white and gay) flocked to Pride House despite its location in a tourist locality and thus disregarded opposition to the games, further consolidating the Canadian state's negation and erosion of Indigenous rights.

The tourism of the Olympic Games was focused on commodification not only of Canadian culture but also of the Indigenous, inviting the appropriation and consumption of the racial Other (O'Bonsawin 2010). Many of the Olympic souvenirs and garment images relied on characters and caricatures appropriated from various Salish and Inuit nations (Bourgeois 2009; O'Bonsawin 2010). Queer participation in the Olympics did not acknowledge Indigenous peoples but partook in the national project of appropriating and consuming indigeneity. In her seminal essay "Eating the Other," bell hooks (1992, 22) writes, "From the standpoint of white supremacist capitalist patriarchy, the hope is that desires for the 'primitive' or fantasies about the Other can be continually exploited, and that such exploitation will occur in a manner that reinscribes and maintains the status quo." Commercializing Indigenous cultures for a primarily white settler consumer during the 2010 Olympics reinscribed the relations of power between settlers and Indigenous peoples, replaying a colonial script in which the "primitive" (body, space, and culture) belongs to white settlers.

Among other noted issues of concern to anti-Olympics protestors were sponsorship of the 2010 games by documented human rights violators and alleged war profiteers, including Bombardier, General Electric, Dow Chemical, and Coca-Cola, and apparel manufacturing by companies alleged to use sweatshop labour. Anti-Olympics activists also alleged that Vancouver had turned into a militarized zone due to an influx of military and police personnel as well as the contracting of surveillance to the Honeywell company for more than $30 million (Privacy Commissioner of Canada 2009). Although queer participants in Pride House may have sought to distance themselves from these surveillance and military operations because they did not see themselves as actively engaged with either, this understanding attempts to delink queers from oppression. Pride House was undeniably linked to the 2010 Winter Olympic Games, whose military and surveillance technologies sought to defend the "Olympic zone" and keep the anti-Olympics protestors from disrupting the celebration, queer or otherwise.

Although I situate settler colonialism as the underpinning mode of domination and control in Canada, Olympic colonialism operated in conjunction with multiple forms of oppression: labour exploitation in garment manufacturing and the use of migrant labourers by hotels, gentrification through forcible removal of homeless people and sex workers from the zone, and corporatization through sponsorship support from corporations involved in global human rights abuses. The 2010 Olympics' pinkwashing allowed the gentrification that took place in downtown Vancouver to be hidden, particularly from the international community, in spite of anti-Olympics protests that sought to disrupt the celebratory tone of the games. The centring of Pride House in the media both as "the first Olympic Pride House" and as one endorsed by the international human rights organization ILGA counteracted the claims of human rights abuses against Indigenous peoples evidenced in the popularized hype surrounding Pride House as a signifier of Canadian progress.

Conversely, gentrification and forced evictions, among other human rights abuses, were extremely well known and publicized during the 2008 Beijing Summer Olympic Games. In the Western imagination, the presumed answer to the question "what human rights do the Chinese have?" is none, or at least none that "we" already have. Canada is able to escape allegations about its own human rights abuses by positioning rights violations as characteristic of communist (i.e., repressive) states such as China rather than gay-friendly liberal democracies such as itself. This stance operates much like Israel's pinkwashing, which places greater attention on human rights abuses in surrounding "Islamic" countries, especially on the so-called "gay executions" in Iran, thus directing attention away from Israel's occupation of Palestinian territories. Western states such as Canada utilize China for juxtaposition, painting it as a repressive political space apart, one that has committed appalling human rights abuses that Canada would not.

Conclusion

I consider the 2010 Winter Olympic Games to mark a major epistemic shift in Canadian queer politics toward the collusion of LGBT rights progression with state interests and discourses of settler colonialism, nationalism, gentrification and poverty, corporatism, and militarism. A large number of queer actors in Canada consciously and willingly partook in advancement of state projects, namely those involving not only settler colonialism but also neoliberalism and consumer capitalism. I situate homonationalism both in epistemic terms and within a trajectory of settler colonialism intended to eliminate the Indigenous peoples of Turtle Island.

In Canada these queer politics and the nation building of the white settler society are deeply interconnected. Pride House, through its colonial invitations to settle and belong, extended an invitation to willing queers to imagine themselves as national subjects. The queer figure, categorically white and cisgender, least of all Indigenous, was extended an explicit role in this incarnation of the white settler project; without objection, rather than shifting or imploding the national figure, queerness here shifted to homonationalism. Already complicit in the state project, the homonational figure was now specifically invited and expected to partake in settler colonialism. In turn, Indigenous rights at the 2010 Winter Olympic Games became figured as being in opposition to LGBT rights and space. Yet as I have argued throughout this chapter, Indigenous rights

Sonny Dhoot

continue to challenge the settler state, thereby disrupting homonationalist claims to belonging.

Elaborating on Puar's (2007) discussion of US homonationalism, we might note that many Canadian sexual and gender queers performed an "unqueering" (or "dequeering") of themselves by allowing their assimilation into the nation, whereas Indigenous peoples' refusal to assimilate and their unwillingness to recognize the settler state's legitimacy performed "queer" (De Genova 2010). This performance of queerness was seen in how Indigenous resistance destabilized naturalized borders, colonial laws, liberal rights discourse, blood and hereditary norms, family formations, and most of all the sovereignty of the Canadian nation-state. Inclusion of queers in the Olympics through homonationalism relied on decades of police violence against Coast Salish peoples and their eviction from the Vancouver area, making this exclusion a necessary part of LGBT history. This was a major shift away from queer histories that reveal opposition to police targeting of LGBT people (see also Gentile and Kinsman, this collection; and Fink, this collection).

This chapter has focused on the 2010 Winter Olympic Games for two reasons. First, Pride House was the initial attempt at pinkwashing in Canada following a rise in homonationalist discourses about issues such as same-sex marriage. Subsequently, pinkwashing was employed by politicians who declared their support for LGBT refugees in order to keep out undesired groups.[8] Second, the 2010 Winter Olympics highlighted the settler project, a reality that too often becomes forgotten or simply negated as disparate from the discussion of LGBT rights or from "war on terror" discourses when in fact these issues are inseparable from the colonial state's genocidal project and goals. After all, Canada has not stopped being a white settler society in regards to immigration reform, LGBT rights, environmental concerns, or "war on terror" discourses – the white settler project remains the foundation of Canada.

I point out the issue of ongoing colonial projects in Canada because it becomes difficult for groups to make claims against the state for human rights abuses when it upholds them elsewhere – especially somewhere that is temporally and spatially specific to Canada and other white Western nations. Nonetheless, with the 2010 Winter Olympic Games, a collusion took place that meshed queer discourses with settler colonialism, nationalism, gentrification and poverty, corporatism, and militarism. This chapter outlines the Canadian practice of pinkwashing while also contributing to the mapping of Canadian homonationalism as linked with settler colonialism.

It is outside the scope of this chapter to suggest solutions beyond abstractly rejecting these settler-homonationalist rights claims that allow for the continued denial of Indigenous rights. However, both Morgensen (2011b) and Riggs (2006) advise that non-Indigenous queers challenge this problematic relationship by looking at Indigenous rights and self-determination as the starting point in order to place the question of collective rights within a historical context. This was my starting point for analyzing Pride House. As Sunera Thobani (2002) succinctly states, "We have to recognize that there will be no social justice, no anti-racism, no feminist emancipation, no liberation of any kind for anybody on this continent unless aboriginal people win their demand for self-determination."

It is not uncommon to hear that Canada has been a human rights defender, but such rhetoric risks obscuring centuries of genocidal colonialism. The "washings" in Canada, like pinkwashing in this analysis, will always be useful for the settler colonial project, as it lies at the heart of what must be concealed and denied.

Notes

1 Several mainstream and LGBT news sources have made this point (see Gray 2012; and G. Smith 2012).
2 An earlier version of this chapter was presented at the Canadian Sociological Conference in June 2012.
3 The Pride House website contained a document entitled "Chalk Talk: Inclusion of Transgender Athletes on Sports Teams," authored by well-known transpolitics author Pat Griffin. The article has a celebratory tone and educational aspect regarding "transgender" participation in sports. Another key celebratory component is the International Olympic Committee's "Stockholm Consensus," a report declaring that "transsexual" people can participate in Olympic games. However, transpolitical discussions concerning this "inclusion" seem to ignore the extent to which transsexual participation in the games requires strict hormone and genital guidelines and does not rule out the invasive policing measure of gender testing, let alone break the gender binary.
4 See the subsection "Call for Inquiry into Death of Harriet Nahanee" in Government of British Columbia (2007).
5 I situate Pride House's provision of "immigration and refugee experts" as part of settler colonial discourses because of the implied invitation to settle on contested and unceded Indigenous territory, which Indigenous peoples continue to claim. However, I do not situate all forms of migration as a settler colonial *logic of elimination;* for example, Alain Tom (2009), of the Native Youth Movement, stated during an anti-Olympics speech, "We believe that immigration is a human right; everybody has the right to live here." What I am emphasizing is that Pride House's creators understood themselves as rightfully responsible for allowing settlement on Coast Salish territory and, in facilitating immigration, attempted to erase Coast Salish communities.
6 One notable exception to the absence of Two-Spirit figures from the 2010 Winter Olympics and Pride House was the participation of Sandra Laframboise, an "Algonquin–Cree Metis Elder to the Two Spirited People," who provided a "blessing" during the ribbon cutting

for the Pride House Whistler opening ceremony. I do not want to dispute or interrogate the intentions of Laframboise in participating in Pride House, but I do want to point out several items for consideration based on the information available. Laframboise is an elder of the Two-Spirit community in urban Vancouver, and she is a trinational Indigenous person whose national belonging spans from what is now Alberta through what is now Ontario. Laframboise's participation is described by Pride House only in terms of the "blessing" she provided, with no information as to its contents. I make this last point because elders usually provide blessings that welcome nonmembers onto their territory, and Laframboise gave her blessing on Squamish and Lil'wat territory despite being from elsewhere. It is possible that she was asked to give a blessing by the Squamish or Lil'wat, but this request is not indicated anywhere. Bourgeois (2009) claims Indigenous inclusion in the Olympics was intended to ensure Indigenous peoples did not disrupt the games. Thus the Indigenous opposition to the games alongside the inclusion of a Two-Spirit Indigenous elder who blessed contested space is highly problematic, and this inclusion alone should not legitimatize non-Indigenous queer participation in the games or Pride House. Likewise, although a number of gay organizations participated in the event or acted as partners, hosts, or sponsors, no Two-Spirit organizations were present in any of these capacities. At the "Pride at Toronto 2015" workshop that took place on 23 November 2012 to strategize about the inclusion of a Pride House at the Pan-American Games, Dean Nelson explained the blessing in this way: "Someone approached us about doing this ... [We] found a Two-Spirit person ... to do a sage-ing and blessing of Pride House ... [It's a] very West Coast thing" [room erupts in laughter]. Later, when Nelson was questioned about the Indigenous opposition to the 2010 Winter Olympic Games and the responsibility of LGBT people, he paused and then said, "I don't know how to answer that." After another extended pause, Nelson stated something like, "We included a First Nations person to bless Pride House." Thus I am even more skeptical that Pride House's inclusion of Laframboise was meant to be a critical engagement with Indigenous peoples. Rather, I believe that Pride House appropriated the blessing as an Indigenous practice to legitimize itself.

7   "Comments: Mike, [Vancouver, BC,] May 15, 2009 at 10:13pm" (in Hainsworth 2009).

8   Since 2010 the minister of citizenship, immigration, and multiculturalism, Jason Kenney, has continuously pushed for the participation of LGBT refugee organizations in the governmental restructuring of the refugee program by positioning undesired and unwanted refugees as "false claimants" who take away spaces from "legitimate" (LGBT) claimants. Pinkwashing is evident both in the lack of attention to LGBT rights as the issue and in the greater concern with the refugee program's restructuring and its exclusion of "illegitimate claimants." See Kenney's letter to the editor "Kenney Responds to Immigration Story" (2012), Andrea Houston's article "Jason Kenney Defends Gay Refugee Email" (2012b), and Danny Glenwright's editorial "Tory Embrace Just for Show" (2012).

4

Disruptive Desires
Reframing Sexual Space at the
Feminist Porn Awards

NAOMI DE SZEGHEO-LANG

> We watch and talk about our porn in public. We won't do it quietly;
> we won't do it in private. Just like we won't talk about our sexuality in hushed,
> shameful whispers. We'll do it *in public*, proudly.
>
> **– Tristan Taormino, "Opening Address," Public Provocative**
> **Porn Panel, Feminist Porn Awards 2011**

Public.Provocative.Porn: The Year's Best in Feminist Film is an annual event that takes place as part of the Feminist Porn Awards (FPA) in Toronto, Canada. It features porn screenings of FPA-nominated films in public theatres, alongside panel discussions on topics surrounding feminism, porn, art, and representation. Started in 2006 by the feminist sex shop Good For Her, the FPA celebrate pornography that challenges dominant, mainstream depictions of sex and sexuality while offering complex, multifaceted representations of women and other marginalized people. Originally conceived as a way to "recognize erotic

---

AUTHOR'S NOTE: In the years since this chapter was first written, there has been a proliferation of work on feminist porn as a topic of scholarly and cultural analysis. The Feminist Porn Awards have continued to grow and adapt with encouragement from ongoing industry, community, and sociopolitical conversations; this evolution, as I argue, is one of their strengths. The annual Feminist Porn Conference has established itself as an important addition to critical conversations, and there is an increasing wealth of published writing on the topic of feminist porn.

filmmakers who are creating hot, sexy, woman-positive porn," the awards have since grown to highlight a broad diversity of "ethical, feminist smut" (GoodForHer.com n.d.). Each year, a jury comprising members of the FPA organizing committee and people invited from the community award films, performers, producers, and websites for achievements ranging from "Sexiest Short" and "Most Deliciously Diverse Cast" to the "Smutty Schoolteacher Award for Sex Education" and "Heartthrob of the Year." A combination of playful humour and insightful intellectualism, the awards and the works they foreground offer alternatives to widely proliferated (mis)conceptions of those working in porn industries and present opportunities to shift engagements with visual representations of sex and desire. By celebrating feminist porn, the FPA are an important intervention into mainstream pornography's stereo-typical and marginalizing representations, but they also operate on a broader scale to challenge normative state regulations of homonormative and homo-nationalist public sexual space.

"Feminist porn" is a term that has been taken up to describe a loose as-semblage of pornography and explicit imagery that interrupts dominant and often exploitative production standards. The growing practice of naming some porn "feminist" is a relatively new phenomenon with a long history, as many of its main tenets and goals draw on other delineations of past and present porn movements, such as alt porn, indie porn, queer porn, postporn, and woman-positive porn, to name a few. Although there is no universally accepted set of criteria for what makes a piece "feminist" *enough* or "pornographic" *enough* to be included in the category, feminist porn generally begins from a process-centred belief that we do not need to eliminate porn and the sex industry, as some fervently argue, but that we *do* need to work to change it both from within and without.

In this chapter, I take up the Feminist Porn Awards to explore the potential of feminist porn to challenge state-sponsored regulations of sexuality. I argue that through their focus on pleasure, desire, agency, and boundary-expanding representations, the FPA simultaneously unsettle normative conceptions of sexual citizenship and disrupt homonormative and homonationalist narratives. Although the work of the FPA is certainly not exhaustive or all-encompassing, and is always and importantly contested, the FPA function on multiple levels – local, interlocal, national, and transnational – to force public visibility and attention in order to disrupt borders and boundaries between "public" and "private" realms of sex and sexual representation.

The pervasive racism, marginalization, and disempowerment found within many mainstream porn productions were major driving forces behind the creation of the FPA. Good For Her owner Carlyle Jansen and the original FPA organizers wanted to recognize people who have chosen to make porn differently and publicly support their work. According to their website, the FPA encourage filmmakers to submit "anything that reflects eroticism," although to be considered for an award, entries must meet at least two of the following criteria:

1) Women and/or traditionally marginalized people were involved in the direction, production and/or conception of the work; 2) The work depicts genuine pleasure, agency and desire for all performers, especially women and traditionally marginalized people; 3) The work expands the boundaries of sexual representation on film, challenges stereotypes and presents a vision that sets the content apart from most mainstream pornography. This may include depicting a diversity of desires, types of people, bodies, sexual practices, and/or an anti-racist or anti-oppression framework throughout the production. (GoodForHer.com n.d.)

Beyond these broad requirements, there are no specificities that must be met in terms of identities, sexual acts, embodiments, or sexual dynamics represented (the exception, of course, being the minimum legal age of consent). These criteria have been shifting and will likely continue to shift as conversations persist and ways of demarcating what constitutes a challenge to dominant stereotypes in porn become increasingly nuanced.

The lack of definite boundaries for what may or may not be considered feminist porn allows for expansive and productive potential. Within the murky waters of incoherent or incomplete categorization lie potent possibilities for imagining and reimagining what "better" porn might look like. The FPA are part of larger artistic and political movements that seek to imagine and create new sex-positive and people-positive pornographies. Feminist porn directs conversations away from longstanding moralistic debates about censorship or abolition and toward a focus both on the modes of production and on the ethics of engagement with porn and sex(ual) representation. In this piece, I explore the conceptual and physical spaces that are opened up when we adopt a starting place that no longer treats "feminism" and "porn" as mutually exclusive categories. Positioning the two as incommensurable denies a world of political reworking and shuts down invaluable lines of thought. Many people were engaged in discussions around these issues prior to the creation of the FPA, and women and feminists were making porn long before the mid-2000s, but the awards

Naomi de Szegheo-Lang

have fostered an important opportunity to critically engage issues of explicit sexual representation and sexual performance.

It would seem that more of this space is slowly being created in feminist communities. However, despite this push, there has also been a resurgence of anti-porn and sex-negative publications by authors like Sheila Jeffreys and Gail Dines. This chapter joins a renewed and growing response in academic scholarship to such works and contributes to a body of knowledge that rejects calls to abolish the porn industry in favour of critically reconsidering and reconstructing its terms.[1]

The FPA have been transformed from a one-day celebration and awareness-raising night into a relatively large-scale annual production consisting of multiple fundraising events throughout the year. A network of feminist porn lovers and porn makers is supported through the FPA, and extensive international conversations have been sparked. After several years, it is clear that the FPA have made their mark on public dialogue around possibilities for empowerment and nonexploitation in porn. Although they are not exclusively nor explicitly queer, the FPA are a project of queering dominant paradigms and rupturing normalizing imperatives; in these interventions, they create space for critical dialogue and re-presentation. Through these disruptions, the FPA demand a public engagement that reframes possibilities for sexual citizenship by unsettling normative constructions of desire, intimacy, and national (un)belonging.

In the following sections, I expand on this claim through three interrelated discussions. First, I map out ways that constructions of the ideal subject-citizen are organized through regulations of sexuality in "public" and "private" spheres. I contemplate how the awards recentre sexuality and sexual representation and situate themselves outside of the proverbial and physical "home" rather than remaining complicit within it.[2] In blurring the lines of public-private divides, the FPA contest normative ideas around citizenship and sexual participation in public discourse. I argue that by drawing sexuality and sexual representation into public space, they force a visibility that challenges current heteronormative, homonormative, and homonationalist practices.

I then consider the mobilizing potential of affect and affective attachments, notably the role of desire in feminist porn production. I contemplate how (re)centring desire at various points in the production process may disrupt normative systems and promote new engagements with normative sexual citizenship, agentic sexuality, and marginalized bodies. I conclude with a consideration of critical community building through the FPA. In drawing focus away from regulating borders and boundaries, the FPA shift energy toward new and fluctuating creativities and community constructions, and in distancing themselves from neoliberalism's preference for individualizing models of personal success, the FPA facilitate a valuing of collaboration, political and artistic exchange, and community-building projects.

Throughout this chapter, I highlight some of the disruptions in both discursive practices and lived experiences of homonationalisms that have occurred at the FPA, drawing on the development of collaborative communities that can be either tangible or not, that are based around desire and around feminist world making, and whose projects are intimately bound up in reimagining terms for sexual engagement and explicit sexual representation. I draw out connections between sexual depiction, queer (re)formulations, and homonationalist state-sponsored space, while exploring what might be at stake in shifting porn's terms of engagement.[3]

Public Space, Private Sex: Blurring Bounds at the FPA

Speaking out about feminism and porn, art and politics, the FPA have been framed by organizers and attendees alike as a refusal to remain quiet and invisible when it comes to desire, pleasure, and sexuality. A major element of the awards has been their role in facilitating public recognition of and engagement with so-called "non-normative" sex and sexual images. Performances and screenings have run alongside public dialogue at FPA events from the beginning, starting with the inaugural roundtable discussion, where feminist porn makers considered issues in the creation of pornography and sexually explicit material. In pushing early public engagements with "private" sexualities, the FPA have sparked ongoing, international debates and controversies over possibilities for creating and recreating porn genres.

Homonationalisms, and citizenship more broadly, are deeply embedded in considerations of sexuality and sexual representation, racialization, and settler colonialism. In their influential essay "Sex in Public," Lauren Berlant and Michael Warner (1998) draw out deeply entrenched citizenship narratives through a discussion of sex and sexuality. They articulate a tension that exists in the social construction of the ideal neoliberal subject-citizen: the "proper" and "acceptable" citizen is expected to keep sex acts (especially so-called non-normative ones) contained within private spheres, yet one's recognition as a full citizen also requires public visibility and active participation in public domains. Dominant ideas of citizenship, therefore, both demand and remain dependent on accessing an engagement with the state that is necessarily and exclusively normative and therefore largely desexualized. These regulations of

Naomi de Szegheo-Lang

citizenship are exacerbated and further solidified in homonationalist spaces, where any dissent is positioned as anti-national, as dangerous, and often as terrorist (Puar 2007).

As a sort of precursor to discussions of homonationalism, Lisa Duggan (2003, 50) has put forward the term *homonormativity* to signal practices that belong to a privatized, depoliticized gay culture based in domesticity and material consumption. According to Duggan, a homonormative gay politics "does not contest dominant heteronormative assumptions and institutions, but upholds and sustains them" (ibid.). Within neoliberal frameworks, "the new homonormativity" further solidifies links between domesticity and privatized sex, patriotism, and access to the "free market" (Duggan 2002, 179). Within this structure, many gay and queer people adopt dominant modes of being – complete with the colonial, racist, homophobic, and sex-negative qualities of each. The more "acceptable" of marginalized people are called on to act as agents of the state, policing themselves and others within seemingly similar social circumstances. Picking up on the ways that homonormativities prioritize national(istic) participation, homonationalisms further centre appeals to national belonging for certain gay and queer subjects.

Homonationalism rests on the promise that those who adhere to the normative values of sex and sexual practice will eventually be granted state acceptance and support, whereas those who cannot or will not adhere are denied the same approvals. It is within this context that mainstream activist energies and resources are often directed toward making appeals to "human rights" (i.e., appeals for official acceptance from the state), and certain segments of sexually marginalized populations are drawn into this narrative and continue to propagate it. Members of marginalized communities must consistently negotiate tensions between making precarious lives more livable and participating in state projects that (continue to) leave the most vulnerable at the bottom of the priority pool, notably people who are racialized or Indigenous, who are under- or unemployed, who have mental or physical health concerns, and who engage in sex work. This "trickle-down" approach rewards those who are willing and able to successfully keep their "private" activities separate from their public and working lives and, again, penalizes all others.[4] Perhaps unsurprisingly, this pits those who will and/or can remain quiet about their sexuality and sexual expression against those who will not and/or cannot. The ongoing effects of colonialism, classism, ableism, and homophobia mean that many people may not have a choice to begin with; marginalized bodies are repeatedly and consistently assigned a "perverse" meaning and are subsequently denied agency (Butler 2008; Erickson 2009; Puar 2007). These types of "divide and conquer" tactics have long been cultivated by dominant structures, yet their pervasiveness resonates with renewed fervour in contemporary rainbow nationalisms and neoliberal pressures.

Within the context of neoliberal citizenship, Berlant and Warner (1998, 553) make links between normalizing sexual imperatives and affective experiences that become attached to them. They argue that feelings of relation such as intimacy – both as an affective attachment and as a cultural construction – are increasingly narrated as private connections and are linked to privatized sex, coupledom, and family, while being distanced from work and (normative) public engagement. In contemporary sex-negative and erotophobic worlds, fear and disdain become fixed to bodies that blur the lines between intimate feelings and public lives. Sexual bodies, desiring bodies, and consenting bodies – especially when they belong to already marginalized people – invoke particularly harsh sanctions in attempts to control and manage their scope of visibility. There is resistance to be found, then, in asserting agency and taking control over whom and what is made visible and under what circumstances.[5]

In refusing to allow sex, porn, and desire to remain locked within private realms, the FPA resist dominant ideals of quiet and polite citizenship. These resistances actively complicate what is expected of subject-citizens in "public" and "private" sites, pulling content across borders and piercing existing boundaries between the two. An ever-growing number of events held in conjunction with the FPA offer forums for critical engagement with feminism and activism, while exploring the transformative potentials of sex. This process works toward a powerful reimagining of a queer sexual citizenship that does not depend on state narratives and nationalist rhetoric but resists easy identification and prefers the development of messy conceptual frames and indefinite spatial delineations.

Similarly, the term "feminist porn" is continually being (re)defined by the content that is taken up under its name. The scope and foci of the FPA shift slightly each year depending on submissions and attendees, and they remain in perpetual conversation with themselves. Tensions and dissent within producer, performer, and viewer communities resist easy categorization of content, which ensures unsteady and expanding meaning over time. Although the concept of feminist porn is more widely accepted now than it once was (e.g., the FPA have been profiled by national and international newspapers and by independent and informal news sources), feminist porn still comes under heavy scrutiny and debate. This tension, however, is productive, a crucial element in resisting its settling into static conceptions of (just) another form of "alternative" porn. Because terms often circulate and become mainstreamed to the

Naomi de Szegheo-Lang

point of losing the dynamic meanings they were initially taken up to indicate, the productive potential of "feminist porn" is retained by the FPA's commitment to maintaining a level of instability and incoherence.

These circular processes are critical to maintaining a politics of resistance; there is danger in anything becoming too comfortable with itself. Legacies of colonial and neocolonial systems insist on clearly (often falsely) delineated categories with the aim of management and control. This biopolitical project consistently plays out through bodies, which come to stand in for the nation and national borders.[6] Access to "private" and "public" experiences are necessarily bound up in the state regulation of bodily movement, sexuality, and affective deployments.

Marginalized bodies are frequently placed within a false dichotomy of being either desexualized or hypersexualized and are positioned as always already perverse (Erickson 2009; Puar 2007). These systems are clearly linked to investments in dominant neoliberal nationalist rhetoric and in the reification of borders between "public" and "private" spheres. In addition, marginalized people are still disproportionately the target of consistent and repeated portrayals that signal unworthiness and an inability to express desire. The FPA challenge these dichotomous constructions in prioritizing productions that offer multiple representations of agentic sexuality and active consent across a range of bodies, identities, sexual interactions, and desiring practices.

Desiring Bodies Desired

Although sexuality often factors into demarcations of "public" and "private" space, acknowledgment of the affective role of desire is curiously absent from nationalist rhetoric. Interrogating this silence is a worthwhile endeavour. What role might desire, both spoken and unspoken, play in the (re)framing of space? Because of its attention to bodily relations, desire is often framed as a particularly "messy" topic and is frequently replaced with sanitized considerations of sex in normative concepts of sexual citizenship. When it is addressed, it is most often heedlessly attached to sexual acts, to "orientation," or to listless mentions of attraction. These translations, however, only attempt to concretize (and control) an affective relationship that is, at its core, unfixed.

The FPA, along with much of feminist porn more generally, value the role of complex and manifold desire throughout the process of production. Prioritizing desire along with active agency, sex positivity, and pleasure resists the sanitized sexualities that often come to permeate the ideal subject-citizen. Creating and screening sexually explicit images that represent nondominant and/or queer desire interrupt the inactive depictions of marginalized people that circulate within homonationalist frameworks. In many FPA-nominated films, marginalized bodies are positioned both as desirable and as actively desiring – no small feat among the narrow scope of representation within traditional mainstream pornography.

In mainstream productions, it has been standard for marginalized people to face severe limitations and to be contained within "exceptional" spaces of representation.[7] Desire for marginalized bodies is often positioned as existing only within the realm of fetish or exoticized "niche markets" and is devalued accordingly (Erickson 2007). The bodies and interactions of performers, as well as the sexual acts performed, are generally marked through the simplified taxonomies used in the categorization of porn scenes on DVDs and online, with race, size, and gender being most commonly demarcated if and when they deviate from white, small, and curvy, cisgendered (i.e., nontransgendered), heterosexual, and female. Often, the further away from this ideal (potential) performers are, the more restricted their performance opportunities become.

Loree Erickson, a self-identified "queer femmegimp pornstar academic" and winner of "Sexiest Short" at the FPA in 2008 for her film *Want,* discusses the impacts of such strict limitations of representation for people with disabilities in "Revealing Femmegimp" (2007). Erickson positions her own work as an interruption of widely circulated ideas about people with disabilities being "unsexy" and necessarily incapable of sexual desire or agency. She interrogates the production of shame that occurs through these narratives and argues that "one of the main effects of shame is to keep us isolated and separate from our bodies/selves, and from each other." She goes on to explain how "this isolation and separation from others and ourselves keeps us from unlearning the current body politic and discovering new ways of being in the world" (ibid., 43). Through the regulation of desires, she argues, social action, activist organizing, and dissenting mobilizations are quelled. Erickson discusses the necessity of shifting the existing record and of creating narratives that position typically "undesirable" bodies both as desirable and as actively desiring.

These types of dissenting representations are especially important given the deeply Eurocentric nature of the bulk of mainstream porn. All too often, marginalized bodies are considered to be inherently disruptive (Erickson 2009). Presenting active desires and engagements of people of colour, Indigenous people, and otherwise "transgressive" bodies is a radically important political project; it is a political act for people with little control over how they are represented to (re)claim the power of production (Erickson 2007, 47). Director Nenna, winner of "Most Deliciously Diverse Cast" in 2011 for *Tight Places:*

A Drop of Colour and winner of "Hottest Dyke Film" in 2012 for *Hella Brown: Real Sex in the City,* emphasizes that productions featuring casts composed mostly or entirely of people of colour, and made by people of colour, are still far too difficult to find (HotMoviesForHer.com 2012). Similarly, Tobi Hill-Meyer, winner of the "Emerging Filmmaker Award" in 2010, discusses problems of representation(s) for trans women in sexually explicit film, noting that a vast number of films and scenes that feature trans women continue to be created by cisgendered and white producers (QueerPornTV 2011; Taormino 2012). Although even cisgendered and white people working with trans and racialized bodies might work to diversify existing representations, both Nenna and Hill-Meyer stress the importance of placing the bulk of the power of such representations in the hands of those who have been marginalized under pervasive systemic oppressions.

Drew Deveaux, a performer in several films, including Hill-Meyer's *Doing It Ourselves: The Trans Women Porn Project,* and winner of "Heartthrob of the Year" at the 2011 FPA, picks up on these ideas and expands upon what she positions as great transformative potentials in sex and pornography. Deveaux claims that "porn has a lot of educational potential" and "a lot of potential to really change, and be a tool for, activism" (HotMoviesForHer.com 2011a). She sees possibilities for dismantling cissexism, cisnormativity,[8] and other forms of systemic oppression through explicit sexual imagery. According to Deveaux, "the bedroom is the last frontier of social justice" – a measure of the possibilities for and limitations of desire, personal interaction, and broader representational practices.

The intersections between Deveaux's assertions and those of Erickson and others indicate that bedroom borders offer a way to look at community borders and, further, that they are implicated in and reflective of national borders as well; there is a flow of desire between micro, local, and national space. Porn, in general, threatens the supposed order of things by bringing an act that has been increasingly privatized and individualized – sex – into public spheres of business markets and capital gain. When combined with the active engagement of people who have been constructed as disruptive just by virtue of their existence, feminist porn is imbued with a vast power to transform relations.

Live, in 3-D!

Further to centring desire generally, many of the productions highlighted at the FPA also make an effort to prioritize performer desire rather than existing solely for that of viewers. Productions often trace, reflect, and record the kinds of sex that performers have in their own lives and/or want to be having, while frequently providing opportunities to play out scenes of performer fantasy and desire. In this intersection of various desires and pleasures, these productions walk an interesting line between "real" representations of sexuality and consumer desire for "authenticity" in the images they consume.[9]

This creation of space is a deliberate move for many filmmakers. Producer-director of many winning FPA titles Tristan Taormino, for instance, articulates clear personal production ethics for her projects. She is one of several people who involve performers in planning scenes and who highlight active desires of those on film. She includes interviews with performers throughout her DVDs and encourages performers to speak for themselves where possible. Extended interviews are a common feature of many productions that are highlighted at the FPA. Shine Louise Houston and Pink and White Productions, responsible for an extensive list of films as well as for the popular sites CrashPadSeries.com and HeavenlySpire.com, include many nonsex clips of performers and production crews on their member sites and in a publicly accessible online video stream. QueerPorn.TV (created by performer-producers Courtney Trouble and Tina Horn), too, features online bios and performer interviews, as well as links to performer Twitter feeds and other social media. These interactive platforms show people involved in porn to be outspoken, articulate, and dynamic in the work they create, and they allow for a variety of critical public engagements with porn performers and content producers.

Taormino explains the importance of this dynamism in an interview with J.D. Bauchery of HotMoviesForHer.com (2010). She positions her directorial strategies as especially important given that sex workers often circulate in public discourse as two-dimensional figures who are consistently undervalued and dehumanized. In having stars discuss their fantasies, motivations, and choice of co-star(s) on screen, her productions actively interrupt dominant constructions of porn performers as service workers who are solely directed by those working behind the camera. Acknowledging, and interacting with, performers as skilled labourers is central to Taormino's approach. This is one of the foundational values in her version of "ethical porn" production (which she likens to a type of "organic, fair-trade" porn), where production sets are stocked with everything from performers' preference of toys and safer-sex products to nutritious snacks and other items that make working conditions as attentive and comfortable as possible. For Taormino, this is one way of recognizing that porn performers work physically demanding jobs that can and should be approached with the same progressive politics as other labour and employment practices – even though, and perhaps especially because, this work involves sex and desire.[10]

Naomi de Szegheo-Lang

Desire is undeniably complex and manifold; a realistic engagement with desire again requires an approach based on nondelineation and destabilized conceptual boundaries to allow for its complex ebb and flow, layers, counterlogics, and incoherences. In valuing sexual interactions that are attentive to performer desire, feminist porn creates an ambiguated archive; in hosting and recording a cross-section of these scenes, the FPA end up tracing an unofficial and always incomplete map of community engagements, while strengthening community development of their own.

Desiring Community

Not only do the FPA offer an opportunity for in-person discussion and debate, but at FPA events it is also common to find resource sharing, artistic collaboration, and interlocal and international community support. Interestingly, although in many ways the awards are constructed around desire, they also resist emotional coherence and host a diversity of relations (e.g., socially, culturally, and politically) to sex and sexuality. The FPA attract people from many different social worlds; despite several pre-related community members who attend regularly, there is no one "type" of person who gathers each year (other than, one might assume, those who are in some way interested in feminist porn). Of course, any community has its own exclusions, and I do not mean to suggest that the FPA are somehow an exception. However, it would be fair to assume that the diversity of participants reflects equally diverse investments and reasons for attending, as well as a multitude of relationships to porn, feminism, desire, public space, sociality, and representation.

Because of the still relatively small numbers of performers and producers involved in feminist porn, these productions also tend to map out community bonds, friendships, relationships, and partnerships of various kinds. The desire to develop sex-positive, pleasure-positive communities indicates another form of national dissent – one that rejects the persistent devaluing of collaborative endeavours, responsibility, and care that is often found within neoliberal and homonormative modes of relation. There is good reason for national systems to uphold discursive silences around desire: desire threatens the normative order of things. In short, desire disrupts.

The push toward models of individual success and production is intimately bound up in the proliferation of homonationalisms; the way that certain, "more normative," subjects are placed against the most disruptive (and therefore the most violently resisted) often breeds a culture of competition, hostility, and suspicion. Through feminist porn, however, possibilities for artistic, political, and desiring communities are expanded, reframing interactions and further exploring important conceptual space. Many people involved in feminist porn express a desire to participate in (feminist) forms of world making. In fact, many openly express wanting to change the world – one porn at a time. The FPA work on multiple levels to foster spaces of recognition, networking, critical celebration, and community building through pleasure and desire.

These spaces of potentiality might be thought of as communities of desire. They could be placed within and stand alongside various alternatives: communities *through* desire, communities *with* desire, communities *for* desire, desiring communities, and so on. The FPA provide a complex and critical opportunity for reimagining and resignifying space, for drawing focus away from clearly delineated borders and boundaries, and for encouraging an energy shift toward new creativities and collaborative constructions.

Since their inception, the FPA have become a gathering site for many sex-positive queers and feminists – an ever-growing collection of people – and negotiating the intricate connections that sometimes arise in such close-quartered spaces seems to have become par for the course at these events. Although such interactions come with their own set of complications, the ways that desire for or within certain communities mobilizes people, or the ways that embodying desire relates to desiring bodies, pleasure, passion, and erotics, should not be underestimated in this conversation: with desire and the making of new worlds comes intense affective investment.

The awards offer space to model new ways of relating to and around sex, intimacy, desire, and creation. There is often overlap or crossover between porn performers and porn makers; many performers have produced content, and many content producers are former or current performers. Many people cite the inspiration and support of the FPA as leading to the realization of projects; for example, QueerPorn.TV was conceived at the FPA in 2010, and Toronto local N. Maxwell Lander started creating content after FPA encouragement in 2011. The kinds of collaboration that occur between and among performers, producers, directors, and other content makers again blur the bounds of compartmentalized relations, all the while embracing the messiness of "appropriate" roles within private and public spheres.

Other commitments that blur or conflate these realms are similarly devalued or dismissed, as with nonprofit and social workers, artists, activists, and those who perform various forms of affective labour. Perhaps it is no coincidence that many feminist porn makers take up one or more of these other roles as well. Each has a particular set of contexts and considerations, but the individuals in all of these roles face a general refusal or withdrawal of support for their work that leads to devaluation and restrictions. Projects like the FPA reinstate some of the public support that has been denied by mainstream normalizing narratives.

Conclusions

As a critical celebration and engagement with feminist porn, the FPA do several things. To start, they draw awareness to porn productions that can be identified as "feminist" in some regard, as laid out by the organizers and jury. They also allow for many ground-level possibilities for engaging with these bodies of work, including developing archives of feminist porn and community archives of desire,[11] sparking conversation and debate around what makes (or could be qualities of) porn that is loosely recognized as "feminist," "nonexploitative," "ethical," "indie," "queer," and so on, and encouraging more people to create collaborative and diverse representations of sex and sexuality. However, perhaps one of the FPA's most valuable contributions thus far has been in their demand for public presence and their fostering of visibility, their pushing conversation forward, and their reframing of discourses around porn and feminism – a discursive shift.

The focus of the FPA on ethics and engagement rather than on the always and exclusively negative aspects of porn encourages a move away from what Eve Sedgwick (2003) has called paranoid readings, a type of overinvestment in criticism, and toward more nuanced ameliorative, or reparative, readings. Kath Albury (2009, 649) draws on Sedgwick to ask how even "flawed or imperfect" porn might provide opportunities to move from dualistic either/or approaches to more productive and complex analyses of pornography and sexual representation.

Instead of turning away from negative and potentially harmful portrayals, feminist porn turns toward them in order to confront them head-on. Rather than responding to negative aspects by rejecting the whole genre, feminist pornographers have disidentified with the format, (re)making it consciously and with intention.[12] The FPA celebrate such disidentifications; they are a critical project in reimagining that highlights realistic engagements with the "bad feelings" that arise from dominant portrayals in porn, while giving space to hope and futurity in refiguring sexual representation.

The FPA open lines of discussion and sustained engagement through the conscious creation of space for complex, and often subtle, nuanced representations of various marginalized people. Still, it is crucial to ask how we might continue to take seriously the ways that biopolitical state projects reinforce homonationalisms and further marginalize those who have been made most vulnerable. The sexual policing of bodies is deeply embedded in normative colonial systems and national histories, and a multiplicity of tactics and strategies is needed to address the multiple levels on which homonationalisms operate. More work must always be done to decolonize and challenge the logics of neo-liberalism, settler colonialism, (homo)nationalisms, and erotophobia. Although decidedly (and with self-awareness) nowhere near enough to address the per-vasiveness of these issues on their own, the FPA and the communities they support are one step toward unlearning and denaturalizing deeply held norma-tive assumptions and discursive oppressions.

The awards offer a space where such questions might be taken up by ex-panding the representation of marginalized people and by repurposing public space as sex-positive, sex-worker-positive, body-positive, and anti-oppressive. The physical and conceptual borders that are permeated by the FPA have im-plications that reach far beyond the porn industry; these interruptions are connected to the disruption of *all* borders, including gendered, raced, classed, colonial, and national ones. They target nationalist ideologies of sex, sexuality, and sexual representation, while unsettling relations between citizenship and normative notions of privatized sex. The work of feminist porn and the FPA supports a critical project of reimagining that continues to reinvent and remake itself, while ultimately feeding into a feisty feminist movement that accedes no bounds.

Notes

1 Examples of recent sex-positive and sex-worker-positive publications are *The Feminist Porn Book: The Politics of Producing Pleasure* (Taormino et al. 2013) and *New Views on Pornography: Sexuality, Politics, and the Law* (Comella and Tarrant 2015).

2 For a similar discussion of challenges to sexual citizenship and privacy in the context of the Toronto Fetish Fair, see Wahab (this collection).

3 To think through the set of dissenting spaces that make up the FPA, I must also consider personal experiences and the role of my own communities. I write this piece from a situated position, approaching it as an insider in some ways and as an outsider in many others. I am a white, able-bodied, middle-class, sex-positive, and sex-worker-positive feminist queer who has participated in various forms of sex(ual) counterpublics, including porn perform-ance, public sex, nude and erotic modelling, and other queer-sex activisms. I have, at dif-ferent times, been more and less involved in these spaces. Although I have modelled and performed, my personal involvement with porn and with the FPA has remained relatively limited, and I have not thus far defined myself, nor have others defined me, primarily through my engagement with these realms. In a world that is heavily invested in policing borders of all kinds – including borders between those who would/could/do perform sex work and erotic labour and those who would/could/do not – I offer recognition and respect to those for whom this is not the case.

4 Attorney, educator, and trans activist Dean Spade (2009) has articulated the flawed logic behind such "trickle-down" approaches to human rights and protections. He has joined others in making a call to shift activist strategies toward prioritizing care and attention for the most vulnerable first, with the understanding that such interventions will benefit all people, from the most disenfranchised upward (what he terms "trickle-up" social justice).

5 For further discussion of the politics of visibility in porn, see L. Williams (1999).

6 For a discussion on nation, national borders, bodies, and blood, see Dryden (this collection).

7 For a more in-depth discussion of the limitations faced by racialized porn performers, as well as shifting possibilities of representation, see Hoang (2004), Miller-Young (2014).

8 "Cissexism" is a term used to indicate "the belief that transsexuals' identified genders are inferior to, or less authentic than, those of cissexuals" (Serano 2007, 33). Cisnormativity firmly upholds a binary gender system and refers to "the expectation that all people are cissexual, that those assigned male at birth always grow up to be men and those assigned female at birth always grow up to be women" (Bauer et al. 2009, 356). Both terms point to systemic supports for such views, as well as the privileges and barriers that are created in allowing these essentialist and essentializing notions of gender to continue unchecked.

9 For further discussion, see Attwood (2007). Fiona Attwood's case study of online community sites in the late 1990s and early 2000s examines consumer demands for "authenticity" in sexual representation. She looks at new "sex taste cultures" and highlights the way(s) that commerce and community are becoming increasingly intertwined as sexual display and participation infuse more aspects of community building in online life (ibid., 441). In her discussion, she touches on consumer demand for porn that reflects contemporary real worlds (or the appearance of real worlds) and consumer desire for porn that fits into existing practices of media consumption and interactive technologies (ibid., 452).

10 For a discussion of these, and other, elements of "organic, fair-trade" porn production, see Taormino et al. (2013). For further discussion of sex work as labour in national and transnational contexts, see van der Meulen, Yee, and Durisin (2010), Kempadoo (2003), and Brock et al. (2000). For community resources, research, and action projects that are driven by sex workers and geared toward improving the working and living conditions of all those working in the sex industry, see the Montreal-based organization Stella (chezstella.org) and the Toronto-based organization Maggie's (maggiestoronto.ca).

11 Other projects, such as the Feminist Porn Archive and Research Project, headed by Bobby Noble and Lisa Sloniowski at York University, have also started taking on the digitizing and archiving of woman-positive and/or feminist porn in an attempt to preserve this aspect of feminist histories.

12 For more on disidentifications, see Muñoz (1999).

5

Monogamy, Marriage, and the Making of Nation

SUZANNE LENON

It is March 1899, and in a courtroom in Fort MacLeod, Alberta, a man named Bear's Shin Bone is criminally charged for entering into a polygamous marriage with two Kainai women. Viewed as a test case following the new (1892) Criminal Code's provisions prohibiting polygamy, *R. v. Bear's Shin Bone* is one element in federal government initiatives to refashion Indigenous kinship structures to fit a Christian, patriarchal, monogamous family model.

Flash forward 106 years to 2005. Canadian politicians pass the Civil Marriage Act, which gives same-sex couples the right to marry. In so doing, they cement monogamy's privileged place as the nation's normative family-sexual structure. In public discourse, support of same-sex marriage operates as a metonym of *what* Canada as a nation stands for and what it means to *be* Canadian.

Six years later in November 2011, the BC Supreme Court releases a *Reference* decision that upholds the Criminal Code's provisions prohibiting polygamous marriage. The court asserts that polygamy is antithetical to the value of gender equality, which is part of Western civilization.

These three vignettes highlight the state's vested and enduring interest in determining who can form a family and which family forms count as legitimate. Land, blood, and economies of capital, labour, gender, race, and affect are ties that bind body to family, family to nation, nation to body. Marriage law in

Canada is but one route through which the state regulates, manages, and sediments such ties in the service of nation building. Our kinship and intimate ties, then, are never only private matters. Rather, they might be thought of as "intimate publics" (Wiegman 2002).

The practice of polygamy, whether given public attention in news stories about the openly polygamous community living in Bountiful, British Columbia, or treated as a central storyline in popular television programs such as *Sister Wives*, *Big Love*, and *Breaking the Faith*, is a current example of such intimate publics, one that, I argue, is entangled in histories of race, colonialism, empire, and civilizational discourses. The 2011 BC Supreme Court *Reference* decision on polygamy (hereafter, the *Polygamy Reference*) reveals these histories as enduring in the present. As Angela Davis (2008) remarks, "Histories never leave us for another inaccessible place. They are always part of us." This chapter seeks to illuminate sets of historical relationships – settler colonial, racial, imperial – that join across time to profoundly condition the content and meaning of this legal decision on polygamy.

The *Polygamy Reference* began with the laying of criminal charges against Winston Blackmore and James Oler, two leaders of the Fundamentalist Church of Jesus Christ of Latter-Day Saints (FLDS) in Bountiful, British Columbia, who openly practise polygamy as a central tenet of their faith. The community of Bountiful has long been the subject of investigation by the Royal Canadian Mounted Police; concurrent to this, the attorney general of British Columbia had actively sought legal advice from three different special prosecutors to determine whether Blackmore and Oler could be charged for violating the Criminal Code's prohibition against polygamy[1] (section 293) without such a charge being interpreted as violating their freedom of religion as guaranteed under the Canadian Charter of Rights and Freedoms (hereafter, the Charter). In 2008 the two men were arrested only to have the charges against them quashed by the BC Supreme Court in 2009, on account of what appeared to be an overly aggressive approach by the attorney general of British Columbia in pursuing a prosecution. Instead of appealing this decision, the attorney general decided to seek an advisory opinion from the BC Supreme Court, in order to determine whether and to what extent section 293 is consistent with rights guaranteed by the Charter.[2] Known as a "Reference," this is a way for courts to hear complicated questions with respect to the constitutionality of the government's laws in a fairly expedited way. While often viewed as authoritative on the point of law, the opinion given is advisory only, meaning that governments are not bound to act upon it (Calder 2014, 218). The parties to the *Polygamy Reference* were the Attorney Generals of Canada and British Columbia who argued that section

293 should be upheld. An *amicus curiae* (friend of the court) was appointed to present the opposing view. Additionally, there were submissions from eleven interveners and over ninety affidavits and reports from both expert and lay witnesses. The reference hearing was held before Chief Justice Robert Bauman and in November 2011 he issued his decision upholding section 293 as constitutional. He judged that although the Criminal Code violates freedom of religion and affects liberty interests of children between the ages of twelve and seventeen who marry into polygamy (guaranteed under sections 2(a) and 7 of the Charter, respectively), such a violation is justifiable because the pressing and substantial objective of section 293 is the prevention of harm to women, to children, and to the institution of monogamous marriage (para. 5, 904).[3]

As I will show, what is striking about the *Polygamy Reference* decision is how explicitly its discursive narrative evokes a civilizational ethos in which polygamy emerges as a threatening spectre of degeneracy. This compelled Justice Bauman to state that both Parliament and the courts had a responsibility to "draw a bright line" that would explicitly reflect the pre-eminence of monogamous marriage as a value inherent to Western civilization and society (para. 1040-41); and section 293 *is* this bright line. Notably, same-sex marriage is enfolded within this delineation of monogamy's "bright line." Couples in committed same-sex relationships figure as civilized subjects who safeguard the material and symbolic "life" of Canada from the inherent harms posed by polygamous marriage. The *Polygamy Reference* thus mobilizes a homonational critique of polygamy in its deployment of same-sex marriage to index the constitutive borders of Western civilization. As chapters by Dhoot and Awwad in this collection make evident, the ascendancy of homonationalism does not have to be enacted by lesbians and gay men alone but can be taken on by the nation-state itself. Law is one site where this occurs, and this chapter examines points of homonational collusions exercised through the *Polygamy Reference*.

However, critiquing this legal decision as homonationalist requires foregrounding homonationalism not as an epithet but as a field of power. In this chapter, I illustrate the relations of power at play that enabled the *Reference* decision's homonationalist claims to be made in the first place, namely settler colonialism, racialization, and empire. My reading is a palimpsestic one, in that I understand the "time" of marriage law in Canada as bearing the visible traces of its earlier forms. The three opening vignettes highlight the historical continuities of marriage law and its investments in sexual modernity, which is at once colonial, racialized, and imperial. This chapter suggests that the homonationalism evident in the *Reference* decision is both informed and enabled by these sets of historical relationships.

Suzanne Lenon

The first part of the chapter examines how the "truths" of polygamy are produced through a discourse of harm that ultimately idealizes monogamous marriage in an ahistorical manner. In particular, I consider how the court arrived at a critique of polygamous marriage through a disavowal of settler colonialism, an act that simultaneously naturalizes the Canadian nation-state within a historical trajectory of Western liberal democracy. The second section examines how processes of racialization and empire further enable the homonationalism of the *Polygamy Reference*. I examine the metaphor of contagion, which sanctions polygamy's truths, drawing attention to the racial (and racializing) narrative of the *Reference* decision, particularly with respect to immigration and to how Bountiful, both as a place and as a narrative, might be thought of as a story of whiteness. It is against the spectre of polygamy's contagious effects that same-sex relationships become enfolded into the biopolitical mandate of preserving monogamous marriage and, by extension, Western civilization. The *Polygamy Reference* strikes me as an anxious piece of writing; that is, white anxiety over sex and reproduction (both of populations and Western/Canadian values), over immigration, over national "life" and well-being. My analysis contends that the discourse of harm and trope of contagion together come to shape the meaning of section 293 as a "bright line" in ways that sustain racialized and settler (homo)national formations of Canada.

Conceptualizing Polygamy's Harms: "There Is No Such Thing as Good Polygamy"

In the *Reference* decision, the various "truths" about polygamy are produced through a discourse of harm. Evidence from the social sciences and scientific experts, together with testimony from lay witnesses, overwhelmingly establish polygamy's inherent truth: that it "is inevitably associated with sundry harms and these harms are not simply isolated to criminal adherents but *inhere in the institution itself*" (para. 1343, emphasis added). Polygamy's harms, both current and anticipated, include increased rates of violence against women, reduced gender equality across society, higher infant mortality rates, an escalation in crime rates due to an anticipated large pool of unmarried men, poverty, welfare fraud, a weakened democracy, and a decline in national wealth (GDP). According to the expert evidence in evolutionary psychology submitted to the court, crime rates, for example, would increase if polygynous polygamy[4] were decriminalized due to the creation of a pool of unmarried low-status men unable to find wives (paras. 505–7). Indeed, monogamous heterosexual marriage is understood as making "men much less likely to commit crimes such as murder, robbery and rape" (para. 509). The court sided with the proposition that "monogamous marriage suppresses men's criminality" (para. 510). In other words, it civilizes men.[5]

An intriguing patriarchal property logic underlies this argument: despite suggesting that polygamous marriage is bad patriarchy for the high incidences of violence against women that it engenders, the argument implies that the privilege polygamy assails is male; that is, it limits men's "access" to women, who implicitly figure as property to be distributed among men. Since women are presumably a civilizing force, maintaining their availability for men is key to minimizing male aggression and violence. As feminist scholar Lori Beaman (2014) has argued, this notion of "surplus men" distracts from broader economic, race, and class inequalities that may produce such groups of men in the first place, and does not address the propensity to engage in war among nations that are not polygamous (150). Ultimately, the court determined that polygamy's harms "can be generalized and expected to occur wherever polygamy exists," including in polyandrous or same-sex polygamous relationships (para. 14, 1045). To the extent that polygamy may not be inherently harmful, Justice Bauman determined that *the risks* of its social, economic, and political harms are considered serious enough that criminalizing all polygamous marriages is not viewed as a disproportionate response (para. 1220).

"Truths" about monogamy are produced in equally essentializing terms yet with very different effects. Monogamous marriage is represented as a key historical factor in the development (and continued well-being) of Western civilization, democracy, and political equality, including gender equality. The institution of monogamous marriage is foregrounded as that which is *"naturally* designed to respect gender equality" (para. 214, emphasis added). Gender equality within monogamous marriage is not understood as the outcome of fierce feminist legal, political, and social struggle but is produced as an inherent feature of and within monogamous marriage. Justice Bauman does concede that monogamous marriage is not a uniformly positive experience for everyone. He briefly speaks to the harms arising out of monogamous marriage, such as violence against women and children, but in so doing remarks that these seem "beside the point" (para. 543). Disavowing the violence and the numerous inequalities legally and socially produced by the institution of monogamous marriage becomes a way to successfully construct polygamy as its absolute antithesis. Monogamous marriage does not afford unique protection from gender inequality and harm. Feminists have long critiqued the gendered, racialized, sexualized, and economic nature of inequalities and violences that inhere

Suzanne Lenon

within the institution of heterosexual, monogamous marriage (see Boyd 2013; Cott 2000; and Pateman 1988). Yet in this *Reference*, only polygamy is subject to special critique.

In short, the "truth" about monogamous marriage that circulates widely throughout the *Polygamy Reference* is that it best ensures "paternal certainty and joint parental investment in children. It best ensures that men and women are treated with equal dignity and respect, and that husbands and wives (or same sex couples), and parents and children, provide each other with mutual support, protection and edification through their lifetimes" (para. 884). Again, a logic of patriarchal property glimmers in the implication that monogamous marriage best ensures "paternal certainty" over man's property (in this case, his children), one intertwined with the neoliberal, market-infused language of "investment" in familial relations. Monogamous marriage can be understood here as offering an aspirational route to that "moral-intimate-economic" form of life Lauren Berlant (2011, 2) calls the "good life," with its fantasies of upward mobility, security, enduring reciprocity, and durable intimacy. Add to this that monogamous marriage best ensures the self-realization and moral uplift (i.e., edification) of its family members, it becomes clear that "the negative and the positive aspects of the polygamy prohibition are two sides of the same coin" (para. 885). That is, section 293 of the Criminal Code "abates the harms to individuals and society associated with polygamy, and it protects and preserves monogamous marriage, the institution believed to advance the values threatened by polygamy" (para. 885). In the context of such objectives, the court can assert that "there is no such thing as so-called 'good polygamy'" (para. 1343).

This statement is telling, not only for the way the court fails to make explicit the distinction between polygamy as an inherently exploitative institution and the way it exists as a variable practice between individuals but also for the ways it handled competing truths about polygamy's endemic and inherent harms. Law and its citational practices construct particular forms of knowledge that masquerade as grand "Truths" in the shape of norms (Osterlund 2009, 96). My aim here is not to determine the truth or falsity of the evidentiary record submitted to the court. Rather, it is to point to the interlock of truth and power that effectively delegitimizes some knowledge claims and authorizes the resilience of others. Justice Bauman, for example, was faced with expert evidence submitted by the *amicus curiae* cautioning against facile acceptance of stereotypical and uniform portrayals of what are in fact quite heterogeneous experiences of women globally living in polygamous communities.[6] Such evidence sought to counter totalizing claims about the oppression of women by highlighting mutuality and women's agency within polygamous relationships. The court was fairly dismissive of such feminist evidence, finding it sincere but somewhat naïve (para. 752).

The *amicus curiae* also entered expert evidence arguing that Christian beliefs in the primacy of monogamous marriage, together with anti-Mormon sentiment, had originally propelled the Canadian Parliament to write anti-polygamy legislation in 1892.[7] The court rejected this by maintaining that Parliament's prohibition on polygamy was motivated largely by secular concerns with perceived harms to women, children, and society. The aversion to polygamous marriage "has always been seen as addressing the risk of harm to women and children" (paras. 1088–89). However, the handful of reported Canadian cases that have interpreted this provision do not mention this objective.[8] Moreover, as some Canadian feminist research argues, section 293 is in fact punitive to women, as it applies to *anyone* over the age of eighteen; in other words, women, too, can be criminally charged under the polygamy provision, and feminist legal scholars have expressed reservation that this may in fact impede women from leaving abusive polygamous relationships (Bailey et al. 2005).

As Margaret Denike (2010b, 140) notes, there is plenty of historical evidence to suggest that what really troubles the Western imagination about polygamy has less to do with ensuring personal and societal relations of gender equality than with making sure that such relations are not tarred with the brush of barbarism or "foreign" cultural practices. While much of the contemporary anxiety about polygamy is articulated through the language of gender equality, the racialized roots of anti-polygamy legislation in both Canada and the United States run deep. Nineteenth-century anti-Mormon discourses often analogized Mormons to Muslims and polygamy to harems. Together with slavery, polygamy figured in the United States as one of the "twin relics of barbarism" (Gordon 2002). In a leading anti-polygamy case of the late 1800s, *Reynolds v. United States* (1878), the US Supreme Court remarked that until the establishment of the Mormon Church, polygamy was "almost exclusively a feature of the life of Asiatic and of African people" (Ertman 2010; Gordon 2002). Similar to the *Polygamy Reference* discussed in this chapter, the *Reynolds* decision marked polygamous marriage as antithetical to Western civilization. There was a series of increasingly harsh laws targeted at the territory of Utah, the aim of which was not only to root out the practice of polygamy but to punish the Mormon Church through a legal assault on its members, its holdings, and its political power (Rifkin 2011, 165). As Martha Ertman (2010) has argued, a critical component of such legal and political campaigns was to constitute polygamy

Suzanne Lenon

as "race treason" – that is, as an imminent threat both to the nation's moral and racial identity and to the political order of a Christian nation-state.

Canadian anti-polygamy legislation arose out of cross-border pressure from the American government to address polygamy practised by Mormons who were migrating from Utah to southern Alberta in the late 1800s to flee this persecution. It contained a clause targeting Mormons that was not removed until amendments were made to Canada's Criminal Code in 1954 (Bailey et al. 2005, 23). This legislation perhaps derives less from the threat posed by Mormons to the Canadian moral order than from ongoing challenges to narratives of settler sovereignty posed by the persistence of Indigenous peoples on their lands (Rifkin 2011, 165). As historians have noted, Canadian government officials were concerned that the Mormons arriving in southern Alberta – that is, occupying and settling on Blackfoot territories – would encourage the Blackfoot to continue to practise polygamous marriage and they would learn not only that what was understood as polygamy among the Blackfoot was not yet illegal (Carter 2008, 205–6), but that such kinship formations persisted in spite of efforts of the Department of Indian Affairs and missionaries to impose British norms of lifelong, Christian, heterosexual marriage.[9]

Sarah Carter's (2008, 13) historical research reveals that until the late nineteenth century, measures aimed at eradicating what was understood as polygamy among Indigenous peoples in Canada remained tentative and cautious, both due to the fear that a prosecution for polygamy would not hold up in court and because of the resistance of Blackfoot people to interference in their domestic affairs. But with the 1892 anti-polygamy provision, the Department of Indian Affairs more actively pursued a more forceful reconfiguration of Indigenous kinship structures (Carter 2008). In fact, a notable feature of the arrests of Winston Blackmore and James Oler of Bountiful is that they marked the first time that the anti-polygamy provision had been used against the specific religious minority that it was allegedly drafted to target. Until now, the only conviction has been against an Indigenous man, Bear's Shin Bone, who was brought before a judge at Fort MacLeod in March 1899 for forming a polygamous marriage with two women of the Kainai Nation. The judge in the case determined that the marriage customs of the Blood (Kainai), which allowed for more than one wife, were contrary to the Criminal Code.[10] Upon conviction, Bear's Shin Bone stood at risk of five years' imprisonment or a fine of five hundred dollars. As Carter (ibid.) has argued, this case was both the effect and culmination of a decade of such efforts by the Department of Indian Affairs, which also included withholding rations and annuities, placing second wives in residential schools, and subdividing land on the Kainai Reserve into small lots to deter large extended families and promote nuclear breadwinner families. In many ways, then, the Bear's Shin Bone case is representative of the shifting terms of recognition by the settler Canadian state of Indigenous marriage customs between Indigenous peoples. Where these customs violated central Euro-Canadian, Christian beliefs they were increasingly condemned in court cases, with the force of criminal law, as was the case with Bear's Shin Bone (Backhouse 1999a).

In the *Polygamy Reference,* the *amicus curiae* submitted expert evidence that contextualized section 293 as a tool of settler colonialism in order to make its case that the provision is historically bound up with mainstream Christianity and thus infringes upon religious freedoms. Justice Bauman, however, ultimately situates *R. v. Bear's Shin Bone* as but one example in the long arc of Western civilization's efforts to eradicate polygamy. This discursive move produces Canada as a Western liberal democracy unmoored from its enterprise as a white, settler colonial nation-state. Such an unmooring naturalizes settler colonialism as a condition of our present. The disavowal of *R. v. Bear's Shin Bone* as settler colonial obfuscates the state's investments across time in regulating legitimate family forms. Yet such investments are not *completely* elided as Justice Bauman, when speaking of the pre-eminence of monogamous marriage to Western culture, avows that "we have come, in this century and in this country, to accept same-sex marriage as part of" the institution of monogamous marriage (para. 1041).

Herein lies the palimpsest of this court decision. The haunting presence of *R. v. Bear's Shin Bone* in a contemporary legal text that steadfastly normalizes monogamous marriage as the privileged condition of sexual modernity evinces Patrick Wolfe's (2008) positing of settler colonialism as a structure, not an event – that is, as a complex social formation and as historically continuous. For Wolfe (ibid., 102), the phrase "logic of elimination" marks "the multifarious procedures whereby settler colonial societies have sought to eliminate the problem of Indigenous heteronomy through the bio-cultural assimilation of Indigenous peoples." He writes that negatively the logic of elimination "strives for the dissolution of native societies. Positively, it erects a new colonial society on the expropriated land base. Settler colonizers come to stay" (ibid., 103). The colonial history of marriage law(s) in Canada that glimmers in the *Polygamy Reference* and marriage law's continuous construction of settler-national modernity through sexual and kinship formations bespeak this logic of elimination. Moreover, there would be no *Reference* decision, with its attendant panics about polygamy (and indeed no "Canada"), if settler colonialism was not at all times historically continuous.[11]

Suzanne Lenon

As a pervasive and continuous power relation, then, settler colonialism conditions the inclusion of same-sex marriage in the *Polygamy Reference* as exemplary of Canada's latest iteration of sexual modernity. The gesture of homonational inclusion through the register of progress evinced in Justice Bauman's avowal of same-sex marriage as a key component of the institution of monogamous marriage "performs" Canada as exemplary of liberal govern-ance (Morgensen 2011a). The chapter now turns to the ways this homonational inclusion interlocks with processes of racialization and the logic of empire.

Defending the (Homo)Nation against Polygamy's Spectre

The various "truths" about the harms of polygamy discussed in the previous section are sanctioned through a trope of contagion that finds its power in what Michel Foucault (2003, 249) calls "biopolitics" – that is, a form of power centred upon the life of a population. As Foucault (250–53) argues, sexuality is the precise point where the body and the population meet, the point where disci-plinary power over bodies and regulation of populations are articulated with and through each other. The norm of monogamous marriage that both precedes and engenders the *Polygamy Reference* circulates between the discipline and regulation of polygamous family-sexual formations *as* criminal. The discipline of individual bodies by law (e.g., in the laying of criminal charges against the two men from Bountiful) exceeds such bodies, in that its regulatory effects also pertain to the body social. In this sense, the numerical forecasts and statistics employed by the expert evidence to measure, predict, and subsequently produce polygamy's harms are technologies of power centred upon life and intervene in the health of the population as a whole.

Craig Jones, one of the lawyers for the attorney general of British Colum-bia, eloquently, if not dramatically, sums up this trope of contagion. Discussing the history of Bountiful's openly polygamous community in his book about the *Polygamy Reference,* Jones (2012, 49) writes,

> Harold Blackmore didn't understand it, but he was releasing into his isolating incubator in the forested interior of BC a behaviour coded within our DNA for millions of years. It proved to be a force that he would not be able to con-trol ... Polygamy is a powerful, primitive force; it is always there: it breathes; it waits. And when it is released, it grows and consumes.

Justice Bauman foregrounded evolutionary psychology expert evidence which posited that, without criminalization, a *nontrivial* increase in the incidence of polygynous polygamy was "quite plausible" given that it "could catch on in a complex society such as Canada" (para. 555, 1290). The biopolitical anxiety raised by the spectre of contagion comes to be located in particular bodies so as to distinguish populations who might optimize the "life" of the nation (Canada) and those who might endanger it. Here, the trope of contagion becomes thoroughly racialized. Craig Jones's characterization of polygamy as a "powerful primitive force" reveals the racial thinking that ties monogamy to a civilized sexual modernity. Further, in the *Polygamy Reference,* it was suggested that should polygamous marriage be allowed, Canada would end up being the Western destination of choice for those practising polygynous polygamy, particularly from Africa and the Middle East. The expert witness conveyed to the court that "fertility is always higher in polygynous communities. It's just robust. So these communities are going to grow faster and merely by population demographics they will expand faster than monogamous communities" (para. 555). Siding with this evidence, the judge wrote, "It requires no leap of imagination to see how immigrants from these countries (Africa & Middle East [*sic*]) might view Canada as an especially desirable destination were polygamy not prohibited" (para. 560). It requires no leap of critical imagination to see at work in these statements the image of the racial Other assailing Canada's border, threatening "our" modern (read: civilized) values of gender equality and monogamous marriage (see Razack 2000). Justice Bauman contends that there is a real "possibility of an increase in immigration-based polygamy" (para. 573). Moreover, he held that there was the risk that "people from other cultures and faiths which practice polygyny already resident in Canada ... might take it up were it not prohibited. Here I refer to the same groups mentioned earlier in the immigration context" (para. 575). Reproduction and fertility rates function here as "technologies of security" against both external and internal threats to the population and as a way of regenerating one's own (national) race (Foucault 2003, 256–57; Puar 2007, 34).

It is important to note here that the court heard expert evidence contending that polygynous polygamy among Muslims in Canada was neither widespread nor a mainstream phenomenon (para. 429, 745). How, then, to explain this concern over which populations might immigrate to Canada if polygamy were decriminalized? Here, the racialized discourse of contagion interlocks with the civilizational logic of empire in a post-9/11 geopolitical context. I propose that a fear of the cultural-racial Other as Muslim haunts the *Polygamy Reference,* as it does anxieties over polygamy more generally. I want to offer two examples of this. First, temporally overlapping with the *Polygamy Reference* was the highly publicized trial of the Shafia family murders,

Suzanne Lenon

in which Mohammed Shafia, his wife, and son were found guilty of four charges of first-degree murder and conspiracy to commit murder in the deaths of four female members of the family (the first wife and three daughters) in Ontario in 2009. Although much of the news coverage focused on the issue of "honour crimes," the fact that this was *also* a Muslim polygamous household was used in the media to further pathologize the family as "outside" of Canada and its values (Razack 2008; see also Gyulai 2009).[12] As Canada does not recognize valid foreign polygamous marriages for the purposes of immigration, the Shafias' polygamous family formation *within* Canada's borders further confirms discourses of deceit and betrayal that often animate Islamophobia. The deaths of these four women were used more recently as a narrative backdrop at the Conservative government's announcement of Bill S-7 this past November (2014). Called the "Zero Tolerance for Barbaric Cultural Practices Act," Bill S-7 amends various pieces of already existing legislation in a bid to purportedly protect women from the practices of polygamy and forced marriages.[13] In his announcement speech, the Minister of Immigration and Citizenship, Chris Alexander, said:

And we all know the tragic story of the Shafia family ... This tragedy touched many Canadians, including myself, including all of us. As a government, as a society, we must work tirelessly to make sure that what happened to Zeinab, Sahara, Geeti, and Rona Shafia never happens again on Canadian soil ... That's why our government is pleased to announce our intention to table legislation *today* that makes it clear to *anyone* who may doubt how serious we are that we do not, under any circumstance, accept or allow the propagation, support, or enactment of barbaric cultural practices on Canadian soil. The Bill ... will show quite clearly that our Canadian values do not extend to barbaric acts. Our government will continue to stand up for all victims of violence and abuse and take necessary action to prevent these from happening on Canadian soil.[14]

Similar to the *Polygamy Reference,* Minister Alexander's speech and Bill S-7 rely on a racialization of patriarchy that erroneously locates polygamy as a "cultural" issue ignoring the statistics and lived reality of violence against women that happens daily in Canada across "cultures." Moreover, the minister's speech obfuscates the ongoing murder and disappearance of Indigenous women and girls "on Canadian soil." His speech elides the gendered violence that the settler state requires to make this soil "Canadian" in the first place. The use of the concept of "barbarism" conflates racial and geopolitical boundaries, and we need to be mindful of the ways in which the Muslim woman's body is used to articulate Western superiority. As Sherene Razack (2004b, 168) writes, "We cannot forget for an instant the usefulness of her body in the contemporary making of white nations and citizens." In this instance of white nation making, it is worth noting that this phrasing of "Canadian soil" was repeated six times in the Minister's twelve-minute speech. Such an insistence and repetition works as an assertion of settler sovereignty that seems to forget that plural marriage has always-already been – *and is* – part of "Canadian soil."

This leads to the second example of my argument as to why the racial Other as Muslim haunts anxieties about polygamy. Again, this example occurred during the time period of the *Polygamy Reference* when the federal Minister of Justice at the time was speaking about Bountiful. Feminist scholar Lori Beaman remarks that in the minister's brief, there is a rapid transition to Muslims, polygamy in Muslim communities, and immigration. Why, she asks, if the minister was being asked about polygamy, specifically in relation to the situation in Bountiful, was there a need to talk about polygamy among Muslims (quoted in Chan 2011, 25)?

Although one answer to this question lies in the Orientalizing dynamics of Islamophobia, another answer lies in the whiteness of the Bountiful story.[15] Media representations of the community of Bountiful often portray it as a space frozen in time, from which women need to be saved. As Angela Campbell (2009) remarks, visual and written news accounts of Bountiful routinely depict the women of this community as submissive, silenced, coerced, and isolated; their traditional dress and the number of children often shown following or clinging to them suggest conservatism and exploitation (ibid., 185–86). Such media accounts of Bountiful as cultural Other could be understood as following the histories of the racialization of Mormons as nonwhite, discussed in the previous section. Yet it is important to consider how Bountiful, as a fundamentalist Mormon religious community, might also be shielded by its whiteness. This is not to suggest that the community has not come under the surveillance of state authorities; it has. Such surveillance is what procedurally led to the *Polygamy Reference*. Yet it is important to consider that the protective privileges offered by the white racial norms of Canadian citizenship explain why Bountiful's existence has been allowed to continue for decades. Would a Muslim polygynous community (or even an Indigenous one) be allowed to exist for such an extended period of time? Might Bountiful's "bad" and excessive patriarchal relations be assuaged, in part, *through* its whiteness? The easy slippage from Bountiful to a focus on polygamy among Muslims that Beaman points to – and

Suzanne Lenon

Minister Alexander's wilful forgetting that polygamy has long been practised "on Canadian soil" – are both enabled precisely because Bountiful is racialized as white, and its colonial settlement on unceded Ktunaxa territories[16] remains unspoken.

Returning to the trope of contagion embedded in the *Polygamy Reference*, it is against the backdrop of biopolitical anxieties over immigration, sex, and reproduction that racialization, as structured by white supremacy and a logic of empire, conditions the homonational gestures of inclusion found within the *Reference*. A national (monogamous) lesbian-gay subject becomes enfolded into the biopolitical mandate to preserve monogamous marriage and, by extension, Western civilization. Such a sanctioning comes from the unlikeliest of sources. The conservative women's organization REAL Women of Canada has long been opposed to legalizing same-sex marriage on the basis of deeply held beliefs in the patriarchal, heterosexual family as the privileged site for the raising of children. As but one voice in the cacophony of conservative opposition, the group has consistently maintained that children are, in fact, at harm if raised in same-sex relationships because such relationships "are not and can never be functionally equivalent to opposite-sex marriage" (Landolt 2004a). Because of this, REAL Women has argued that the legalization of same-sex marriage will erode the nature of monogamous marriage and ultimately lead to the unravelling of society (Landolt 2004b). In a rather surprising move, however, REAL Women's submission to the BC Supreme Court for the *Polygamy Reference* states that although same-sex and opposite-sex conjugal (but nonmarital) unions "may differ from traditional heterosexual marital relationships, there *is substantial functional overlap*" and "there is *no evidence* that harm is associated with them" (REAL Women of Canada 2011, para. 2.6.1.6, emphasis added).[17] However contradictory this statement is, it should not be interpreted as the group's sudden conversion to unequivocal support for lesbian, gay, and queer people's lives. Rather, the import of such a statement, however contingent and hesitant such a recognition may be, speaks to Jasbir Puar's argument that homonationalism is not an identity nor an attribute but rather a field of power into which we are all interpellated (Puar 2013a).

This interpellation is further echoed in Justice Bauman's view (para. 1041) that section 293 of the Criminal Code draws a "bright line" to reflect

> the pre-eminent place that the institution of monogamous marriage takes in Western culture and, as we have seen, Western heritage over the millennia. When all is said, I suggest that the prohibition in s. 293 is directed in part at

protecting the institution of monogamous marriage. And let me here recognize that we have come, in this century and in this country, to accept same-sex marriage as part of that institution. That is so, in part, because committed same-sex relationships celebrate all of the values we seek to preserve and advance in monogamous marriage.

Although Justice Bauman does not explicitly outline which "values" of monogamous marriage same-sex relationships preserve and advance, one might surmise that these cohere around what polygamy is uniformly believed *not* to entail: equality, romantic love, privacy, neoliberal citizenship, consumption, and relations of contract, autonomy, and consent. In fact, Justice Bauman rejects the "slippery slope" argument, which holds that the legalization of same-sex marriage will inevitably lead to the legitimization of polygamy. In its opinion, this "alarmist view ... misses the whole point" because monogamous same-sex and heterosexual marriage share the same "doctrinal underpinnings" (para. 1042). In other words, monogamous same-sex marriage is now part and parcel of the temporal and spatial modernity of the West. The trope of polygamy as (primitive) contagion, expressed in the racial and implicitly imperial terms of immigration, profoundly structures the court's own homonationalism so as to demarcate sexual modernity and a civilized nation. It animates the enfoldment of monogamous same-sex couples into the white modern settler nation-state. The "bright line", then, that section 293 is mobilized to safeguard *is* the colour line.[18] Because of this, rather than be seduced by its promise of inclusion, the homonationalism waving its flag at us through the lines of this *Polygamy Reference* should stand more as caution, not as celebration.

Conclusion

Given this chapter's critical analysis of the *Polygamy Reference,* it should not come as a surprise to read that the court assuredly asserts that the state *does* in fact have "business in the bedrooms of the nation" in its defence of the institution of monogamous marriage from attack by polygamy (para. 1042). This is a play on the words of former minister of justice Pierre Elliott Trudeau, who famously stated, in the context of decriminalizing homosexuality in 1969, that "the state has no place in the bedrooms of the nation." The privacy offered in such a gesture is, as Puar (2007, 124) has argued, a gift of recognition with many strings attached, circumscribed as it is by gender, race, citizenship, class, and colonization. Which bodies and which family forms, precisely, can inhabit this gift? Which bodies and which family forms have not inhabited this gift?

Suzanne Lenon

In line with Angela Davis's evocation that histories never leave us for another place, the *Polygamy Reference*'s explicit evocation of *non*privacy as a social good evinces the palimpsestic interlock of settler colonial, racial, and imperial relations of power that gave rise to the *Polygamy Reference* in the first instance and that enable its own homonational critique of polygamy. This chapter offers an analysis of the ways these relations of power steadfastly shape the meaning and content of section 293 and the *Reference* more generally. Such historical relations continue to thickly weave the institution of monogamous marriage as (Western) sexual modernity into the persistence of white nation making.

Notes

1 Section 293(1) of the Criminal Code reads,

   Every one who

   (a) practices or enters into or in any manner agrees or consents to practice or enter into

      (i) any form of polygamy, or
      (ii) any kind of conjugal union with more than one person at the same time, whether or not it is by law recognized as a binding form of marriage; or

   (b) celebrates, assists or is a party to a rite, ceremony, contract or consent that purports to sanction a relationship mentioned in subparagraph (a)(i) or (ii), is guilty of an indictable offence and liable to imprisonment for a term not exceeding five years.

2 *Reference re: Section 293 of the Criminal Code of Canada, 2011, BCSC 1588 [SO97767].* The *Reference* considers two questions (para. 16):

   (a) Is section 293 of the *Criminal Code of Canada* consistent with the Canadian *Charter of Rights and Freedoms*? If not, in what particular or particulars and to what extent?
   (b) What are the necessary elements of the offence in section 293 of the *Criminal Code of Canada*? Without limiting this question, does section 293 require that the polygamy or conjugal union in question involved a minor, or occurred in a context of dependence, exploitation, abuse of authority, a gross imbalance of power, or undue influence?

3 However, the court also held that section 293 is *not* consistent with the Charter to the extent that it includes within its terms children between the ages of twelve and seventeen who marry into polygamy or conjugal unions with more than one person at the same time (para. 1359). In other words, the law is valid and enforceable except that it cannot criminalize minors involved in polygamous marriages. In March 2012 the attorney general of British Columbia announced that the province would not ask a higher court to review the outcome of the *Polygamy Reference* (see Keller 2012). In August 2014, BC's Criminal Justice Branch approved polygamy charges against Winston Blackmore and James Oler as well as other family members, alleging the unlawful removal of children from Canada with the

intention of committing sexual crimes. As this chapter goes to press, the outcome is not yet known (Judd 2014).

4   Polygamy is a kinship-family structure that contains both polygynous (one man, multiple women) and polyandrous (one woman, multiple men) forms. The *Polygamy Reference* holds that section 293 is directed at both heterosexual polygyny and polyandry, as well as at "multi-party same-sex marriages" (para. 1037). However, it is *polygynous polygamy* that is of central concern in this legal case.

5   This echoes similar arguments made by William Eskridge (1996) and Andrew Sullivan (1996) that monogamous same-sex marriage is a social good for the ways it civilizes gay men.

6   Angela Campbell's (2005, 2009, 2010) research is notable in this regard. For instance, she has conducted interviews with twenty FLDS women who are or were Bountiful residents. Her study casts Bountiful as a heterogeneous and dynamic social and political space where at least some women are able to wield considerable authority. Their stories are inconsistent with the dominant legal and social narrative about polygamy and its harms to women.

7   The first criminal prohibition against polygamy was enacted in 1890 when the offence was added to the *Act Respecting Offences Relating to the Law of Marriage*, R.S.C. 1886. The provision was included in Canada's first comprehensive Criminal Code in 1892 as sections 278 and 706. It was later amended to be section 273.

8   *R. v. Labrie* (1891); *R. v. Bear's Shin Bone* (1899); *R. v. John Harris* (1906); *Dionne v. Pepin* (1934); and *R. v. Tolhurst* (1937). The 1937 case was the last reported attempt to use this section, when it was held by the Ontario Court of Appeal that a man who left his wife and was living in an adulterous relationship was not committing the offence of polygamy. In this case, the courts concluded that the anti-polygamy provisions in the Criminal Code do not apply to adultery (Drummond 2009).

9   Canada inherited an English common law (i.e., judge-made) definition of marriage as part of its colonial foundations. In *Hyde v. Hyde and Woodmansee* (1866) 1 L.R. P. & D. 130, a case concerning the breakdown of a polygamous marriage in Utah, the judge held that "marriage in Christendom is understood to be the lawful union of one man and one woman for life to the exclusion of all others" (para. 134). Since 2005, however, civil marriage in Canada has been defined as "the lawful union of two persons to the exclusion of all others" S.C. 2005, c. 33, s. 2 [*Civil Marriage Act*].

10 *R. v. Bear's Shin Bone* 1899 Carswell NWT 32, 4 Terr.L.R. 173, 3 C.C.C. 329.

11 I would like to thank one of the manuscript's anonymous reviewers for this point.

12 I would like to thank Eve Haque for drawing my attention to this point.

13 Bill S-7 proposes amendments to admissibility provisions under the Immigration and Refugee Protection Act. If a permanent resident after landing in Canada through a sponsorship stream or otherwise begins or resumes a polygamous relationship, they could be found inadmissible on this basis alone, without requiring evidence that the person misrepresented their situation or has a criminal conviction. If found to be inadmissible, the permanent resident could then be subject to removal. A foreign national who practises polygamy in their country of origin who seeks temporary residence will be found inadmissible if they try to enter Canada with only one spouse at the time of seeking entry. Bill S-7 also amends the Civil Marriage Act and other provisions of the Criminal Code as a means of targeting forced marriages (South Asian Legal Clinic of Ontario, n.d.).

14 Video excerpts of this speech can be found at http://www.cbc.ca/news/politics/feds-brace -for-backlash-over-new-immigration-rules-banning-polygamous-forced-marriages -1.2824320.

15 I would like to thank one of the manuscript's anonymous reviewers for this point.
16 For more information on the Ktunaxa Nation and its ongoing treaty negotiations, see http://www.ktunaxa.org/who-we-are/.
17 I would like to thank Lisa Lambert for bringing REAL Women's submission to my attention and Lisa Lambert and Michelle Bennison for their research assistance with this chapter.
18 I would like to thank OmiSoore H. Dryden for this point and for all of the discussions that have informed our collective labour in editing this book.

6

Homonationalism at the Border and in the Streets
Organizing against Exclusion and Incorporation

KATHRYN TREVENEN AND ALEXA DEGAGNE

Work in the field of queer theory highlights the myriad ways that some LGBT people, queers, and feminists are recruited into racist and imperialist projects – whether they involve policing the boundaries of citizenship and nationhood, justifying the occupation of Palestine, or pursuing wars in Afghanistan and Iraq. Scholars such as queer theorist Jasbir Puar have examined the shifting regulation and mobilization of homonormative subjects, arguing that the temporary or partial inclusion of certain queer subjects within national projects has helped both to define the borders of the nation and to reinforce racialized and queered exclusions. Puar (2007, xi) examines not simply how homonormativity works to distinguish between the "good gays" and the "bad queers" but also how queerness "as a process of racialization informs the very distinctions between life and death, wealth and poverty, health and illness, living and dying." She thus argues that LGBTQ communities need to be vigilant about the ways that countries such as the United States, Israel, and Britain use "gay rights" to portray themselves as more civilized or humane than their Orientalized enemies. Queer-disability theorist Robert McRuer (2006) further argues that it is a defining feature of neoliberal states to present themselves as progressive by demonstrating their "flexibility" about the inclusion of a small segment of normative and compulsorily able-bodied queers – using this flexibility to further regulate and exclude communities whose members are less "well behaved," "productive," and "adaptable."

In this chapter, we continue the project of "disrupting queer inclusion" that this volume undertakes by examining the articulation of homonationalism in response to two different sites of state power: immigration control and policing. By looking at two different organizations – Egale Canada and No One Is Illegal (NOII) – we first examine protests and discussions regarding changes to the Canadian citizenship study guide *Discover Canada: The Rights and Responsibilities of Citizenship*, proposed by Conservative immigration minister Jason Kenney in 2010. In particular, we examine the ways that these different groups challenged the proposed exclusion of LGBTQ rights and communities within the broader context of Canada's regulation and policing of immigration, refugee claims, and citizenship. The second section of this chapter discusses how queer citizens relate to the police and policing by examining the responses of two different LGBTQ organizations to a violent attack against an Edmonton woman, as well as by briefly discussing debates around the police presence at the Ottawa Dyke March in 2011. We suggest that different queer organizations, large and small, are grappling with the implications of homonational critique by questioning and challenging their relationships with the police. We argue that an interlocking analysis is necessary in responding both to the debate over the citizenship guide and to the cases in Edmonton and Ottawa so that queer rights and inclusion are not being fought for at the expense of communities who are excluded, overpoliced, or exceptionalized through regimes of citizenship, policing, immigration regulation, border control, and refugee asylum.

In pursuing this project, we use an interlocking theoretical lens to undertake a critical discourse analysis of press releases, statements, blogs, and newspaper articles concerning the citizenship guide controversy as well as the case of Shannon Barry, the Edmonton woman who was attacked. We also combine our discourse analysis with participant observation in Edmonton (Alexa) and Ottawa (Kathryn) at community meetings, panel discussions, protests, and rallies. Sherene Razack (1998, 11) elaborates an interlocking analysis as an attempt to "find a language that captures the simultaneity of systems of domination and the many ways in which they mutually constitute one another." She further explains that "each system of oppression relie[s] on the other to give it meaning, and that this interlocking effect could only be traced in historically specific ways" (ibid., 12). Interlocking systems of domination thus both require each other and help to secure each other in specific and shifting ways.

An interlocking analysis reveals the ways that three different cases situated in different places in Canada – one centred on a Government of Canada publication, one on the response to a violent attack in Edmonton, and one on the challenges of organizing a Dyke March in Ottawa – are connected by state attempts to incorporate, "protect," and maximize the productivity of some queered citizens, while excluding and targeting other queered citizens. The three cases thus reveal the diverse sites of homonational politics in Canada and offer possibilities for resisting or disrupting homonational state strategies. In all three cases, resisting homonational politics of incorporation meant that organizations or communities had to closely examine who was being excluded and deliberately "underprotected" or targeted by the state or by police services and that they had to organize from a position that resisted a "single issue" analysis.

We situate our work within a methodological and theoretical frame shaped by interlocking analysis but attend to the cautions raised by Jasbir Puar, Robert McRuer, and queer theorist Lisa Duggan about the challenges of interlocking analysis – particularly if it becomes locked into a rigid or essentialist understanding of identity. We are guided by Puar's theorization of homonationalism as a way of thinking about the impossibility of separating queerness from racialization and about the way that this combination slates some queered bodies for life and others for death.

As a way of signalling the fraught and productive solidarities that compose the communities we discuss, we shift between using "LGB," "LGBTQ," "LGBT," and "queer" to refer to different organizations and communities. Wherever a group or organization describes themselves, we have respected the identification they use. When there is no designation, we have chosen a description that seems to best describe the issues to which the group responds. We use these various appellations to point to the fluid and contested solidarity between lesbian, trans, queer, bisexual, and gay people. As they are often lumped together under the umbrella "LGBTQ," a focus on homonationalism allows us to examine how individuals and communities are underrepresented or excluded within this umbrella.

Homonationalism at and in the Borders

In March 2010 homonational tensions erupted when the media revealed that in 2009 Immigration Minister Jason Kenney's office had asked that references to same-sex marriage be removed from a study guide for potential citizens titled *Discover Canada: The Rights and Responsibilities of Citizenship*. When the story broke, a diverse group of organizations and communities protested the exclusion. Among them were Egale Canada and No One Is Illegal (NOII). The different reactions from these groups highlight the fraught stakes of homonational acceptance and neoliberal inclusion.

Egale Canada, Canada's highest-profile national LGBT organization and instrumental in many civil rights struggles (notably the fights for equal marriage and trans rights), responded to stories about the citizenship guide in a primarily

Kathryn Trevenen and Alexa DeGagne

conciliatory manner. Executive Director Helen Kennedy told the Canadian press that she had met with Kenney in December 2009 to complain about the omission but that she was "hopeful and optimistic that we're going to get it fixed" (Beeby 2010). In contrast, activists and community organizers from NOII critiqued the study guide exclusion while confronting Minister Kenney at speeches in Montreal and Ottawa, and they continued to put forward a critique of the racist, sexist, and homophobic policies of the Conservative government during the Toronto Pride Festival and G20 protests in the summer of 2010. In this way, not only did NOII protest the exclusion of gay and lesbian Canadians from the guide, but it also connected the Conservative government's marginalization of queers in the study guide with its repressive crackdown on protestors, its "tough on crime" agenda, and its increasing focus on "protecting" national borders from "illegitimate" refugees.

After some media attention, protests from the public-sector unions CUPE and PSAC, and protests from different organizations, the guide was changed and reprinted in 2011 with these lines: "Canada's diversity includes gay and lesbian Canadians, who enjoy the full protection of and equal treatment under the law, including access to civil marriage. Together, these diverse groups, sharing a common Canadian identity, make up today's multicultural society" (Government of Canada 2011, 13). Interestingly, the guide also contains a picture of Canadian swimmer Mark Tewksbury, who won a gold medal for the 100 metre backstroke in the 1992 Summer Olympics. Under the picture of Tewksbury in the guide, a caption reads, "Mark Tewksbury, Olympic gold medalist and prominent activist for gay and lesbian Canadians" (ibid., 26). What is striking about Tewksbury's inclusion in the guide is what kind of "gay subject" he represents. Here, Robert McRuer's analysis of the complex ties between compulsory able-bodiedness and compulsory heterosexuality is helpful. McRuer argues that neoliberalism requires and produces bodies and subjects that can respond with flexibility to moments of crisis. Importantly, like those homonationals who are shown to be incorported into the nation in Puar's analysis of homonationalism, ideal flexible subjects are not simply able-bodied and heterosexual but also *tolerant*: "Neoliberalism and the condition of post-modernity, in fact, increasingly needs able-bodied, heterosexual subjects who are visible and spectacularly tolerant of queer/disabled existences" (McRuer 2006, 2). This flexibility, most commonly expressed in Canadian contexts in the language of "diversity," "multiculturalism," and "accommodation," reaffirms the superiority of the dominant culture or society. In this crisis (the challenge to the citizenship guide), Mark Tewksbury is the "spectacularly" able-bodied, white, patriotic, gold-medal-winning, gay, male, flexible body. And as such, he is positioned as an ideal subject for inclusion in the citizenship guide. Through his image not only are the interests of the state portrayed, but the narratives of Canada as a tolerant and civilized nation are also reinforced.

After the reprinting of the guide, Egale stated that "Egale Canada is pleased that the new guide accurately reflects the current climate in Canada. Nonetheless, its obvious omission of our trans population highlights the urgent need to pass Bill C-389[1] before the next election, in order to ensure the rightful inclusion of trans people within Canada's human rights regime" (Egale Canada 2011b). Egale's statement importantly raises the issue of the visibility and rights of trans people, a population that continues to be denied some of the limited legal protections that LGB citizens enjoy. However, as queer scholar and journalist Ariel Troster (2011) argues, Egale's positive response to the guide is problematic in light of the other changes that the government made to the guide – changes that were never challenged by Egale and that were not revised in the reprinting. These changes included language implying that instead of being indigenous to Canada, Aboriginal peoples are "believed to have migrated from Asia." Troster (ibid., 40-41) links these changes, which are reflective of Conservative government attempts to undermine Indigenous land claims, to long-time Conservative advisor Tom Flanagan, who argues in his book *First Nations? Second Thoughts* (2000) that First Nations people were Canada's "first immigrants." Egale's response also naturalizes and reinforces the idea that inclusion in a guide that articulates a Conservative vision of Canadian nationalism is automatically a good thing for *all* queers – many of whom are targeted for exclusion from the nation in other ways.[2] In effect, Egale's response allows Prime Minister Stephen Harper's government to appear tolerant *and* flexible; by reinstating gays and lesbians in the guide, the broader Conservative politics of national inclusion and exclusion goes unexamined.

In their response to gay and lesbian people's exclusion from and reintroduction to the study guide, Egale demonstrates a problematic "single issue" focus that plays into the government's homonational tactics. By praising the fact that the guide "accurately reflects the current climate in Canada," Egale ignores the myriad protests against the Harper government forwarded by Indigenous, anti-colonial, and anti-racist organizations that challenge the dominant ideologies of citizenship and multiculturalism currently functioning in Canadian immigration policy. Similar problems exist with an Egale press release of 3 May 2011 titled "A Canada for 'All Canadians,'" issued immediately after the election of a majority Conservative government. In the release, Egale takes up Stephen Harper's claim that "we are and we must be the government of all Canadians." Egale comments that this ideal must be "raised as a standard" and that it "demands the dedication of every community and every individual in the country." In response to Harper's promise to reduce crime and make streets safer, Egale says,

> For members of Canada's diffuse and diverse LGBTQ community and their allies, the first litmus test of this and the Prime Minister's promise to "stand on guard for all," will be the explicit inclusion in the crime-prevention agenda of measures to protect trans Canadians from hate crimes, hate speech and discrimination by continuing the unprecedented work of the outgoing Parliament towards recognizing equality rights based on gender identity and expression. (Egale Canada 2011a)

As we discuss below in our section on policing, Egale's endorsement of Harper's crime-prevention agenda supports the protection of *some* LGBT citizens from hate crimes at the expense of people who will be targeted by the racist, transphobic, homophobic, and anti-poor "tough on crime" reforms that the government supports – most notably the omnibus crime bill.[3] Again, Egale's analysis of and response to the Conservative government's policy changes reflects a "single issue" politics that Dean Spade challenges in his scholarship and organizing. He explains that "single issue" politics often assume that "fixing" a single issue like discrimination against gay and lesbian people creates a benefit that "trickles down" to people facing multiple vulnerabilities or systems of oppression. Spade contrasts this with the framework used by the Sylvia Rivera Law Project, which centres "the people who are facing the worst vulnerability because this kind of justice only trickles up, it never trickles down" (Spade 2011). A trickle-up model might press an organization like Egale to consider how "tough on crime" reforms affect trans sex workers who are vulnerable to police surveillance, harassment, and violence – a community of trans people who might not fall into the group "protected" by hate crime legislation and the police.

Egale has also commented on Conservative government immigration and refugee policy, issuing a statement in response to Bill C-31.[4] The statement highlights the ways that "the lesbian, gay, bisexual and trans community stands to be disproportionately affected by the proposed changes because some of the countries that produce the largest number of claims based on sexual orientation will undoubtedly be considered safe" (Egale Canada 2012). As with previous statements highlighting the importance of advocating for trans rights, this Egale release focuses attention on an important issue: the specific ways that LGBT refugee claimants from so-called "safe" countries will be affected by Bill C-31. It does not, however, attend to the myriad ways that the Conservative government is intensifying the divisions between insiders and outsiders at the borders of the Canadian nation – divisions that depend on complex processes of both queering and racializing to make the divisions between worthy citizens and excluded "others."

Bill C-31, titled "Protecting Canada's Immigration System Act," continues a trend in Conservative government policy making that has led to harsher immigration requirements and to more invasive surveillance and fear mongering around the "invasion" of Canadian borders by immigrants and refugees (NOII–Toronto 2011). This bill would give the minister the power to place countries on the safe-country list without consultation, would eliminate appeals for some refugees, and would allow more invasive and extensive collection of biometric identification data. The reason for introducing this bill, as Mr. Kenney explains, is that "too many tax dollars are spent on bogus refugees" (Baluja 2012). This claim relies on what both Sherene Razack (1998, 2008) and Yasmin Jiwani (2007) identify as "common sense knowledge" or "common stock knowledge" that circulates throughout narratives of Canadian security and nationalism. The idea that there are hordes of (deceptive and greedy) "bogus refugees" seeking to take advantage of the (generous and fair) Canadian immigration system works to justify increased surveillance, regulation, and refusal of refugee claimants. The "bogus refugee" thus joins the "queue jumpers," "the terrorists," and the "dependants" – racialized figures, positioned as threatening, who wait at Canadian borders looking for a gap in security or an excess of the mythological Canadian softheartedness, a mythology belied by the falling numbers of refugees actually accepted into Canada (NOII–Toronto 2010).

We again compare Egale's response to Conservative government immigration and crime policies with NOII's analysis of who gets targeted by the nation for death or assimilation. In its document "Ten Reasons to Stop Harper's Conservatives," NOII references job losses; "austerity" cuts to social assistance, childcare, and education; resource extraction on Indigenous lands; privatization of essential services; military missions and occupations in Afghanistan, Libya, and Haiti, as well as support for Israeli apartheid; criminalizing the poor; an aggressive anti-refugee campaign, including migrant detention and expansion of migrant-worker programs; and attacks on organizations promoting queer-sexual liberation and cuts to women's advocacy groups (NOII–Vancouver 2011). In this list, and through events like "Undoing Borders: Queer Discussions on Im/migration and Criminalization" (NOII–Toronto 2012), NOII gives us an example of how "anti-homonationalist" analysis and organizing could be done. NOII's analysis encourages us to see LGBTQ communities as non-homogeneous communities comprising people with different kinds of privilege,

Kathryn Trevenen and Alexa DeGagne

differential access to services and rights, and different specific histories with the police, borders, and the state – people whose life and death, and visibility and invisibility, are tied to homonational strategies pursued by the state.

NOII's analysis does not separate sexuality from other distinctions that feed the inside-outside politics of Canadian borders (both literal and metaphorical). Just as trans people are "too queer" for inclusion in the citizenship guide, Roma refugees targeted by Minister Kenney are queered by racist "gypsy fiction" that associates Roma people with laziness, sexual promiscuity, crime, and misogynist cultural or social practices (Berger and Rehaag 2012; Nerenberg 2012).[5] NOII's protests against the Harper government allow us to see that without attention to the interlocking systems of queerness and racialization, wealthy, white LGB citizens are encouraged to think that inclusion in the citizenship guide gives them a stake in protecting "their" borders and civilization from "bogus refugees." We see similar stakes in the next section as we examine debates among LGBTQ organizations about resisting or co-operating with police services in Canada. In both cases, despite the different geographical spaces, certain queers are re-cruited into "protecting" some form of the nation to which they are encouraged to think of themselves as belonging.

Homonationalism in the Streets

North American LGBTQ history is strongly shaped by relations between diverse groups of LGBTQ people and various police organizations. It was, after all, the 1969 police raids on the Stonewall Inn in New York that famously contributed to rising political action and the modern gay-liberation movement. Retellings of the Stonewall Riots, however, often omit the fact that poor queer and trans people of colour initiated and sustained the anti-police riots and then created a sophisticated analysis of police violence against many communities (D'Emilio 1992). Before and after Stonewall, there were many police raids on gay, lesbian, and gender-nonconforming establishments in the United States and Canada. Riots erupted in Montreal in 1975 and Toronto in 1981, for example, as queer people in both cities pushed back against heightened police harassment of gay businesses, organizations, and media (Kinsman and Gentile 2010). These riots against the police are depicted as critical and galvanizing moments in which queers and gender-nonconforming people fought back in collective ways against the regulatory bodies of the state.

The acceptance and precarious protection of *some* LGBTQ people – what Puar (2007) terms *sexual exceptionalism* – has several implications that are pertinent to relationships between LGBTQ people and police forces. Whereas some white and affluent LGBTQ people are able to avoid violent or oppressive interactions with the police, many people remain vulnerable to police regulation and violence because they are positioned within a targeted segment of the population whose members face increased police intervention due to their race, gender identity, immigration status, income level, housing situation, and/or occupation. Policies and laws aimed at protecting LGBT citizens, namely anti-discrimination and hate crime legislation, have certainly offered some people important and necessary protections around employment, pay, housing rights, harassment, and violence (M. Smith 2008; T. Warner 2002). But these laws and policies are also tools that are frequently used to target and punish queers who are sex workers, activists, people of colour, Indigenous people, and street-identified people. As Yasmin Jiwani (2002, 69) explains, Canadians need to look critically at which communities are "over policed and under-protected." Gary Kinsman and Patricia Gentile (2010, 433) have argued that,

> at the same time that this [heteronormative] integration is taking place, other queers are being excluded as too queer, too irresponsible, and not respectable enough to be part of this nation. Certain more "respectable" middle-class queers are coming to be invested in the defence of national security ... This group forgets the historical experience of the Canadian war on queers and comes to "otherize" some queers, people of colour, and various groups seen as security threats.

In the face of these tensions, Canadian LGBTQ organizations and communities have debated how and when they should co-operate with or resist police services. To explore the links between homonationalism and policing, we briefly examine responses to the Edmonton Police Service's handling of the 2010 homophobic attack on Shannon Barry. In this case, local LGBT and queer organizations have reacted in different ways to police neglect, protection, abuse, and/or mistreatment of sexually marginalized citizens.

Edmonton's Shannon Barry Case

On 16 April 2010 Shannon Barry, a white lesbian living in Edmonton, was on her way home when four men attacked her. The men called Shannon and her friends "dykes and faggots" before kicking Shannon in the face, leaving her with a broken jaw, a crushed left eye socket, and facial nerve damage (Rusnell 2010b). News of the attack spread quickly through Edmonton's LGBTQ community. Media and public attention grew exponentially, however, once it was revealed

Kathryn Trevenen and Alexa DeGagne

that the Edmonton Police Service (EPS) had seriously mishandled the case: the police were slow to respond, waited five days to file a report, and did not initially identify the attack as a potential hate crime.[6]

The Edmonton Sexual Minorities Liaison Committee (SMLC) intervened in the Barry case as an intermediary between Barry and the EPS. The SMLC is mandated to represent the needs of Edmonton's LGBTQ community in relation to the EPS. During the Barry case, the SMLC defended the actions of the EPS officer and the police chief and attempted to speak on behalf of Barry to media and the EPS (Ruddy 2010b). As a result, many within Edmonton's LGBTQ community questioned the effectiveness of the SMLC as an advocate for the city's queer and sexually deviant citizens, many of whom continue to be the targets of police regulation and harassment.

In the weeks that followed the attack, some members of Edmonton's LGBTQ community formed the Community Response Project (CRP).[7] The CRP was created to craft a "queer, systemic response to the recent assault against Shannon Barry (and others)" (Ruddy 2010a). We argue below that the CRP put forward an interlocking analysis of violence and the police response that did not focus on sexuality in isolation but attempted to challenge and complicate hierarchies and exclusions that are manifest through sexuality, gender, race, citizenship status, and income. The CRP did this, we argue, by situating the police response to the attack within a specific context that included examining the overpolicing and criminalizing of Edmonton's Indigenous communities, the limitations of hate crime legislation, and the prison industrial complex in Canada.[8] CRP members challenged the SMLC's claim that the majority of Edmonton's LGBTQ community believed in working within the criminal justice system and depending on hate crime legislation to combat homophobic violence in the city. The CRP problematized Canadian homonational politics, as its members attempted to resist incorporation into formal institutions that continue to neglect and punish individuals who are not "ideal citizens."

In the months following the Barry attack, the SMLC and the CRP debated, among other issues, the implications of developing a better relationship between the Edmonton Police Service and Edmonton's queer community. At a media scrum six days after Barry was attacked, Edmonton police chief Mike Boyd reported that he was conducting an internal review to determine whether the attending officers should be reprimanded for mishandling the case. In the scrum, the chief referred to the relationship between the queer community and the EPS as "excellent" and said that the service treated hate crimes as a "very, very important concern" (Ruddy 2010a). Kris Wells, co-chair of the police liaison committee for the GLBTA community of Edmonton, acknowledged that the EPS initially mishandled the Barry case and stated that the SMLC was working with the EPS to determine whether the officers' mishandling of the case was an isolated incident or indicative of systemic problems within the police department[9] (ibid.). Ultimately, Wells said, the SMLC "is trying to build a relationship based on mutual respect and trust between the police and the queer community" (ibid.). In response, founding member of CRP Michelle Thomarat (2010) wrote that many people in Edmonton's queer community did not agree with Boyd's assertion that the relationship between the EPS and the queer community was "excellent." Thomarat explained that, "for many people, increasing their feelings of security in their neighborhood would mean decreasing police presence, not increasing it." The CRP argued that attempts to foster a better relationship with the EPS actually reinforced the dominance of the criminal justice system at the expense of people within the community who were targeted by the police for harassment and surveillance.

Statements from the SMLC argued that LGBTQ citizens needed to work with police in order to increase their safety and security. The SMLC prioritized the arrest and prosecution of the accused attacker, and made the case for tougher hate crime laws and a heightened police presence in Edmonton's queer communities. Upon hearing news of the attack, Edmonton mayor Stephen Mandel said, "The kind of people that committed the horrific attack on that individual – what can you say about those kind of people in the city? They are just not welcome" (Rusnell 2010a). Two days after the mayor's comments, the EPS charged a fourteen-year-old boy[10] with aggravated assault in relation to Barry's case (Sands 2010). Echoing Mayor Mandel's sentiments, Wells told the *Edmonton Journal* (ibid.), "The most important thing for the community ... is the announcement that there is an individual who is in custody and charged with the assault ... Now that an individual has been charged and is in custody, our community can breathe easier." CRP member Robert Nichols (2010) replied to Wells, "It is neither the case that the most important thing to come out of this is that a 14-year-old is in custody, nor that his being charged means the community can 'breathe easier.'" Nichols argued that the arrest of a single person, especially a fourteen-year-old boy, did not make marginalized people feel safer and that Mayor Mandel's declaration that people like the attacker were "just not welcome" was emblematic of a criminal justice system built on individualized victimization and punishment – one that rendered invisible the complex intersections of subtle and daily oppression and violence that characterized many people's experiences in Edmonton. In a *Vue Magazine* column, CRP member Thomarat (2010) wrote that although members of the SMLC may have seen the Barry case as an "isolated incident," others within the queer community – who had lived

Kathryn Trevenen and Alexa DeGagne

with homophobic, transphobic, and racist violence on a daily basis – were not surprised by the Barry attack.

The CRP disagreed with the SMLC's "single issue politics" assertion that Edmonton's entire LGBTQ community was a homogeneous group facing uniform discrimination and violence on the basis of sexual identity. In the days following the attack, Kris Wells, the chair of SMLC, told *Xtra!* that "hate crimes are message crimes. They don't just target an individual victim, but they target an entire community, and that's why they need to be treated with all seriousness ... Many gay, lesbian, bisexual, trans-identified persons are wondering 'Could I be the next target?'" (Ruddy 2010a). In their response to the case, Wells and the SMLC cast Barry and "gay, lesbian, bisexual, trans-identified persons" as an identifiable group of "good citizens" who are in a constant state of potential attack and victimization based simply on their sexual identity. The presumption is also, then, that once sexuality protections and rights are granted, these citizens will attain security and inclusion under Canadian law. As with Egale's response to the citizenship guide and Conservative immigration policy, the SMLC's commitment to legitimizing the police services and Canadian law is complicit in reinforcing the distinction between people and communities who are worthy of protection and inclusion and those who are not.

In distinction to the "single issue" approach, Lucas Crawford and Carmen Ellison (2010), members of the CRP, argue that the SMLC's model of hate crime legislation, police interference, and punishment fails to account for people in Edmonton who are most targeted by police and societal violence. Crawford and Ellison argue that supporters of tougher hate crime laws and of increased police surveillance and intervention are largely the most privileged and protected members of the LGBTQ community and that the SMLC's logic ignores how the gender, race, and income (of the victims and the accused) engendered the attack. Crawford and Ellison (ibid.) state that "the sort of violence that falls under the Criminal Code is, of course, unacceptable, but many people – including some in the lesbian, gay, bisexual, transgender and queer (LGBTQ) community – experience invisible, subtle, or extreme violence regularly, owing to multidimensional lives marked by race, ethnicity, wealth, religion, mobility, and gender."

CRP members Crawford and Nichols (2010) point to the fact that Indigenous LGBTQ and Two-Spirit people are overrepresented in the criminal justice system in Alberta and Canada (see also Fink, this collection) and argue that "resources are better devoted to supporting marginalized communities – for whom unequal social conditions put individuals at higher risk of entering the criminal justice system. Right now 60 percent of the prairies' federal inmates are Indigenous people, and LGBTQ people – particularly transsexuals of colour – are victimized by the criminal justice system in great number." Here the CRP links the criminalization and overpolicing of Indigenous people to rhetoric around protecting white LGBTQ people from homophobic hate crimes. Like NOII's critique of the Harper government's omnibus crime bill, the CRP's critique of "police-based" solutions highlights how systems of domination based on race, class, and sexuality interlock to target poor, queer, and racialized subjects for death or violence.[11]

We argue that the analysis put forward by the CRP highlights how uncritical LGBTQ support for hyperpolicing and harsher sentencing (through hate crime legislation or support for the government's omnibus crime bill) reinforces the notion that queers, and other marginalized people, need to depend on the state and support the ostracization and punishment of undesirable citizens or threatening "outsiders" like the "bogus refugees" who try to take advantage of Canadian healthcare or welfare systems.

The critique of both the police services and the criminal justice system that the CRP developed in response to the discussion around the Shannon Barry case is arguably part of a broader conversation in queer communities across Canada. A similar analysis shaped the 2011 Ottawa Dyke March, whose organizing committee decided not to apply for a permit for the march and therefore not to have an official police presence marshalling the march. This decision was made in consultation with (among others) people of colour, trans people, activists, sex workers, and queer Muslims – people within queer and nonqueer communities who feel unsafe around police officers. Leslie Robertson (2011), a queer activist and ally member of POWER (Prostitutes of Ottawa/Gatineau Work, Educate, Resist), explained in her speech before the march that rejecting a police presence and building solidarity with sex workers, refugees, street-identified people, and other members of the Ottawa queer community who were being harassed and targeted by police were crucial undertakings, especially since the police were trying to pinkwash themselves as friends of LGBTQ citizens. Robertson highlighted the particular importance of the decision that summer, in light of recent cases of police violence against detainees in the cell block, the labelling of HIV-positive gay men as sexual predators, ongoing Ottawa police sweeps being conducted to "clean up" neighbourhoods where sex workers and drug users lived and worked, the history of police violence against G20 protestors, and the fact that the Dyke March ended in Dundonald Park – where street-identified people were routinely harassed by police.

Robertson's comments emphasized the slippery homonational politics being negotiated by the organizing committee. On the one hand, some members of the lesbian and queer community felt less safe with the absence of a permit and

Kathryn Trevenen and Alexa DeGagne

official police presence – an understandable concern given the high level of violence and intimidation that some members of the community face while walking down a street. But on the other hand, the Dyke March Committee felt that it would potentially be compromising the safety and comfort of people who visited the park if it brought police there and that it would be ignoring and marginalizing the many people who would have to stay away from the march if police were present.

After some debate, the march went forward without a permit, but police officers did show up to "marshal," an activity that involved intimidating and yelling at the volunteer Dyke March marshals, verbally harassing them as they walked down the street, and ultimately ticketing one marshal for a traffic violation. The Dyke March Committee responded with an open letter to Police Chief Vern White and the head of the Ottawa Police Services Board. The letter explained that the "decision to march without the police ... honoured the fact that many members of our communities feel threatened and targeted by the Ottawa Police. Many people in our communities are people of colour, street-involved people, HIV-positive people, survivors of sexual violence, and sex workers who frequently experience racial and social profiling" (Ottawa Dyke March Committee 2011). The events at the Ottawa Dyke March not only high-light the pressure that queer communities are under to be "well behaved" and accept paternalistic "protection" and interference from the state (even when they are simply walking down the street) but also demonstrate how important solidarity building is for queer communities. The analysis provided by NOII and the organizing strategies of the Ottawa Dyke March Committee and the CRP draw links between state-sanctioned racism, immigration control, and queered inclusions and exclusions.

Both the protest over the citizenship guide and the debates in the queer community about resisting regulation and police control highlight how different populations are queered and racialized as they circulate through the Canadian imaginary and how they provide the backdrop against which queers are incorporated, policed, and protected, depending on their national standing and "value." In the case of the citizenship guide, we see how "bogus refugees" and fears about "invading" immigrants can be used to recruit affluent white LGBTQ citizens into defending national borders (both symbolically and through policy making) against queered and racialized others. In debates about policing, we see how incorporating some sexually exceptionalized citizens into the category of "protected" encourages some LGBTQ people to advocate for "tough on crime" approaches that reinforce the marginalization and criminalization of Indigenous people, poor people, activists, and sex workers, among others. This analysis demonstrates the importance of resisting the politics of homonational incorporation in Canada by highlighting that despite the appeal and material benefits (for some) that might arise from friendly relations with the state, incorporation will always come with renewed exclusion or surveillance of targeted populations.

Notes

1 Bill C-389 was introduced in 2010 by Bill Siksay, a member of Parliament in the New Democratic Party, to amend the Canadian Human Rights Act to include gender identity and gender expression as prohibited grounds of discrimination. Also, it would have amended the Criminal Code so that crimes committed against people because of their gender identity and/or expression would be treated as hate crimes. The bill died in the Senate with the call of the 2011 federal election. A similar bill (Bill C-279) passed a second reading in the House of Commons in June 2012. Bill C-279 seeks to include gender identity and gender expression in the Canadian Human Rights Act and Criminal Code (Parliament of Canada 2011).

2 For a discussion of Conservative rhetoric, nationhood, and sexual citizenship, see Awwad (this collection).

3 The Conservative government's omnibus crime bill (Bill C-10: Safe Streets and Communities Act) was passed in March 2012. The bill fundamentally changes nearly every element of Canada's criminal justice system by adding new criminal offences, new and increased mandatory minimum sentences, the selective elimination of conditional sentences, increased pretrial detention and harsher sentencing principles for young offenders, longer waiting times before individuals can apply for pardons, and increased barriers for Canadians detained abroad who wish to serve the remainder of their sentence at home.

4 Bill C-31, passed in June 2012, reforms the Canadian refugee-protection system. Conservative immigration minister Jason Kenney argued that the bill would stop abuses of the immigration and refugee systems from foreign criminals, human smugglers, and those with unfounded refugee claims. Critics have said that the bill has many dangerous flaws: it sets impossibly tight deadlines for preparation of refugee hearings and for processing refugee claims, it allows the minister alone to decide which countries are safe, it allows groups of two or more to be detained if the government decides they are "irregular arrivals," it allows children to be detained with their parents or sent to foster care, it allows refugee claimants who are from countries deemed safe or who are deemed irregular arrivals to be denied the right to appeal, and it denies desperately needed healthcare funding to refugees (T. Cohen 2012).

5 Conservative commenter Ezra Levant has said, "These are gypsies, a culture synonymous with swindlers. The phrase[s] gypsy and cheater have been so interchangeable historically that the word [gypsy] has entered the English language as a verb: he gypped me. Well the gypsies have gypped us. Too many have come here as false refugees. And they come here to gyp us again and rob us blind as they have done in Europe for centuries ... They're gypsies. And one of the central characteristics of that culture is that their chief economy is theft and begging" (quoted in Farber, Leipciger, and Rosensweig 2012). Minister Kenney and other Conservative members of Parliament have constantly reiterated the idea that Roma refugees are "bogus" refugees since they do not face "real" persecution and come to Canada merely to take advantage of generous healthcare and welfare programs (Berger and Rehaag 2012).

6   CBC News Edmonton broke the story and reported that the investigating officer "also did not call in the dog team or Air 1, the police helicopter, in an attempt to track the four young men. That is standard procedure for such a serious crime, according to one veteran of the Edmonton force, who spoke on condition of anonymity. He also said department policy requires officers to file reports on the same day, especially in a case involving a serious incident, such as an aggravated assault and potential hate crime" (Rusnell 2010b).

7   The CRP decided that it did not need a constitution, leaders, or a hierarchal structure and comprises Shannon's friends, anarchists, activists, academics, queers, and allies.

8   For a discussion of prisoner justice, see Fink (this collection).

9   In an open letter on 30 April 2010 in response to the EPS's handling of the case, the SMLC (2010) acknowledged the EPS's "timely arrest of the alleged predator" and the police chief's public apology for the "breach in reporting policy by the attending Constable," noting that his statements "demonstrated the gravity in which the EPS has taken our community's concerns." Crawford said that the apology was merely an attempt to appease the queer community and that the liaison committee should have been more critical of the motives behind it. Wells responded that the SMLC had chosen to work with the institution of the police service, rather than against it, in order to keep the EPS transparent (Ruddy 2010b).

10 Details about the attacker, in the media or from police, are limited not only because he was a minor at the time of the attack but also because whiteness (and we believe the attacker to be white) remains an un(re)markable detail.

11 The recent case of Cece McDonald, an African American trans woman, further illustrates the dynamics of sexual exceptionalism and subjectivities targeted for death rather than life. In June 2012 McDonald was convicted of manslaughter after she defended herself against a white man who had assailed her with racist and transmisogynist insults before physically attacking her (Leger 2012). McDonald's experience as a trans woman of colour in the context of a racist, transphobic, and transmysogynist society was delegitimized in court when expert testimony about the life-threatening danger that trans women face was not considered admissible in her trial. Here again, Dean Spade's (2011) trickle-up analysis is needed to combat a "single issue" criminal justice analysis that failed to account for the many factors affecting Cece McDonald's interaction with a violent white man.

7

"A Queer Too Far"
Blackness, "Gay Blood," and
Transgressive Possibilities

OMISOORE H. DRYDEN

> Not only are black subjects always already queer relative to
> normative ideals of the person, but black queers also often seem *a queer too far* for
> much of queer studies and gay and lesbian popular culture and politics.
>
> **- Jafari S. Allen, *Black/Queer/Diaspora at the Current Conjuncture*,**
> **emphasis added**

In Canada the conjunctural positioning of blackness within sexual liberation, sexual exceptionalism, and same-sex state-sanctioned victories frames how these occurrences are desired, imagined, and measured. In fact, the queerness of blackness and the ways that it is deployed has come to frame the "proper," including objects, matter, bodies, and blood. This chapter explores the varying analytics of racialized sexuality, specifically the queerness of blackness, through an exploration of "gay blood" and blood donation. Blood, an assemblage of diverse, complicated, and competing realities, is manifest culturally and productive in creating knowledge, assigning meanings, and provoking emotions in and through bodies. Blood is a complex text, and any interrogations into blood therefore require "queerer modalities of thought" (Puar 2005, 121), specifically where interlocking systems of oppression are taken into consideration.[1] I bring these considerations and modalities of thought to discussions of "gay blood" and black queer subjectivities in Canada. Current discussions undertaken by Egale Canada preclude and foreclose the presence of other politically viable sexual subjectivities – subjectivities that are also already present. The production of places (Canada), spaces (blood supply), and bodies (gay-queer) is bound up with contradiction, specifically when engaging blackness. The conditions of inclusion facilitate blackness as not-belonging through both its visibility and invisibility (McKittrick 2007).

Canadian Blood Services argues that its required donor questionnaire is specifically designed to effectively distinguish between donors who have blood that gives life and donors who have blood that brings death. Canadian Blood Services and the donor questionnaire were established as a direct outcome of the recommendations of the Krever Commission following the crisis in Canada over HIV/AIDS-tainted blood.[2] The donor questionnaire is intended to provide the nation with a safe and life-giving blood supply by asking potential donors a number of questions regarding travel history, medical background, drug use, and sexual encounters. Also included are questions regarding "geographic" locations, ostensibly to determine where one is "from" and where one has been (and for how long), as well as to facilitate the determination of the range and scope of potential sexual contact while "there." The donor questionnaire is designed to facilitate the identification of potential blood-borne diseases, but in practice the questions have been most closely directed at preventing a recurrence of the HIV/AIDS outbreak in the "general" population.

The scope and breadth of the questions on the donor questionnaire[3] are important to note, for each question does not simply exist as a separate and distinct "moment" with its own historical specificity but is also *conjunctural* – connected and hinging upon the others – and thus part of a larger, vibrant discursive exchange. For example, question 19 – "Men have you had sex with another man, even one time since 1977?" – probes sexual practice. Although this question can be separated from the others, isolated, and singularly held up as a question about sexual identity, specifically bisexual and gay sexual identities and their "gay blood," it is part of a chorus of questions that collectively interrogate sexuality and provide insights into sexual identities, their blood, and the national blood supply. One such proximal moment is question 30, which in part reads, "Were you born in or have you lived in Africa since 1977," and "have you had sexual contact with anyone who was born in or lived in Africa since 1977?" This question also speaks to sexuality and provides added significance to the limited and simplified articulation of "gay blood." Constructing "gay blood" to be a necessary component in the national blood supply, as the blood of the nation, separates it from other narratives – other proximal moments – that disrupt the history of the imagined truths of blood in which contemporary narratives of homonationalist "gay blood" reside.

I therefore employ a black queer diasporic analytic to interrogate the homonationalist construction of both "just gay" (Lenon 2005) blood and the donor questionnaire and to seek out transgressive possibilities of the queerness of blackness. This analytic reveals how racialized sexuality is framed within and by the questions in the donor questionnaire and the corresponding mediation and surveillance of life-giving blood. This discordant analytic, like its poststructural associations, is multidirectional and multidimensional, allowing for a shift in gaze that challenges stabilized meanings and fixed binaries. Stuart Hall (1990, 229) posits that this shift in gaze "show[s] how meaning is never finished or completed, but keeps on moving to encompass other, additional, or supplementary meanings." Engaging with this destabilizing practice is necessary for the unsettling and disruption of contemporary homonationalist constructions of ("just gay") blood.[4]

As expressed in the opening epigraph, black queer subjects are both already queer and at once "a queer too far." They are subjects whose blood and bodies are already out of place, in an outer (not here) space, and thus outer-national. The importance of using a black queer diasporic analytic within this contested region known as "Canada" draws on an already present lineage of black queer studies that insists upon potential possibilities for imagining transgressive futures. It is an analytic that takes up racialized sexuality and thus criss-crosses many boundaries. The black queer diaspora exposes the impossibilities of settlement, revealing its continuing and persistent displacement. It identifies a "perpetual unsettlement." Therefore, it is important to consider different approaches and trajectories of belonging that offer greater possibilities for transgressive transformations.

In the first section of this chapter, I speak to how Egale Canada has used blackness to facilitate a framing of a "gay" Canadian subject and homonationalist blood. I then turn to Canadian Blood Services and an examination of nationalist blood narratives, such as blood-protection laws, blood quantum, and miscegenation. These colonial significations of blood have facilitated and informed contemporary narratives of blood safety and purity. The chapter ends with a closer look at the donor questionnaire and the knowledge it produces about blood, bodies, and the queerness of blackness.

Egale Canada: Whose National Organization?

Egale Canada,[5] once known as "Equality for Gays and Lesbians Everywhere," currently describes itself as "*our* national lesbian, gay, bisexual, and trans (LGBT) human rights organization: advancing equality, diversity, education and justice"

OmiSoore H. Dryden

(Egale Canada n.d., emphasis added).[6] This utterance of "our" is animated through the ways that Egale presents lesbian and gay subjects in and through legal interventions to secure equality rights. The parameters of (what makes) a Canadian gay subject emerge through this work, including Egale's intervention with the blood donor questionnaire, thus offering further insights into who and what this subject is. In its mandate to secure equality for "gay people and their families," Egale has pursued a number of goals, including the acquisition and extension of marriage rights.

In the process of securing marriage rights, as argued by Suzanne Lenon (2005), Egale makes use of racial analogy, specifically anti-miscegenation laws. Anti-miscegenation laws dictated that black people were legally prohibited from marrying white people. Through this use of racial analogy, Egale suggests that same-sex couples being prevented from marrying was "just like" the racism, discrimination, and violence black people endured *in the United States*. This analogy has many effects; here I wish to highlight two. First, by focusing on the experience of racism in the United States, both blackness and the realities of racism are overlooked and effectively placed outside of Canada. In addition, the deployment of this analogy productively constructs sexuality and race as separately occurring conditions, with gay bodies then understood as white and black bodies understood as heterosexual. To construct a lesbian and gay subject alongside a black subject is to produce (and declare) a white gay subjectivity. This is the type of process that Allan Bérubé (2001, 246) speaks of in his work on "gay whitening practices." The temporal proximity between the advocating for marriage rights and the advocating for inclusion of "gay blood" facilitates this entrenchment of a gay white subject and Egale's continued participation in "gay whitening practices." Unlike in its work to secure marriage rights, where blackness became an analogy necessary to constructing gay subjectivity and gay humanity, in its work on blood, instead of using racial analogies, Egale *refused* to acknowledge the presence of the queered blackness of blood.

The "just gay" individual upon whom Egale relies is imagined to be a stable and reliable subject (as understood through the practices of marriage and child-rearing, presumed to mirror the tropes of family relations and kinship) and a subject who not only believes *in* the nation but also actively supports the nation (as understood through service in the military and, in this case, the "patriotic" desire to donate one's blood). In turn, it is reasoned that only question 19 can be the primary question of concern in relation to "gay blood."

In general, the work to modify the "gay blood" ban speaks to important concerns of HIV/AIDS and to the desire for participation in the nation as fully included citizens. A modification to the ban would include limiting the terms of indefinite deferral and removing the question all together, thereby no longer targeting men who have sex with men or casting them as endemically diseased and ultimately responsible for the tainted-blood scandal. Thus the continuing prevailing narratives that construct gay life as part of the larger "general public" seem to shift with the acceptance of "gay blood" as life-giving so that it is no longer seen as bringing death and therefore no longer a threat to the nation's safety. In making this argument, Egale actively and definitively distances "gay life" from other questions on the questionnaire, questions that also speak to the lives of queer and trans people in Canada, including question 30.

The manipulation of blackness becomes a device that Egale uses to construct belonging (to gay community) and political subjectivities, which it then ascribes to some while denying it to others. For Egale, question 30, (African) HIV/AIDS, and blackness become much too far afield to be understood as related and as members of "the family." The concern of HIV/AIDS is over a narrow conception of homophobia, one that excludes the important concerns of racialized sexuality and racism. Prioritizing question 19 over other questions facilitates a "just gay" or "gay only" reading of the question that suggests it is not "lived through" forms of racialization (Allen 2012; Bérubé 2001; Johnson 2005; Lorde 1984). And this is an important indication of how Egale animates the "our" in its current motto, "Egale Canada is our national lesbian, gay, bisexual, and trans (LGBT) human rights organization: advancing equality, diversity, education and justice." The exclusion of narratives on racialized sexuality from the work on including "gay blood" in the national blood supply demonstrates its homonationalist deployment.

Other proximal questions on the questionnaire also participate in the dialogue on sexuality, and what these questions articulate must also be considered. When these moments (the other questions) are brought into contact with one another, including question 19, "new" ideas emerge. Borrowing from E. Patrick Johnson (2005, 127), we can describe these meditations as *quare*. Quare is a way of knowing that is viewed, as Johnson argues, "both as discursively mediated and as historically situated and materially conditioned." The proximity of the questions in the questionnaire provides added significance not only because of their connection to continuing significations of HIV/AIDS but also because of how belonging is delimited through the dialectics of racialization, sexuality, and colonialism. The continuity of these "queerer" meditations with other moments on the questionnaire allows for further exploration and interrogation into the dialogues regarding sexuality, "gay blood," and the national blood supply. The blood(ied) system in Canada is a contemporary technology of

OmiSoore H. Dryden

nation building, and thus to know oneself as a blood donor in this system is to entertain, embrace, and engage in the colonialist productions of citizenship.

Canadian Blood Services and the Colonial Signification of Blood

The blood business in Canada is intimately connected to the production of Canadian nationalism. Incorporated in 1909, the Canadian Red Cross Society was an auxiliary to the government's military medical services in wartime and held its first public, nonmilitary blood donor clinic in 1940. With the slogan "Make a Date with a Wounded Soldier" (Picard 1995), Canadians were urged to donate blood, with all donations being reserved for use solely within the military. The formation of voluntary blood donation during and in response to the Second World War effectively configured the practice of donation as one of citizenship and nation making, and by recruiting citizens to identify with Canadian soldiers and then donate blood, it further consolidated the nation. Not only did the practice of donating one's blood become the "Canadian" thing to do, but it also became as archetypically and emblematically "Canadian" as the national anthem and ice hockey. The inception of blood donor clinics, influenced by current scientific and normative social-political narratives of blood, weave together and enmesh race, sex, and gender with cultural contagions. Although "make a date with a soldier" is simply and morally stated, this slogan is deeply gendered, racialized, and I posit, queered.

All blood collected was earmarked for military use. The first blood transfusion recipients were white American and British soldiers, and following the direction of the American Red Cross Society, all blood collected in Canada was racially catalogued with the purpose of ensuring that white soldiers did not receive blood from not-white bodies, as it was believed that not-white blood was inferior to white blood and therefore not fit for white soldiers. In addition, between 1940 and 1942, women who largely ran the clinics were not allowed to donate blood, as it was suggested that women would not be able to handle or manage the physical process of donation. It was not until 1947 when the first peacetime blood donor clinic was held that all blood collected was made available for use by the general public. These blood narratives of racial segregation and gendered exclusion framed early practices of blood donation in Canada and constitute the social determinants of blood, belonging, and inclusion that continue to inform the blood system in Canada today.

The blood system in Canada, as deployed through the Canadian Red Cross Society and Canadian Blood Services, purports to provide a safe blood supply to the nation. As a result of the scandal over HIV/AIDS-tainted blood, the Canadian Red Cross Society was held legally liable for its failure to keep the blood supply safe and as a result was stripped of all responsibilities related to blood donation. In its place, Canadian Blood Services was formed with a mandate that included restoring the public's confidence in the blood system. Under recommendation from the Krever Commission and to fulfil its commitment to providing a clean and healthy blood supply, Canadian Blood Services instituted a screening process that included the use of a donor questionnaire. The questionnaire was specifically designed to identify and distinguish between bodies that have blood that gives life and bodies with blood that brings death. However, blood is much more complicated than these simply stated either-or binaries. Blood, including the blood collected for the purposes of donation, flows amid a much larger field of reference in which "giving life" (turning toward) and "bringing death" (marked for) are but two possibilities.

The work to modify Canadian Blood Services' "gay blood" ban also takes up these considerations of life and death, specifically the push to have gay bodies "folded into life" (Puar 2007).[7] As Michel Foucault (1990, 149, emphasis added) reminds us, there is "a long series of permanent interventions at the level of the body, conduct, health, and everyday life" that receive "their color and their justification from the mythical concern with protecting the *purity of the blood* and ensuring the *triumph of the race*." In line with Foucault, the hermeneutics of blood operates in the management of populations through the categorization (and thus creation) of multiple body types that delimit those of the nation, those outside of the nation, and those considered to be out of place, to occupy outer – (not here) – space, to be outer-national. Nations have laid claim to space and place through the signification of blood. Nations use blood to facilitate the language of lineage, and they use purity to dominate and inform the manufacturing of the nation, national identity, and the body politic.

Canada, through its blood quantum practices, is not the only nation to rely upon blood to produce knowledge about bodies, purity, lineage, and relatedness. The United States through blood quantum and one-drop theory, or miscegenation, and Germany through its blood protection laws are but two notable examples. Blood stories, such as blood protection laws, blood quantum, and miscegenation narrate the constitutive making of bodies and framings of belonging. Although these stories are considered to belong firmly in the past – a different time, place, and/or space – they continue to influence contemporary blood narratives and the politics of blood donation in *this* moment. These historical and contemporary blood theories and practices depend on a physical legibility of identity and on the surveillance of these bodies to ensure that "othered" bodies – those considered impure, "bad," foreign, and dangerous – remain readily identifiable as "Other" and therefore perpetually out of place in the nation, including the blood supply.

The desire to find "truths" in blood facilitated the devastating realities of the Holocaust. Constructed and fictitious narratives of blood purity targeted marginal and vulnerably positioned bodies, marking them for eradication through legislative edicts regarding marriage, procreation, and death. The Law for the Protection of German Blood and German Honour (1935–43) was designed to construct a "master race" by folding specific bodies into life while marking other(ed) bodies for death – that is, by regulating the populace. Narratives of blood purity, born of racist, anti-Semitic, homophobic, and misogynistic constructions and engagements of the body, proved deadly for bodies identified as possessing "Jewish" blood or, as time progressed, "Gypsy," "Negro," or "homosexual" blood. The dehumanization of this tainted Other was deeply systemic and far-reaching, with Canada refusing asylum to fleeing Jewish refugees seeking a safe haven. Citational practices of blood purity discourses, in this case, led to the rejection of the pleas for sanctuary.

First Nations peoples and communities are numerous, diverse, sovereign, self-governing, and self-defining, and they *currently* exist and have existed since before the creation of the limiting borders now understood as Canada. In 1850 the enactment of An Act for the Better Protection of Lands and Property of Indians in Lower Canada provided a blood-based definition of the newly constructed racial category of "Indian," imposing a singular, "just Indian" identity upon diverse peoples. This legal definition declared and created the singular identity of "Indian," which became the basis upon which treaty and citizenship rights were formed. This newly created legal definition was part of a larger concentrated effort of racialization and genocide that dispossessed people from themselves and their surroundings and placed them in the service of colonial nation building. This legislation meant that existing kinship and community lines of relatedness were disrupted (and redrawn). The introduction of blood to signify "Indianness" in effect marked many for death. The results of this blood quantum system are evident today in the continuing repressive legislation that upholds a legal form of apartheid still in existence in Canada (Lawrence 2004, 27).

Blood protection laws and blood quantum are two blood narratives where blood is used to construct white bodies, limit nation-state citizenship, and map the borders of nations through the racialization (and othering) of specific bodies. These bodies, perpetually excluded, are tethered to the nation and necessary for the nation's construction. One last example of a blood narrative regarding "perpetual exclusion" through the racialization of blood and bodies and the construction of whiteness is the "one-drop" rule, or miscegenation.[8]

The one-drop rule is a blood narrative directly constitutive of white and not-white bodies. This narrative posits that a single drop of black or not-white blood thoroughly contaminates the purity of the white body, resulting in its defilement. This one drop of black/not-white blood was a threat to the nation's security, and the regulation of bodies was thus needed to secure and protect the nation. Various anti-miscegenation laws were implemented in the United States banning procreation between the "races" and making interracial marriage illegal. As these laws did not prevent these actions, a further fractionalization of the body was used to mark the levels of defilement that had occurred. Bodies were broken into halves, quarters, and eighths according to their blood quotient. As long as a body had one-half, or one-quarter, or one-eighth "black" blood, it was legally categorized as "Negro." As Debra Thompson (2008, 17) informs us, the racial epithets of "mulatto" (half black and half white), "quadroon" (one-quarter black and three-quarters white), and "octoroon" (one-eighth black and seven-eighths white) were all manifestations of black bodies and were not, in the eyes of the law, nation, and society, the equivalent of white racial identity. It should be noted that some hypodescent laws, in addition to identifying black bodies, also identified Indigenous bodies, Asian bodies, and Filipino bodies and, in some cases, simply referenced "all non-white" bodies (ibid., 2).

Blood "truths" of hypodescent narratives dictate that black ancestry (through black blood) is a powerful queered contaminant (perhaps like present-day HIV/AIDS) that overwhelms white racial purity. The claims of "race defilement" and "race protection" (language prevalent in Germany's blood protection laws) are supported through medicalization and scientific discourse. To claim a white racial identity was to declare one's blood purity *and* one's sexual purity. White racial identity suggested that white bodies were not involved in any "sexual transgressions" that would compromise the safety, security, and purity of whiteness, its blood, and the nation. The effects of the one-drop rule, or miscegenation, continue to impact current understandings of blackness and racialization in North America, including Canada. Blood performativity, as discussed in these three examples, gestures to verbal and nonverbal forms of expression that are taken up legally, politically, and socially and used to imagine, manufacture, and realize the nation. The intimacy between blood, sexuality, and "race" is used in these processes of nation building, with national blood narratives allowing the nation to include and exclude at will. The state surveillance of blood, through colonization and citizenship, access to marriage, and mandates of procreation, dictates the image of the ideal imagined community.

OmiSoore H. Dryden

These national narratives are also transnational since they transcend boundaries, indicating how blood has come to be understood as a barometer of life, death, sexuality, racialization, group belonging, and the limits of citizenship.

Blood stands in as the porous border, where definitions of us and them, insider and outsider, here and there, citizen and Other are forged *and* leak into one another. Demarcating sexualized blood from racialized blood is the attempt to erect impenetrable boundaries in the production and animation of *Canadian* white-blood purity. These stories provide a genealogy of current blood donation practices. It is within this framework of nationalized blood narratives that contemporary "gay blood" discourses reside.

It's in (Hey) You (There!) to Give

One evening while checking out my Facebook (FB) timeline, I noticed a status update by an FB friend who declared that he had become a registered stem cell and bone marrow donor, a program also operated by Canadian Blood Services. He became registered in honour of Black History Month, having responded to a call from Canadian Blood Services for more bodies of African-descended Canadians. He then stated that as a gay man, he hoped to also do his part by one day becoming a blood donor. This is such a captivating queer moment. How are one's perceived inclusion in the nation via the donation of black stem cells and one's exclusion from the nation via the prohibition against the donation of "gay blood" reconciled? How can black "gay blood" be acknowledged in this moment? Racialized sexuality in Canada remains an unresolved anxiety, and the black body therefore persists as a strange, *queerly* positioned body.[9]

The tagline for Canadian Blood Services is "it's in you to give." Used in television and radio commercials, online, and in print, "it's in you to give" is attached to the plea/demand to "book an appointment today." The address "it's in you to give" is used not simply to beckon donors but also to hail national subjects, specifically those who participate in the safeguarding of the nation – in this case, through the gifting of their life-giving blood. Drawing from Louis Althusser (1970), and his discussion of the police officer who calls out "hey you there," I argue that the Canadian Blood Services tagline has people responding to the hail, essentially turning around as if *they* have been personally called and, in so doing, proceeding to engage in the steps required to take up the subject position of donor. However, not all people who respond are actually the object of the hail. Although one may feel that the call "it's in (hey) you (there) to give" is just for them and excitedly begin the process of assessment, the subject position of donor may continue to be elusive. Participating in the assessment process by completing the donor questionnaire may produce surprising results, with the one who responded to the call instead being assigned a different, othered, subject position.

The donor questionnaire is a printed document[10] reminiscent of multiple-choice questions on school exams, with participants invited to provide an answer that best reflects their location, position, and place. The questionnaire is divided into two sections, with the participant filling out questions 1 to 13 directly and questions 14 to 30 being asked *of* the participant by the clinic worker. With the donor-screening process currently employed, after donations have been made, donors may indicate (anonymously) whether their blood should be used or destroyed. At issue here is whether clinic workers are also given a tag that they can place on the bags of donation that indicate their own assessment of whether blood should be used or destroyed. During the Krever Commission it was revealed that nurses who found donors visibly ill or in some way "suspicious" would tag their donation for elimination and subsequent destruction. These practices were sometimes policies of individual clinics and sometimes choices of the individual nurses (Parsons 1995). Although all blood goes through a testing process, according to Canadian Blood Services the tests currently available and in use are unable to capture all strains of HIV, specifically, they note, that of HIV-O, which they determine is geographically specific to Africa, even though there is evidence that this strain is also found within Europe and North America. So perhaps these extra layers of surveillance – personal anonymous confessions and clinic workers' judgments – are understood to capture the blood that passes the testing but may house deathly infection(s) that remain undetectable.

This shift of potential donor from subject to object in the liminal space between questions 13 and 14 is significant for its transition from confession to surveillance. In this space between the two questions, the blood donor moves from the subject of confession to the object of an interrogation that "incites" truth from ("gets" truth out of) participants. But instead of thinking one's self into donor subjectivity, what would it mean to think one's self out of it? In thinking one's self out of these unwelcome inclusions, what type of queer futures become open? What other questions informed by the signification of HIV/AIDS and racialized sexuality, yet outside of homonormative desires for gay inclusion, does the questionnaire hold that may facilitate "new" queerer/quarer forms of knowing? What is the added significance and larger, vibrant discursive exchange of these conjunctural questions?

In addition to question 19 – "Men have you had sex with another man, even one time since 1977?" – I highlight questions 22 and 30,[11] which read,

OmiSoore H. Dryden

22. Female donors: In the last 12 months, have you had sex with a man who had sex, even one time since 1977 with another man?

30. a) Were you born in or have you lived in Africa since 1977? b) Since 1977, did you receive a blood transfusion or blood product in Africa? c) Have you had sexual contact with anyone who was born in or lived in Africa since 1977?

As blackness is produced within and through formations of gender and sexuality (Keeling 2007; Somerville 2000; Walcott 2000, 2003; Wright 2004), once question 30 is made visible as a viable and important queer conjunctural moment, it compels an othered reading of the entire questionnaire – a reading that seeks to identify an outer (not here) space in which the "queer too far" can be found. Such a turn would have blood narratives become unhinged from their biological ties and metaphors of kinship and national relatedness and instead examine what is revealed when different modes of belonging, and perhaps un-belonging, are engaged. Blood pours through and across borders, time, and space. Blood pours from question to question, such as questions 4 (parts d and e) and 12, which read,

4. d) In the last 6 months, have you had a tattoo, ear or skin piercing, acu-puncture or electrolysis? e) In the last 6 months have you had an injury from a needle or come in contact with someone else's blood?

12. Have you ever had an AIDS (HIV) test other than for donating blood?

Questions 18, 24, and 25 also participate in this conversation:

18. At any time since 1977, have you taken money or drugs for sex?

24. At any time in the last 12 months, have you paid money or drugs for sex?

25. At any time in the last 12 months, have you had sex with anyone who has taken money or drugs for sex?

And question 29, the final question to which I attend in this dialogue, asks,

29. In the past 6 months, have you had sex with someone whose sexual back-ground you don't know?

These questions speak to a policing of sex, sexuality, gender, and race that impacts how we come to understand queer and trans life in Canada. Tattoos and electrolysis, contact with someone else's blood, and HIV tests signify suspicious behaviour that is both "unhealthy" and "abnormal." These simplistically worded questions conceal the extensive ways that one may experience these practices and the range of people to whom these questions apply. For example, sex during menstruation (hers, his, or theirs)[12] is not an uncommon occurrence. How is injury from a needle to be determined? Does this include needle play or the self-administering of testosterone? What of the various uses of electrolysis and tattooing, including, for some who engage in these practices, as part of a transition process? And a number of assumptions are made about how knowing one's status is empowering and supportive of one's self, especially within one's sexual life.

Even a cursory glance at these questions suggests a list of behaviours, actions, and bodies that are considered deviant and dubious and thus potential threats to the blood supply. Taken as a whole, the criteria beg the question of who is left if all the people to whom these questions apply are barred from donating blood (even temporarily)? The weight of these questions does not gesture to the possibility of creating a safe blood supply. Instead, it highlights the deep complexity in attempts to do just that. The narratives captured within these questions articulate a particular understanding of sexed, gendered, and racial normalcy *through* citizens with life-giving blood. These questions are an attempt to control the sex of others – to dictate the normal – through the shame of being too "tainted" (too queer, too black, too sexual), and therefore too contagious, to donate blood. The questions that regard sex and money, that require knowledge of sexual history, and that censure casual sex collectively signify the "bringing of death" measured in the blood supply. These questions, then, are not merely an attempt to secure "safe" blood, and they are not primarily about the safety of blood. Rather, when taken conjuncturally, they construct an othered subject who is beyond the boundaries of the proper performance of citizenship and therefore outside the realm of acceptable gayness. In so doing, these questions speak to a fluidity of bodies and situations that ebb and flow and therefore cannot be controlled.

The blood narratives found in the donor questionnaire indicate the "manifest contradictions and intricacies of sexuality" (Eng 2011, 195). The exclusion of these questions from the legal and political demands for the inclusion of "gay blood" marks a specifically notable homonationalist moment, for not only do doctrines of inclusion require the silencing of also queerly framed questions, but they also require an aggressive "unknowing" of how these related blood narratives participate in and alongside historically situated national narratives of exclusion, citizenship construction, and nation making.

What is to be made of the seeming distinctions between the use of "sex" and "sexual contact" evident in the aforementioned questions? No other information

OmiSoore H. Dryden

is offered, either on the donor questionnaire or on the Canadian Blood Services website that would gesture to how these words are being used. Perhaps it is because Canadian Blood Services is also unsure about whether the words are similar, overlapping, or different. Nonetheless, a distinction is evident as "sexual contact" is only deployed in question 30, thus its use must have different parameters than the use of "sex" in other questions. Does the use of "sexual contact" with this question on African blood speak to a particular type of "African" sexual practice? Perhaps it is important to return to the work of Cindy Patton (1990, 25), who has stated, "Much political and social violence is accomplished by collapsing the many cultures of the African continent in the invention [of] 'Africa.'" This collapse of cultures is a necessary step in the construction of a specific "African AIDS" based upon colonialist and racist disorientations of the past centuries. Question 30 mirrors the narratives of racialized contamination found in Patton's work. Arguments in support of this question[13] rely upon an assumed scientific objectivity that is believed to be beyond or outside of its own genealogies of monogeny,[14] polygeny,[15] and miscegenation. Question 30 embodies the discursive articulations of "African AIDS," which are dependent upon the racist tropes of "*the* dark continent" and blackness. These tropes construct Africa as a region where the (black) people are in a perpetual state of development, not yet fully human, and where condom use is nonexistent, medical care is poor and unreliable, and deadly epidemics (known and unknown) are uncontrollable and overwhelming. The racialized science of sexuality and blood demands that a "secret" be uncovered and exposed. Question 30 and the other above-mentioned questions police sex, gender, and race, while working in tandem to construct a queered (always contagious) Other who is mistakenly hailed yet already under surveillance. The practice of pathologizing[16] behaviour and bodies is as fluid and interconnecting as the blood said to hold these bodily "truths."

It was within this framework that I asked my Facebook friend his thoughts about Canadian Blood Services' need for stem cell and bone marrow donations from African Canadians despite its rejection of Africans in Canada from donating blood, my hope being to disrupt the homonormative belief that a mere modification of question 19 would become the site through which black queerness (framed as queerly contagious) would be allowed to enter. The continued push for "just gay" inclusion through the focus on question 19 holds within it a racial history of whiteness, as illustrated by its silence about other also queered blood questions. Yet the accepted belonging of some gays perpetuates the violence against othered queers. What other futures can be imagined if we embrace the ability for blood to disrupt, disorder, and unsettle? The focus on these questions reveals that these discourses of blood facilitate disintegration, and it disrupts the narratives of cohesion that too simply seek and speak to an ideal donor, national, and gay subject.

Blood bodies are always subject to change and cannot be regarded as natural; rather, they experience mediation through different and divergent social constructions. The currencies of blood, the politics of blood donation, and the national narrative of (un)belonging produced by Canadian Blood Services are the location of interrogation of subjugated knowledge that may facilitate a future thinking that allows for interventions with (homo)nationalist inclusion. Canadian Blood Services and its donor questionnaire effectively participate in the cumulative articulations of an ideal blood donor, the person who is free from HIV/AIDS, within larger (national and community) conversations of blood purity and safety. The questionnaire, as a discursive tool, facilitates the production of truths and beliefs regarding donors and also reflects the untenable contradictions demonstrated by my FB friend. So even though it now may be possible (within severely limited conditions) to imagine "safe," HIV/AIDS-free, *gay* blood donors, is it possible to imagine "safe," HIV/AIDS-free, *black/African* blood donors? Or is the queerness of blackness a queer too far?

Blood encounters are simultaneously deeply personal, social, scientific, political, and messy. In taking up the messiness of leaky blood encounters, the seemingly unwarranted simplicity that frames blood in both contemporary blood systems and the Canadian Blood Services' donor questionnaire is disrupted. More directly, messy blood encounters trouble the narrow framing of a "gay blood" ban and "gay inclusion" as understood through contemporary lesbian and gay political activism that has sought to modify this framing, the responses given by Canadian Blood Services in seeking its continuation, and current interpretations of inclusion.

The deployment of blood is a tool of racialization, empire, and the settler colonial project. Consequently, its narratives continue to coerce, persuade, and transform bodies and desires – as seen in the desire to perform the nation through donation of one's blood. Following the direction of Jacqui Alexander and Chandra Mohanty (1997), I argue that the decolonization of blood and blood donation requires that we think ourselves out of these spaces of domination and into something outer-national.

As of July 2015, Canadian Blood Services has modified the donor questionnaire and has removed question 29 (sex with someone whose sexual background you do not know) and amended question 30 to now read, "Togo or Cameroon."

OmiSoore H. Dryden

Notes

1   Here I am thinking of the work asked of us by the Combahee River Collective (1977), Audre Lorde (1984), and Barbara Smith (1983), as well as important anthologies like Cherríe Moraga and Gloria Anzaldúa's *This Bridge Called My Back* (1981) and Gloria Hull, Patricia Scott, and Barbara Smith's *But Some of Us Are Brave* (1982) – historical texts that engage these conversations of racialized sexuality.

2   The federal government established the Royal Commission of Inquiry on the Blood System in Canada, more commonly referenced as the Krever Commission, in 1993. The final report and recommendations of the Krever Commission were tabled in the House of Commons in 1997.

3   The donor questionnaire was modified in July 2013 to reflect the changes to question 19 that limit the deferral period to five years – "Men have you had sex with another man in the last five years?" In this chapter, all questions cited are from the previous donor questionnaire. For all other citations of Canadian Blood Services, see https://www.blood.ca.

4   I extend my appreciation to Suzanne Lenon for the many hours of Skype calls that have helped to generate a stronger and more forthright intervention into the homonation.

5   When founded in 1986 in response to the introduction of the Canadian Charter of Rights and Freedoms (M. Smith 1999), Egale's mandate was to secure legal equality for gays and lesbians, and their families, within and across Canada.

6   In 2012 Egale Canada began the process of changing its website, developing a new format. As a result, information from the "old" site has become more difficult to access and in some cases is no longer available.

7   For similar discussions on the movement of gays into "life," see Lenon (this collection).

8   Miscegenation also impacted whether one was considered authentically Indigenous and/or a member of a First Nation, as happened, for example, with the Cherokee Freedmen (see Byrd 2011; Holland 2000; Miles 2005; and Miles and Holland 2006).

9   For a further discussion, see Walcott (2000, 2003).

10 In 2013 Canadian Blood Services began using an electronic, interactive, touchscreen donor questionnaire with images and voiceovers. Assessment of this new tool is beyond the scope of this chapter. Nonetheless, in December 2013 a new clip on its YouTube channel titled "What is it like to donate blood Here's your step-by-step-guide to blood donation" illustrates a young white man filling out a paper version of the donor questionnaire with no mention of the new interactive touchscreen model. See https://www.youtube.com/watch?v=Vlo1vJo55Tg.

11 The rationale for question 30 is articulated as follows: "1. Geographic Deferrals: People who have lived in certain regions of Africa, who may have been exposed to a new strain of the virus that causes AIDS (HIV-I Group O), are not eligible to donate blood. People who have received a blood transfusion while visiting there or who have had sex with someone that has lived there, are also not permitted to donate blood. This is not based on race or ethnicity but possible exposure to HIV-I Group O. Countries included are: Cameroon, Central African Republic, Chad, Congo, Equatorial Guinea, Gabon, Niger and Nigeria."

12 Menstruation is a practice that happens in various bodies, though cissexism often frames menstruation as a function of *only* female bodies. Thus it is important to signal that bodies that menstruate have diverse gender identities.

13 See note 11. The arguments for this strain of HIV/AIDS are suspect, as it has been framed as "new" for approximately twenty years.

14 *Monogeny* is an eighteenth-century racial discourse, which dominated in Europe and North America and held that human beings were made up of different "races" even though they belonged to the same species. Here "race" and "species," although related, were understood to have different and distinct meanings. Those who were deemed caucasian ("white") were constructed as the original and pure form of human bodies, and all other "racial" manifestations of humans were considered to be corrupted or a polluted derivative. These racial derivatives, it was posited, were the result of geographical and environmental distinctions (Somerville 1996).

15 Beginning in the early nineteenth century, *polygeny*, largely an American scientific school of thought, presumed that different "races" signalled different "species." The "race" of a human body defined its biological and geographical origins (Somerville 1996). The adoption of this school of thought informed the discursive practices of genocide, slavery, and colonialism (Somerville 1996; Wright and Schuhmann 2007). Both the monogeny and polygeny schools facilitated the regulation and supremacy of "white" bodies and the discourse of "whiteness" and, in so doing, developed and affixed a relationship between "race," intelligence, and (sexual) behaviour.

16 My sincere thanks and appreciation are extended to R. Cassandra Lord for her crucial insights and commentary on an earlier draft of this chapter.

8

National Security and Homonationalism
The QuAIA Wars and the Making
of the Neoliberal Queer

PATRIZIA GENTILE AND GARY KINSMAN

This chapter explores a terrain of struggle that dramatizes the social and historical shift within Canadian state formation from queers as enemies of the state to queers as entitled to limited forms of citizenship. Specifically, we start this investigation by contrasting the social and historical construction of gay men and lesbians as national security risks from the late 1950s through to the 1990s, when thousands were purged from their jobs in the public service and the military (Kinsman and Gentile 2010), with how some queers are now deployed in homonationalist defence of national security. We briefly trace aspects of the historical and social transformation of queers from the historical past, when they were seen as national security threats, to the historical present, when some white, middle-class queers (largely but not entirely gay men) are mobilized as defenders of Canadian national security against Arab- and Muslim-identified people, as well as in defence of Israeli apartheid (separation and subordination) policies toward the Palestinians. Mapping its political implications, we explore how this transformation unfolded.[1]

We do this through a focus on queer Palestine-solidarity activism as a crucial rebellion against an emerging Canadian homonationalism. In particular, we focus on the "wars" over the participation of Queers against Israeli Apartheid (QuAIA), a queer Palestine-solidarity group, in the Toronto Pride Parade from 2008 through 2013. In this investigation, we draw attention to both settler colonial and Orientalist moments in the social organization of homonationalism. Although we view settler and Orientalist homonationalisms as having distinctive characteristics, they are also mutually constructed in and through each other,[2] and we must bring them together in our theory and practice. We also suggest ways that homonormativity and homonationalism can be made more useful for activism and social transformation.

Jasbir Puar and Amit Rai (2002) have made a powerful call for disentangling patriotism from sexuality. This critical stance asks queers to stand in opposition to the national security policies designed to bolster the "war on terror" and heteropatriarchal relations (ibid., 130). Central to this call is a rejection of coding gay and queer as white, the West as queer-friendly, and Muslims and Arabs as always heterosexual. This means that the agency of queers of colour must take precedence in the broader critique of the "war on terror." Central to queer organizing must be a challenge to Orientalist homonationalism and how it is immersed in and grows out of settler homonationalism. Puar and Maya Mikdashi (2012) call for activists to recognize Orientalist and settler homonationalism as mutually constructed so as to avoid the pitfalls of social critiques that fail to adequately account for the normalizing and civilizational discourses reinforced and enacted by US, Canadian, and Israeli colonial policies.

In this chapter, we use "queer" as a way of reclaiming a term of abuse that has been used against people identified as queer; as a broader term than "lesbian," "gay," or "bisexual" that can potentially include the experiences of all those in rupture with institutionalized heterosexuality and the two-gender binary system; and as a way of queering or denaturalizing social relations. At the same time, we criticize queer – and not simply lesbian or gay – identifications deliberately since the use of "queer" within queer theory and in other contexts can obscure class relations and struggles as well as racialized relations and anti-racist struggles and can be complicit in forms of homonormativity and homonationalism. We also use "gay" or "lesbian" when doing so is most appropriate for the historical or social context.

From National Security Risks to Homonationalism

How has it been possible for some queers who were constructed in the historical past as threats to Canadian national security to become (in part) defenders of an Orientalist, racialized, and pro-capitalist national security in the historical present? How is it that layers of queer communities can become defenders of the Israeli occupation and oppression of the Palestinians? We can even go so far as to point to the generation of a specifically gay Islamophobia[3] and identification with a white, European-derived civilizational process constructed as being "modern" and in support of gay rights. This has led to the construction of Islam and Islamic fundamentalism[4] as *the* major threat to queers in some sections of gay communities, especially, but not exclusively, in northern Europe. Currents within Western gay organizing even argue that, on a global scale, the main danger facing queers today is Islamic fundamentalism (Puar 2007, 19). In this construction, it is Islamic "sexual backwardness" that is posited as a threat to "us," who are coded as white and "Western" (see also Wahab, this collection).

The following provides an initial sketch of this process of transformation and integration of lesbian, gay, and queer movements in "Canada." First, by the mid-1970s, broader liberationist approaches had shifted toward a more limited strategy based on human rights. Consequently, political organizing became directed toward struggles for formal legal equality with heterosexuals. Fighting for sexual citizenship (Evans 1993) began with the inclusion of sexual-orientation protection in human rights legislation. This then initiated a trajectory of struggle for inclusion within the legal and social forms of spouse, family, marriage, the military, and even national security. The moment of possible radical transformation of these social forms gets subordinated to the moment of inclusion within these existing and heterosexual-dominated, gendered, racialized, and classed social forms. Entrenched at the centre of this campaign was the ideology that "we" (queers) are just like other white, middle-class people. The only difference, it is argued, is that our relationships are based on same-gender love and sexuality. Major gains and important victories were won through these struggles, but they also reshaped lesbian and gay, and eventually queer, movements (Kinsman 1996; T. Warner 2002). By the mid-1980s section 15 (the equality rights section) of the Canadian Charter of Rights and Freedoms (hereafter, the Charter) allowed lesbians and gay men to push forward on formal legal and equality rights but at the same time also moved them away from substantive forms of social equality and liberation.

Emphasizing the Charter led activists to focus on achieving sexual citizenship. Critically examining sexual citizenship struggles asks the question "citizens of what?" This critical approach to sexual citizenship builds on the foundational work of feminists of colour in the Combahee River Collective (1977), Audre Lorde (1984), Angela Davis (1983), and others who showed that gender and sexuality cannot be analytically separate from race and racialization. This insight also clarified that state formation and state nationalism had a clear gendered and racialized character. In differentiating between social moments of homonationalism, we are drawing on the analysis of different forms of racism and racialization that people of colour face in the US, including the construction of racialized and gendered sexualities (see A. Smith 2006).[5]

Indeed, the citizenship articulated in these Charter-based legal struggles is connected to a growing incorporation of gays and lesbians into Canadian nation-state formation and to an identification of this settler colonial state form as the road to their equal rights (Kinsman 2001). A critical analysis of heterosexist and patriarchal social relations that includes an analysis of class relations and racialization paves the way for more profound understanding. Feminist formulations of heteropatriarchy serve as a foundation for this critical analysis (see Lugones 2007; and A. Smith 2011). Scholarship by anti-racist and anti-colonizing thinkers brings heterosexist and patriarchal social relations together so that we can address both the moments of autonomy and the mutual construction between these social relations. These heteropatriarchal relations are also always thoroughly racialized and classed.

The current generation of homonationalism is contextualized within the construction of the "war on terror," which is also another war for hegemonic masculinity and heterosexuality. The "war on terror" is built upon and mobilizes Orientalism. Edward Said (1979) has described Orientalism as an essentialist understanding of people in Arab and Islamic cultures as sharing common characteristics, a perception rooted in an imaginary derived from western Europe and resulting in the "othering" of these people in relation to the "civilized" West.[6] Orientalist practices are linked to a history of imperialism and settler colonialism and cannot simply be read as being about cultural differences. The portrayal of these differences as being "civilizational" (with white Europeans as "modern" and "superior") has become central to Orientalism.

In the current Orientalist construction of this "war on terror," women, gays, and lesbians come to play a special part given the association of being "modern" and "advanced" with the view that women, gays, and lesbians are entitled to limited rights, in contrast to the supposed gender and sexual "backwardness" of the Arab and Muslim world and, by extension, the global South and people of colour more generally. Ironically, Western moral conservatives in this civilizational discourse who would never support feminism or lesbian and gay rights in Canada or the United States champion the rights of women, gays, and lesbians in Afghanistan, Iran, Iraq, and Palestine. As critically elaborated by Julian Awwad (this collection), the Conservative government of Prime Minister Stephen Harper is positioning itself as a defender of gay rights abroad despite its anti-queer internal positions. Declarations by former Foreign Affairs Minister John Baird in favour of Canada's foreign policy position that "gay rights are human rights" and against the persecution of people on the basis of their sexual orientation are contradicted by the Conservative government's actual

Patrizia Gentile and Gary Kinsman

practices and its lack of support for lesbian, gay, bisexual, and trans people in development aid (Larcher 2012).

Since it has a heterosexual (and heterosexist) character, the production of an aggressive, heteropatriarchal, Orientalist, masculine patriotism is detrimental to most queer people. This involves at least two constructions of Arab and Muslim men in relation to "homosexuality." First, it is centred on the concerted effort to emasculate the Islamic "terrorist" by turning him into a "fag." This is based on portraying Islamic and Arab men as monolithically heterosexual, which supposedly makes them vulnerable to devastation through associations with and accusations of queer sexuality and effeminacy (see Engle 2009; and Puar and Rai 2002, 126).[7] This heterosexual assumption does not take into account the diverse social organization of gendered sexualities and eroticism in the Arab and Islamic worlds, "whose ontological structure is [often] not based on the hetero-homo binary" (Massad 2007, 40). Arab and Muslim queers, and others who engage in same-gender eroticism, are thereby set outside their own communities through this construction, producing major problems for Muslim and Arab queers. Second, the "terrorist monster" can also still be conceptualized and sexualized as queer based on earlier Orientalist images of the Middle East that associate the Arab and Islamic worlds with sexual and moral decadence. This association, in turn, links Arabs and Muslims per se with "decadence," including queerness, and exists both in tension with, and at times in combination with, the newer construction of Arabs and Muslims as "sexually backward" and monolithically heterosexual.

The mantra of the "war on terror" that "you are either with us or against us" underlines and helps to sustain homonationalism as well. The homonationalist mobilizations of the "war on terror" do not lead to any increase in acceptance for queers. Queers of colour, in the Middle East and in the West, become targets of the systemic racism produced by heteropatriarchal patriotism. The "war on terror" is generating a racialized, heterosexual, masculinist patriotism in the global North (Thobani 2007) that, among others, is directed against queers, especially against queers of colour.

Participation by people from queer communities in Orientalist national security practices did not happen suddenly but has come about through a series of social transitions in queer movements, communities, and struggles as well as through the legal and social victories gay and lesbian movements have won. These shifts have built on each other. Together and over time, these social transitions and legal victories transformed what was a radical, transgressive social movement into a largely (but still contested) integrationist and accommodationist project. These shifts occurred within a settler homonation-alist context where an earlier opposition to Canadian state national security and sexual policing practices increasingly grew to identify with Canadian nation-state formation based on the colonization of Indigenous peoples. The impact of the Charter of Rights and Freedoms and the struggle for sexual citizenship rights (Evans 1993) were central to this transition.

"Settler homonationalism" is Scott Morgensen's (2011b, 2) resituation of Puar's emphasis on Orientalist understandings of homonationalism and opens new possibilities for grounding this term. "Canada" as a white settler society is built on the history of the colonizing of the Indigenous peoples. Queer iden-tifications with the Canadian nation-state are therefore based on a settler col-onialism and homonationalism since all forms of Canadian nationalism are founded on the appropriation and marginalization of Indigenous peoples. This settler colonialism is also based on the construction of a "modern sexuality" in response to the gendered and erotic practices of Indigenous peoples. With Morgensen (ibid., 42), we argue that "settler colonialism is a central condition of the history of sexuality" in what comes to be called "Canada." Pivotal to this history of sexuality and state formation are a normalized heterosexuality and "deviant" homosexualities (Kinsman 1996)[8] that find their roots in colonizing projects that undermined and transformed Indigenous peoples' social relations, including quite centrally their gender and erotic practices. Orientalist aspects of homonationalism get mobilized within this historical and social context (Morgensen 2011b, 2013). In discussing settler colonialism, Morgensen (2013) argues that the Canadian government's support of Israeli apartheid signals its explicit collusion with Israel's settler colonial rule. A critique of Orientalist homonationalism that is not extended to a critical analysis of settler homo-nationalism is politically limited.[9]

Before proceeding in this exploration, we need some clarification on "homonormativity" (Duggan 2002)[10] and "homonationalism." Both these terms and the analysis associated with them forge a critical path in directing our attention to how neoliberalism, capitalist globalization, and the "war on terror" impact sexual and gender relations and sexual subjectivities. Although "homo-normativity" and "homonationalism" are useful and suggestive terms, we find that they need to be rooted in historical and social practices if they are to be most useful to activists and to transformative social struggles. Without this grounding, the usefulness of these terms as concepts for critical analysis and struggle is limited (see D.E. Smith 1999, 2005). One of our objectives is to signal ways that we can give these terms a firmer social and historical ground-ing in the context of Canadian social and state formation. Making visible the

Patrizia Gentile and Gary Kinsman

class and racialized basis for homonormativity and homonationalism begins to ground these terms (see Floyd 2009; and Hennessy 2000).[11]

Puar's major insights and contributions in *Terrorist Assemblages* (2007) and in other work connect social practices not usually assembled. However, homonationalism has often not been adequately grounded in social relations. Important work toward this grounding was undertaken at the 2013 Homonationalism and Pinkwashing Conference in New York City.[12] In one attempt to address these limitations, we begin to suggest a social, historical, and materialist way of reading and using homonationalism. We clarify that the homonationalism that Puar has most explicated in her work is an Orientalist homonationalism that is especially mobilized in the "war on terror." However, she has also extended its usefulness by engaging with questions of settler homonationalism (see Puar 2013a).

In our view, settler and Orientalist homonationalisms have their own moments of social and historical specificity at the same time as they are combined in the settler colonial projects of both Canadian and Israeli state formation. This engages us directly in the critical interrogation of "investment in settlement," as Morgensen [2013] puts it, both in Canada and Israel. Morgensen speaks directly to this investment in settlement that undermines the work of many solidarity movements in the global North and asks for concerted efforts against these colonial racial formations.[13] Extending to the Canadian context what Puar and Mikdashi (2012) argue in the US context, we also challenge those who fight against settler colonialism in Israel but not in Canada. Puar and Mikdashi also point out the dangers of those organizing in the United States who fail to embrace a critique of settler colonialism in both Israel and the United States as part of their political work. They also criticize those "advocat[ing] for solidarity with the Palestinian cause only if, and because, Palestinian 'queerness' and homophobia shows up on the United States' terms – terms recognizable by global queer identity formations." The emergence of queer, trans, third and fourth gender groupings, and same-gender eroticism in much of the global South does not and will not look as it does in the global North, which must not be seen as the "norm" of "development" inevitably imposed on the global South.

For some, in the context of the use of the Charter, the existing Canadian state form became the vehicle for liberation. Consequently, a white settler homonationalism grew within gay and lesbian communities. In the context of the "war on terror," this sexual citizenship reinforces and maintains Orientalist practices against those defined as racially "other" as well.

Layered on top of settler sexual citizenship were various attempts to manage and contain social responses to the AIDS crisis in the 1980s and 1990s that grew out of queer communities. Early on, gay men, lesbians, and allies responded to state and professional neglect by setting up community-based AIDS groups to provide support and education. ACT UP groups in the United States and Canada and AIDS Action Now! in Toronto mounted protests and resistance against the neglect and regulation of the AIDS crisis. However, by the mid-1990s, state, professional, and corporate strategies of regulation and management of AIDS groups were largely successful in taming this potential challenge (Kinsman 1997). This transformed community-based forms of organizing into increasingly professionalized forms of organizing, with executive directors and boards of directors who sometimes had access to relatively large blocks of government funding compared to others in gay communities. Individual and social groups with professional and middle-class credentials came to dominate these managed and regulated AIDS service organizations. This contributed to shifting the class character of organizing in gay men's communities.

The construction of the "pink market" exemplifies the shifts in social and class relations that we are referencing. The "pink market" generally refers to gay men with "disposable incomes." In effect, a love affair with consumer capitalism and how queers can participate in commodity purchase, consumption, and display has come to define gayness and even queerness in some circles. This also operates as an inclusion-exclusion device in gay and queer community formation. Whereas white, middle-class gay men able to participate in these practices are included, those excluded (or those who can participate only occasionally) include queer youth, queers living in poverty, working-class queers, queers of colour, Indigenous queers and Two-Spirit people, trans people, and others. These divisions are intensified by neoliberal capitalist relations and by the current policies of austerity.

A consequence is a growing privatization of gay and queer sexualities and relationships as earlier public and communal forms of social and erotic interaction are dispersed through the neoliberal undermining of the "queer commons" (Floyd 2009, 208). Pressures for social and sexual respectability and responsibility underscore these shifts. Features of this reality include a replacement of the right to be public and visible with a limited and nontransformative notion of the "right to privacy"[14] (see Kinsman 1996; and G. Smith 1982) and the class-based gentrifications of some communities (Schulman 2012). These outcomes produce further forms of exclusion in gay and queer community formation.

A new middle-class stratum emerged out of AIDS organizing and other major struggles, such as those against the bath raids in Toronto in the early 1980s. This middle-class (and largely white) stratum began to develop its own

Patrizia Gentile and Gary Kinsman

class and social interests autonomously and thus without any responsibility or accountability to a grassroots movement as these mass struggles subsided. Although the grassroots movements and organizing opened up social space and created the social basis for transformation, the new, emerging, white, queer middle class reaped the benefits. With their professional and middle-class credentials, they came to represent the "community" since they could speak the same language as the professional, bureaucratic elites. In this sense, they came to stand over and against gay and queer communities and to also reshape gay and queer politics. They defined a project based on integration into the broader white, middle-class, Canadian state formation. Redefining the gay rights struggle in concert with the other shifts already mentioned helped to solidify this class project. Integration into the broader white middle class provided for a new class politics within gay organizing (which was never named as such), in turn establishing the social basis for what have come to be called "homonormative" practices and for both the settler and Orientalist moments of homonationalism, which enact each other.

Advancing this racialized class project began to erase the social memories of 1970s struggles for gay and lesbian liberation that were intimately intertwined with other struggles for liberation and social justice. "Gay" and to some extent "lesbian" are now theorized as separate from other social struggles and relations, constructing what is gay, lesbian, or LGBT, or even what is "queer." Queerness is actively separated from relations of class, poverty, ability, colonization, and racialization. Gay and "queer" get coded as adult, white, (largely) male, and middle class. This becomes the "common-sense" of gay and mainstream queer politics. This theorizing exemplifies two flawed conceptual assumptions: first, the construction of a false universal queer based on generalizing from the experiences of white, middle-class men; and second, a violence of abstraction where the experiences of queers of colour, Indigenous queers, and working-class queers of racialized and class exploitation are separated from a narrow queer experience of sexuality (which is also coded as white and middle-class).[15] But queer people never live their lives simply as queer or in relation to an abstract sexuality. Queerness is always lived in relation to racialization, colonization, class, gender, ability, age, and other social relations. Our theorizing cannot rip these apart. Instead, we need a way of theorizing that allows us to bring together sexuality, gender, racialization, and class by anchoring them in a critique of settler colonialism and in critical social analysis and practice. Sexuality, gender, race, and class develop in relation to each other and, in a concrete historical sense, are made in and through each other even though they are also specific and distinct forms of oppression. This is a social, relational, and meditational approach. We can now move to locating queer Palestine-solidarity activism within these transformations and struggles.

Queer Palestinian-Solidarity Activism, QuAIA, and the Possibilities of Resistance

Since 2008 a central flashpoint in the struggle against this complicity with the Canadian nation-state and its active support of Israeli occupation and apartheid (Engler 2010) has been the emergence of a vibrant queer Palestine-solidarity activism. This organizing directly challenges the hegemony of Orientalist homonationalism and the racialized practices of the Israeli settler colonial state. It attacks the apartheid character of Israeli state policies toward the Palestinian people, with whom it also builds solidarity. With the growing boycott, divestment, and sanctions (BDS) campaign against the apartheid policies of the Israeli state, the Orientalist portrayal of the Palestinian struggle is becoming increasingly difficult to maintain (see Barghouti 2011).[16] An example of this growth is the tours to Palestine of US feminists of colour and queer activists, which have resulted in their pledges of solidarity with the Palestinian struggle and in their support for the BDS campaign.[17] This solidarity is also a queering of the Palestinian liberation struggle and part of an opening-up of space for Palestinian queers (Schulman 2012). It is for this reason that there is such an organized state and social response to Palestinian-solidarity activism, queer and otherwise. The "wars" fought since 2008 within and around the Toronto Lesbian and Gay Pride Committee over the participation of Queers against Israeli Apartheid (QuAIA) in the Toronto Pride Parade have everything to do with support for *and* subversion of Orientalist homonationalism. Although this flashpoint has been repeated across the Canadian state, Toronto has been the epicentre because of its designation as one of the central sites for rebranding Israel as "gay-friendly."

In 2005, with the assistance of US marketing executives, the Israeli state began a marketing campaign called "Brand Israel" in response to the global Palestine-solidarity movement. As discussed by Sonny Dhoot (this collection) in relation to the 2010 Winter Olympic Games in Vancouver and Whistler, "pinkwashing" is a term coined by activists to conceptualize this rebranding campaign, which portrays Israel as "relevant and modern," thereby redirecting attention from the occupation and oppression of the Palestinians. The Israeli state was coded as belonging to the "modern" West, in opposition to the "backwardness" that Orientalist discourse associates with Arab and Islamic societies. Central to this was an effort to harness the Western gay community by portraying

Patrizia Gentile and Gary Kinsman

Israel as a "gay-friendly" place for tourism (largely focused on Tel Aviv) in an attempt to improve its global image (Schulman 2011).

Orientalist discourses mobilized through the "war on terror" associate Palestinians as "Arabs" and "Muslims" (ignoring the presence of Palestinian Christians) with gender and sexual "backwardness" despite feminist and queer organizing in Palestine and throughout the Palestinian diaspora.[18] Some Western gays misguidedly accept Israel to be a "Western haven" for gays and lesbians in the Middle East, especially as a result of the Israeli state's efforts to rebrand itself as "gay-friendly" in order to counter the growing campaigns of queer solidarity with Palestinians, which undermine the Orientalist framing of the "war on terror" (Luongo 2012). Israel as queer-friendly overlooks the history of opposition to same-gender desire within Israel. Palestinian queers are subjected to the apartheid wall, illegal settlements, checkpoints, the blockade of Gaza, denial of the right of return for refugees, and systematic practices of discrimination even for those who hold Israeli citizenship (Guarnieri 2012).

QuAIA, a Toronto-based group formed in 2008 during the Israeli Apartheid Week activities, actively works to obstruct this rebranding campaign.[19] Membership is composed of veteran and new queer activists. QuAIA's primary purpose is to work in solidarity with Palestinians, particularly Palestinian queers, but it was also formed as a specific response to Brand Israel and pinkwashing. In May 2009 QuAIA organized the conference "20 Years of Queer Resistance from South Africa to Palestine," which made important links between earlier queer solidarity and the struggle against South African apartheid. QuAIA's formation was also based on connections between the Coalition Against Israeli Apartheid (CAIA) and Creative Response, a group of artists, intellectuals, and academics responding to the occupation (see Letson 2011).[20] An organized and visible presence in the Toronto Pride Parade was one of its central mandates.

The Toronto Lesbian and Gay Pride Committee emerged to commemorate the Stonewall Riots of 1969 in the context of the mass resistance to the bath raids and arrests of 1981 and involved activists affiliated with Gay Liberation against the Right Everywhere (GLARE), Lesbians against the Right (LAR), and the Right to Privacy Committee (RTPC), the latter of which organized the resistance to the bath raids. The committee started with a major focus on building lesbian and gay struggles and movements, as well as creating a day for celebration and affirmation of lesbian and gay pride. Since then, Pride Day itself and the organizing group have been transformed by the social and class shifts mentioned earlier, increasing identification with corporate sponsorships, commercialization, mainstream political influence, and the entry of mainstream political parties. Pride Day has largely become an expression of homonormative, neoliberal queer politics. Business opportunities and advertising ventures are often privileged as Pride Day's main objective over creating a place for struggle and resistance against hegemonic heterosexuality. Pride is reformulated for narrowly defined LGBT issues, eschewing the broader social and political struggles in which queers are involved. In this context, public events that are supported and funded by the state, like Pride parades, become sites for the performance of homonationalism. But they can also be places to challenge this homonationalism, with queer Palestine-solidarity activism in Pride marches becoming an important terrain of social struggle. Active supporters of the State of Israel and the Zionist project now participate with their claims that "Israel is a world gay rights leader." Pride Day events are now influenced by right-wing political parties, including the Tories and members of the Liberal Party, as well as by state policies that support the Israeli occupation of Palestine.

Increasingly, Pride events are aligned with an Orientalist and homonationalist approach that actively erases settler colonialism in Canada and Israel. This is about far more than the co-opting of Pride and of queers by another agenda; it is also about the articulation of class and racialized interests taking the form of a settler and Orientalist homonationalism. As a result, "Canada" and Israel are constructed as "advanced" countries on gender and sexual questions as opposed to "sexually backward" cultures like Palestine. Israel cannot be criticized in this configuration as "protector" of human rights, specifically gay rights. QuAIA and university activists during Israeli Apartheid Week are thus constructed as automatically "anti-Semitic" precisely because they criticize the apartheid policies of the Israeli state. When this moniker does not easily stick, there is an attempt to generate a theory of a "new anti-Semitism" defined by being critical of Israeli policies toward the Palestinians in the hope that this will discredit these criticisms (Keefer 2010). Of course, this strategy has itself been criticized by many Jewish activists who argue that deploying this term against claims of human rights violations robs the term of its historical roots in the particular racialization of Jews.

QuAIA's participation in Pride events directly contests and undermines this production and performance of Orientalist homonationalism, suggesting a different articulation of queer struggles. These anti-Orientalist struggles recapture earlier histories of activist and liberationist organizing, including queer support for the struggle against South African apartheid (McCaskell 2010). This is why the group attracts both vociferous organized opposition and widespread support. In 2009 hundreds joined QuAIA's Pride Day contingent, which received further support in following years.

The dispute surrounding the Pride Committee centred on a policy regarding banning the term "Israeli apartheid." This policy would have stipulated that QuAIA could not participate in the event if it used the term, effectively prohibiting QuAIA's presence at Toronto Pride. However, this policy backfired. Support for QuAIA included large numbers participating in a free-speech contingent opposed to the attempted censorship of QuAIA in 2010. That year, QuAIA and its allies mobilized a massive community response, forcing a reversal in the policies of the Pride Board of Directors. However, this only temporarily deterred those on the Pride Committee who opposed QuAIA. The committee attempted to develop a broader and more comprehensive policy aimed at possibly prohibiting QuAIA's participation by introducing a legally defined Dispute Resolution Process (DRP).[21] In this context, QuAIA won a victory in April 2011 when a staff report to the City of Toronto executive declared that use of the term "Israeli apartheid" by QuAIA did not violate the city's anti-discrimination policy. At the same time, QuAIA decided not to participate in the parade that year given the threats by municipal politicians to cut funding for Pride if it did. However, QuAIA did do a banner drop against pinkwashing on Pride Day.

In 2012, in the lead-up to Pride, QuAIA organized a forum on pinkwashing that made important links with the pinkwashing of the Alberta tar sands and with the corporate pink-ribbon culture produced around breast cancer "culture." Connections were made with the neoliberal commercialization, corporatization, and public-relations campaigns involved in these varied forms of pinkwashing, which are aimed to systematically shift social attention away from the roots of environmental devastation, the social causes of cancer, and the apartheid practices of the Israeli state. Regarding the tar sands and Israeli policies, these pinkwashing practices also operate to shift our attention away from the settler colonial projects in both Canadian and Israeli state formation. This suggests that activists need to constantly make connections between different ruling social practices and make as visible as possible the social roots of these problems in contesting varied forms of pinkwashing. There are also both contemporary and historical connections here with the mobilization of "Canadian" national security practices against Indigenous and settler ecological activists, framed as "eco-terrorists" (Kinsman 2012), and against Palestinian activists.

When QuAIA announced it would participate in the Pride Parade, a number of complaints to the DRP were made and some were withdrawn. QuAIA faced a challenge from the League for Human Rights of B'nai Brith Canada, a powerful pro-Israel lobby group. Despite all the problems with the process, the DRP decided there was no merit in B'nai Brith's complaint and that QuAIA did not violate any of the "core missions, or policies, of Pride Toronto," including its anti-discrimination and human rights policies (Houston 2012a; see also QuAIA 2012). This was a major defeat for the pro-Israel forces. QuAIA had a spirited contingent in the parade of about 150 people, following the Independent Jewish Voices contingent. B'nai Brith and others announced that their focus was now shifting to the city and changes to its anti-discrimination policy in order to add use of the term "Israeli apartheid" as a form of "discrimination." This would lead to the withdrawal of city funding for Pride if QuAIA was allowed to participate (Houston 2012c).

In 2013 QuAIA again won a significant victory when, in response to these pressures, city staff reaffirmed that QuAIA did not violate human rights policies and declared that "Israeli apartheid" should not be added to the anti-discrimination policy. Two further challenges to QuAIA's participation under the Pride Committee's DRP were also dismissed (McCann 2013). Significantly, Bernie M. Farber, former CEO of the Canadian Jewish Congress and a leading supporter of Israel, wrote a column in the *Toronto Star* arguing that the strategy of trying to ban QuAIA had clearly not been effective and recognizing the importance of the composition of struggle mobilized by QuAIA in its defence (Farber 2013). QuAIA marched again on Pride Day, this time with a sound truck, music, and dancing. However, Toronto City Council passed a broad and vague motion that could be used at a later point against Pride funding and QuAIA (Salerno 2013). The struggle therefore continues.

Richard Fung (quoted in Letson 2011, 140), an activist in QuAIA, drew some important conclusions from these experiences:

It became obvious that we couldn't separate issues like queer rights from issues like racism or gender. The way those things worked together, the way they fit into a global imperialist framework, could not be pulled apart. So when people ask us, "why are you talking about Palestine when you should be talking about gay rights?" they do violence to something that has always been entwined. Maybe it isn't their intention, but it also says to queers of colour and indigenous queers that their issues and their wholeness are less important than some mythic notion of LGBT rights that exists outside of class, outside of ethnicity, outside of power dynamics that claim gay movements as a space of middle class white gay men.

Fung articulates a powerful argument against neoliberal homonormativity and against both the settler and Orientalist moments of homonationalism. The

Patrizia Gentile and Gary Kinsman

high stakes surrounding the "wars" over QuAIA's participation in Toronto Pride events are about the very direction of these movements and struggles. QuAIA's struggles suggest, at least partially, a way of articulating a trajectory that pushes beyond homonormativity and homonationalism to a perspective where queer liberation is understood fundamentally as also an anti-racist, anti-colonial movement. The QuAIA experience suggests ways of reclaiming the radical roots of queer struggles. At the same time, class struggle has yet to be fully integrated into this analysis, beyond noting that there is a racialized class basis to the homonormativity and homonationalism that queer Palestine-solidarity activists face.

We need to question the racist, colonizing, imperialist, and capitalist limitations and influences on some forms of gay and queer activism. In work primarily directed against the Orientalist moment of homonationalism, such as in queer Palestine-solidarity activism, settler homonationalism must also be specifically addressed. Efforts have been undertaken in this direction, with connections being made between Palestine-solidarity activism and Indigenous struggles. We need to build on and extend these critical links. The inspiring Idle No More mobilizations across the "Canadian" state in 2012 and 2013 did raise the question of the lack of visible queer settler activism in building alliances against racism and settler colonialism. At the same time, important connections of solidarity were built between Idle No More and Palestine-solidarity activists, including queer Palestine-solidarity activists (see US Palestinian Community Network 2012). Queer Palestine-solidarity activism must be activism against settler colonialism in both Israel and "Canada" (Morgensen 2013).

Moving Forward

Our aim in this chapter has been to make visible through an investigation of what we can learn from queer Palestine-solidarity activism how we need to read sexual, racialized, gender, class, and other struggles in and through each other to develop a more comprehensive queer politics that can centrally resist the neoliberal, capitalist politics of homonormativity and of settler and Orientalist homonationalisms. We have attempted to provide a clearer social, historical, and class basis for using homonormativity and homonationalism in queer theorizing and political practice. These concerns need to become central to radical queer organizing and pose special responsibilities for white queers to speak out against national security and to support Indigenous and anti-Orientalist struggles.

Notes

1 In the last chapter of *The Canadian War on Queers: National Security as Sexual Regulation* (2010), we outline how the national security campaigns against queers within Canadian state formation continue in a different form in the current national security wars on "subversion" and "terror[ism]." However, space did not allow us to offer a deeper analysis of these connections. We developed a critical analysis of national security as an ideological practice based on the inclusion of only some groups within the nation and the exclusion of others. In the context of the war on queers, lesbians and gay men were expelled from the nation and defined as a threat to the "nation," as heterosexuality was relationally constructed as the normal and safe sexuality at the centre of Canadian social and state formation. In the "war on terror," Arab- and Islamic-identified people are expelled from the fabric of the nation and constructed as a terrorist-related "threat," whereas a white, Christian-derived culture is placed at the centre of what is considered "Canadian." These nationalist deployments also bring into relief the heteropatriarchal and white settler colonialist roots of Canadian state formation. This chapter continues this exploration and draws on some of Gary Kinsman's newer work for his forthcoming book *The Making of the Neo-liberal Queer*, which explores the historical and social emergence of the neoliberal queer in the "Canadian" context from the 1970s to the historical present.

2 On our use of a mediational analysis, which recognizes both the distinct moments and the mutual construction of social relations, see Bannerji (1995).

3 The formulation of "Islamophobia" is limited since it is built on analogies with homophobia. Although homophobia creatively reversed the construction of lesbians and gay men as mentally ill by problematizing the responses of heterosexuals, this strategy maintained the individualized focus of psychological discourse. "Homophobia" has created barriers for theorizing gay oppression by failing to make connections with broader social relations. Some of these limitations are carried into Islamophobia, which can tend to be individualized and pathologized as outside historical and social relations.

4 Clarifications regarding Islamic fundamentalism are required here. In some areas of the Arab and Islamic world, the democratic and radical left had either been wiped out by state repression or rendered ineffective prior to the uprisings of the Arab Spring. Here the forces of resistance to Western influence often took on an Islamic form. As Tariq Ali (2003, esp. 114–53) suggests, this generated a clash of fundamentalisms: Western, pro-capitalist, Christian-identified fundamentalism was set against various forms of Islamic fundamentalism. The new radical and democratic forces unleashed by the Arab Spring have only partially shifted the Orientalist ways that these struggles are portrayed in the West, with developments in Egypt and elsewhere being used to reconstruct Islam as a major danger. We are opposed to all forms of fundamentalism since they draw on essentialist, asocial, and ahistorical foundations. Fundamentalism is the reassertion of a fundamental, or pure, religion, culture, or identity against other, supposedly inferior, cultures, religions, or identities. It involves a fixed and ahistorical approach to the world that removes culture, religion, sexuality, and identity from their social and historical contexts and from class and social struggles. Associating all of Islam with fundamentalism, however, is a major danger that must be avoided. For instance, we reject the premise that Islam in general is more hostile to queers than fundamentalist currents in Christianity. Christian fundamentalism, moral conservatism, and neoliberal capitalist fundamentalism pose far greater challenges to queer movements in the "West" than does Islamic fundamentalism.

5 On the Combahee River Collective, see its powerful "Statement" at http://circuitous.org/scraps/combahee.html.

6 In cultural studies, Orientalism is sometimes used without being situated within broader class, gender, racial, sexual, and other relations. Here our use of Orientalism is historically, socially, and materially grounded.

7 Puar and Rai (2002) report that, shortly after the 9/11 attacks, posters appeared in Manhattan depicting turbaned caricatures of bin Laden, who was being penetrated anally by the Empire State Building, and the words "The Empire Strikes Back" or "So You Like Skyscrapers, Huh, Bitch?"

8 This book is in need of a critical reading to deepen and extend its only limited challenge to settler homonationalism.

9 Morgensen's (2011b, 27) critical interjection demonstrates the importance of grounding and historizing Puar's initial conceptualization with a critical analysis of white settler homonationalism. Morgensen shows that even what he calls "queer radicals" can be limited in their challenge to settler homonationalism.

10 Lisa Duggan (2002) did not invent the term "homonormative," but she did introduce its applicability as a critique of neoliberal forces within the queer community (see Murphy, Ruiz, and Serlins 2008).

11 Marxist scholars, such as Rosemary Hennessy (2000) and Kevin Floyd (2009), offer insights for grounding homonationalism and homonormativity through their investigations of capitalist social relations and the commodification and reification of queer social and political practices. Unfortunately, Floyd's book is limited in this regard by his reliance on regulation theory (on Floyd, see Drucker 2011).

12 See http://homonationalismconference.eventsbot.com.

13 For suggestions on how white-settler queer activists can work toward a comprehensive and effective solidarity with Palestinian queers, see Morgensen (2013). See also Puar and Mikdashi (2012).

14 This is in contrast to the transformative use of right to privacy in the Toronto response to the bath raids in the early 1980s.

15 On the problems with the construction of false universals and the violence of abstraction, see Bannerji (1995).

16 The BDS campaign is based on the successful BDS campaign against apartheid in South Africa. Its mandate involves action against the illegal occupation, including the apartheid "security" wall and the illegal settlements, against the denial of the right of return for Palestinian refugees, and against discrimination directed at Palestinian citizens of Israel.

17 On this support, see Abunimah (2011) and http://www.pqbds.com/2012/01/27/246/. See also Schulman (2012).

18 Links to Palestinian queer organizations are http://www.pqbds.com; http://www.alqaws.org; and http://www.aswatgroup.org.

19 Israeli Apartheid Week is a global event held in March in support of the Palestinian struggle and the BDS campaign against the Israeli state's apartheid policies.

20 See also the QuAIA site at http://queersagainstapartheid.org. We write this chapter as queer Palestine-solidarity supporters.

21 For a critique of the Dispute Resolution Process, see Queer Ontario (2012).

9

Don't Be a Stranger Now
Queer Exclusions, Decarceration, and HIV/AIDS

MARTY FINK

Prisons and Exclusions

As the Canadian government's "tough on crime"[1] agenda propels prison expansion, homonationalism offers a framework to identify connections between incarceration and white settler colonialism. As a historically rooted practice that continues to directly target Indigenous populations, Canadian incarceration exemplifies nationalist narratives of assimilation, civilization, and governance. Prisons effectively function to disperse and contain Indigenous populations and to sustain structural inequalities between Indigenous and non-Indigenous subjects. Because prisoners are regarded as disposable and antithetical to the nation, the prison offers a space from within which to investigate overlapping imaginings of Canadian and of queer identity. I argue that Canadian homonationalism arises in direct relation to Canadian settler colonialism and histories of genocide. This chapter demonstrates how processes of incarceration exert control over gender and sexual norms by imposing racialized narratives of who does and does not belong within the Canadian state.

In this chapter, I also examine how cultural production challenges narratives of who is excluded from queer movements and also from national belonging. Comprising artistic materials designed by incarcerated queer and trans inmates and circulated by Montreal's Prisoner Correspondence Project (2009–12), this cultural production offers a venue through which to connect the exclusion of criminalized, racialized, Indigenous, disabled, and HIV-positive bodies to the trajectories of both queer and prison-expansion agendas. The cultural work of the Prisoner Correspondence Project challenges homonationalist exclusions, promoting queer community building and HIV/AIDS activism. An analysis of these cultural productions also prompts inquiries regarding how racialization and settler colonialism affect coalition building and activist movements inside prison and out.

With HIV infection rates inside prison nine times higher than outside prison, and with incarceration rates that disproportionately target Indigenous people and people of colour, activists and theorists are correct in their declaration that "prison abolition must be one of the centres of trans and queer liberation struggles" (Stanley 2011, 3). Theorists including Ruth Wilson Gilmore (2007, 6) expose the racialized practices whereby "breathtakingly cruel twists in the meaning and practice of justice" have been written into the penal code, as well as how community-based activists of colour have worked to counter state-sanctioned carceral practices. Understanding how incarceration results from overlapping systems of nationalism, colonialism, and administrative violence, and how the current state of incarceration amounts to the rapid and uncontested rise of HIV and hepatitis C infection, it becomes salient to shift queer agendas away from a desire for homonational belonging in order both to critique the national project of prison expansion and to identify incarceration's roots in ongoing practices of settler colonialism. Recognizing those locked inside prisons *as* members of queer communities and as also deserving of safety and inclusion necessitates intervention at the levels of culture and representation.

Through an investigation of cultural and archival materials, this chapter also considers how prison space functions to restrict certain bodies from national participation and access to state resources, including employment, citizenship status, and health. Cultural materials also preserve the historical relationship between queer movements and prison organizing. Although the 1980s and 1990s brought about a series of collaborations bridging queer and HIV/AIDS organizing inside and outside of prison, contemporary mainstream LGBTQ movements have notably erased prisoners and struggles for decriminalization from their political agendas. Such exclusions have also transpired along gender and racial lines, as mainstream gay movements have increasingly dismissed issues of medicalization and criminalization as pertaining only to transgender communities since the removal of homosexuality from the *Diagnostic and Statistical Manual of Mental Disorders (DSM)* in 1974. This watershed moment created a rift between queer and trans organizers who were previously united in fighting these causes in the period preceding the Stonewall Riots of 1969 (Stryker 2008, 97). Mainstream LGBTQ organizations remain complicit in and at times even responsible for the pathologization and criminalization of transgender and gender-nonconforming youth, particularly low-income and nonstatus queer and trans people of colour (Bernstein Sycamore 2008, 283). Racialized youth are frequently committed through "the front doors of the system," are detained and punished for the length of their hair, the fit of their clothes, consensual sexual desires, and friendships with other queer youth, and are taught that their genders and identities are "wrong," "sick," and requiring cure (Ware 2011, 79).

Resisting these processes of criminalization, this chapter looks to cultural production as a site of intervention against carceral and national exclusion. The art and writing distributed by the Prisoner Correspondence Project uncovers the capacity of self-representation and DIY publication to resist the removal of prison issues from queer agendas. In asking why incarceration should be framed as a queer issue, and why queer politics should include the struggles of racialized, Indigenous, and criminalized queer and trans inmates, cultural production offers new possibilities for connecting current movements to a history of in-prison AIDS organizing, resistance to police brutality, and unification between incarcerated and nonincarcerated queers. The cultural materials of the Prisoner Correspondence Project thus reimagine queer sexuality apart from homonationalist punitive measures that remove racialized and Indigenous bodies from Canadian national and cultural space.

HIV/AIDS Activisms and Cultural Production: Histories of Prisoner Solidarity in Ontario and Quebec

Although health is often understood through a biomedical framework, queer and trans survival can also be sustained through the domain of culture. Cultural production contests narratives that fabricate national belonging by omitting those who are HIV-positive, disabled, racialized, Indigenous, undocumented, impoverished, or incarcerated. As community-based organizations for HIV prevention – including AIDS Project Los Angeles and AIDS Action Now (AAN) Toronto – have recognized, telling queer and trans youth to use condoms and practise safer sex remains a hollow message if such materials fail to represent and affirm the identities of those dually excluded from queer and national movements. HIV prevention, these activists and health educators have shown, is not only about intervening in sexual behaviour or sexual acts but also requires understanding desire and sexuality as linked to experiences of racism, migration, colonization, diaspora, cissexism, poverty, and other complex facets of identity that converge to render sexuality and sexual desire far more complex than what people do or do not do in bed. Such prevention efforts, as a result, offer ground-breaking forms of HIV/AIDS education for queer and trans youth that include the production of culture (e.g., photography, poetry, fiction, and public art) as a means of affirming and supporting queer and trans survival (Ayala, Husted, and Spieldenner 2004; Monkman 2011). For instance, Kent Monkman's (2011) poster for AAN Toronto's *Poster/Virus* public-art series presents an epic landscape where Monkman's iconic "Miss Chief Eagle Testicle" beholds a pair of wrestling angels. Directed at Prime Minister Stephen Harper, the poster's hot pink caption reads, "The Creator Is Watching You Harper!" – thus pinning HIV prevention not on the individual but on the Canadian state and its colonial history.

As such cultural productions demonstrate, Indigenous artists and activists continue to creatively expose these connections between colonialism and criminalization, as the production of media and art remains a crucial facet of Indigenous activist movements. The Idle No More website, for instance, documents a collection of media and iconic images that have been central to the organizing and archiving of this movement.[2] As Leanne Simpson (2013) identifies, a main challenge of the Idle No More movement is that mainstream media have "boxed our peoples inside the confines of the same recycled stereotypes it insists upon invoking." In identifying the explicit racism present within a host of major Canadian journalism pieces covering the movement, including the *National Post* and the *Globe and Mail*, Simpson showcases sites of Indigenous resistance that speak back to these mainstream narratives via cultural self-representations. Simpson notes that in addition to the constellation of grassroots news reporting authored by Indigenous writers and academics, "We have also seen an artistic outpouring, including podcasts, edgy logos and posters, zines, pamphlets, solidarity concerts, short films, poetry and new music by DJs, rappers and singer songwriters, including new tracks by A Tribe Called Red, Cris Derksen, Derek Miller and Star Nayea." Such cultural productions – like Derksen's album *The Collapse* (2013), whose blending of instrumental cello, electronic mixing, and queer vocal stylings culminate in its final track, "Our Home on Native Land" – exemplify how artistic self-representations of queer gender and sexuality are tied to struggles for bodily sovereignty and to the larger Indigenous movement building that is already taking place.

Similarly, the Native Youth Sexual Health Network creates artwork and poster campaigns that draw direct links between settler colonialism, incarceration, sexualization, and violence in the lives of Two-Spirit and all Indigenous people. Media arts and project co-ordinator Erin Konsmo (2013) recently launched a series of poster campaigns addressing the ways that sexual health is necessarily tied to a knowledge of Indigenous histories and how public institutions have attempted to erase these histories and cultures. The online #HeartOurParts campaign describes its central processes being as rooted in self-determination and the creation of culturally safe reproductive and sexual-health materials that are being distributed online and otherwise. Poster slogans, including "Indigenous Sovereignty Starts in This Body" and "My Favourite Condom Flavour Is ... Frybread," frame the production of artistic materials addressing sexual health as "a way of community survival." In "Knowing Our Cultures, Knowing Our Bodies: Indigenous Youth Reclaiming Health, Rights, and Justice," Konsmo identifies that "our bodies are a space where we can actively resist colonization and do cultural resurgence. In many of the similar ways we do that with land." Bodily knowledge, the poster campaign reflects, "can be learning how to describe our body parts in our Indigenous languages, finding ways of expressing our sexuality through arts, songs and dance." Drawing connections between colonialism, survival, and sexual health, Konsmo links health activism to decolonization: "We are taking back control of our bodies as a process for rebuilding our nations."

These culture-based prevention efforts are also framed explicitly within the context of prison. Cultural production can represent prisoners, who face both the highest rates of HIV infection and the lowest access to condoms and other prophylactics and who are (not coincidentally) the same populations repeatedly told by cultural narratives and by the law that their gender identities, queer desires, sexual practices, and national presence are quite literally illegal. John Greyson's (2011) poster in the AAN series features an enlarged image of Harper's face against a fiery sky as he is poked through the barbed wire of a prison fence by a pair of naked anamorphic penguins wielding a giant syringe. The poster's caption reads: "Prick: [prik] *noun* / 1. How HIV spreads in prison without condoms or clean needles / 2. Someone who spends $2 billion on prisons while trashing harm reduction and attacking safe injection sites." As these cultural productions suggest, creating HIV/AIDS- and harm-reduction strategies by, for, and with affected, criminalized, Indigenous, and HIV-positive youth expands understandings of who is included as Canadian, as queer, and as deserving of access to health.

Comprehending the exclusion of queer and trans inmates from healthcare access, from LGBTQ movements, and from national belonging also motivates a historical investigation of Canadian prison organizing dating back to the onset of the AIDS crisis. Responding to the HIV/AIDS pandemic, Canadian inmates, including Peter Collins (who today remains an activist and also remains incarcerated in Ontario), established peer-education and HIV-prevention programs to halt the transmission of the virus while supporting inmates living with the stigmas of HIV infection and with AIDS. For instance, in 1991 Collins organized alongside a coalition of prisoners, ex-prisoners, activists, agencies, and individuals to bring to national attention a concrete program for HIV prevention inside prison entitled "HIV/AIDS in Prison Systems: A Comprehensive Strategy" (Dias and Collins 2009). During this moment, a host of organized and interconnected communities outside prison, including AAN and Prisoners' HIV/AIDS Support Action Network (PASAN) in Toronto and the AIDS Coalition to Unleash Power (ACT UP) in Montreal, placed themselves in solidarity with the movements initiated by queer and trans organizers in prison. Central to the movements outside prison was the sense that in-prison death rates as well as prisoner access to condoms and clean needles were struggles central to activist agendas of nonincarcerated queers. This solidarity was, for instance, demonstrated by several public "die-ins" by ACT UP Montreal from 1990 to 1993 wherein activists wearing prisoner jump suits and grim reaper gowns lay dead on the street to call media attention to the blackout of concern about inmate health.

Archival documents and news footage from this historical moment similarly attest to the Montreal gay and lesbian community's related demand for a decrease in police violence within its gay village. Responding to a violent and homophobic police raid on Montreal's queer Sex Garage club on 15 July 1990, a sit-in was held in front of the precinct the following day. Demonstrators sported placards featuring slogans like "Police: Professional Gay Bashers," and queers spoke out against acts of police brutality based on perceptions of "how we looked" (Herland 1990-91). Following a series of continued protests throughout the year, on 15 July 1991, queer activists returned to the front of the precinct to conduct a "kiss-in" to mark the brutal and excessive violence as well as to address the charges laid against the fifty-six peaceful demonstrators that had yet to be dropped. These actions also effectively publicized homophobic violence by gaining control of the media. In an interview with a local news station, ACT UP member Karen Herland (ibid.) declared, "They have the money, they have the power, they can get away with it, but we're just here to let them know that we know they're getting away with it." Recognizing policing as a civil threat to queers, the anniversary of the Sex Garage raid became an annual Pride March to counter police violence, entrapment, brutality, and community dislocation. By extension, HIV/AIDS-activist movements, led by the same demonstrators protesting the Sex Garage raid, located incarcerated queers and imprisoned HIV-positive individuals as displaced members of their own communities, thus linking the momentum of in-prison organizing to the outside movement's opposition to the police. In contrast, contemporary calls by gay business owners for an increased police presence in Montreal's gay village (Burnett 2011) position gentrification and policing as forces that literally remove queer and trans people marked by poverty, disability, race, and criminalization from public space. Whereas *queerness* was once positioned as an impetus to oppose this policing and erasure – as epitomized by the Sex Garage raid – its contemporary meaning has shifted within a gay village that struggles toward corporatization, state-sanctioned relationship models, racial homogenization, and collusion with the police.[3]

Compounding these forms of national segregation, queer and trans prisoners are further excluded by mainstream LGBTQ movements. As Dean Spade (2011, 33) argues, mainstream LGBTQ movements' rights-based goal to attain liberal acceptance transpires at the expense of these movements' own exclusions, specifically the omission of prisoners as well as low-income and racialized populations (see also Mogul, Ritchie, and Whitlock 2011, 117; and Sudbury 2005, xxi). These movements' identification with gay respectability relies on distinguishing their membership from tropes of the unrespectable queer in need of intervention. Such exclusions parallel those outlined in Sunera Thobani's analysis of Canadian citizenship mythologies. As Thobani (2007, 250) explains, for the white Canadian national to secure a position of belonging, indigenized and racialized Canadians must in turn be imagined as unassimilable into the national body and therefore deserving of civil exclusion. Like the respectable queer, the white Canadian national relies on processes of exclusion to maintain an exalted status. Because these citizenship narratives render Indigenous sovereignty and immigrant belonging as legally and nationally inconceivable, the status (legal and otherwise) of racialized and Indigenous people within Canada's borders also remains conditional (ibid.).

Through an analysis of mainstream Canadian media and the operation of social services, Thobani (2007, 223, 124) accordingly calls attention to how such divisions between Aboriginal and Canadian, immigrant and national, are sustained along the lines of gender. Homonationalism provides a conceptual framework to demonstrate further how middle-class whiteness is similarly embedded in tropes of the socially assimilable (and correlatively unassimilable) queer. Canadian homonationalism thereby arises in direct relation to these histories of Canadian settler colonialism. Such racializing and white supremacist projects remain not merely incidental outcomes of incarceration but also fundamental markers of the Canadian state. As demonstrated by Indigenous activists, including the cultural makers of the Native Youth Sexual Health

Marty Fink

Network, self-representations by queer and trans communities whose members transgress such respectabilities can thus counter this process of national exclusion enacted by mainstream media. Cultural production becomes a venue through which to reject such goals of exalted inclusions by rescripting institutional and narrative processes of national and sexual homogeneity.

Keep in Touch: The Prisoner Correspondence Project's Cultural Productions

Responding to these processes of exclusion, Montreal's Prisoner Correspondence Project provides a case study of cultural production that dually operates to build harm-reduction strategies in response to national exclusion and to reintegrate prison activism within contemporary queer movements. As a pen pal program that matches incarcerated queer and trans people with similarly identified people on the outside, the Prisoner Correspondence Project operates under the mandate that breaking isolation and creating networks of interpersonal support both calls attention to and mediates the harms of disappearing, dislocating, and incarcerating members of queer and trans communities. In addition to co-ordinating the pen pal program, the Prisoner Correspondence Project offers a steadily expanding library of resources that pen pals can request and contribute to, spanning topics from coming-out to hormone access, safer injection, safer tattooing, smut and erotica, punk zines, safer sex, and legal advice.

Through its mandate and its daily operations, the Prisoner Correspondence Project recognizes how processes of racialization and colonial violence that confine bodies within prisons also justify their continued segregation along gender and sexual lines. The isolating conditions that queer and trans prisoners face increase the necessity of a support-based pen pal program. For instance, if cellmates are so much as rumoured to demonstrate queer leanings or intimate relationships, they are separated and moved to different units. All forms of physical affection from hugging to handholding can become forbidden in prison, as can any type of organizing that might be construed as political. Many prisoner-led HIV/AIDS-activist groups from the early 1990s, for example, have since been disbanded by prison administrations under the guise of anti-gang laws. Other formal and informal gatherings between inmates like HIV/AIDS peer-education meetings now often take place without funding or institutional support. Many institutions, additionally, place queer, trans, and gender-nonconforming inmates in solitary confinement (a common punishment measure in prisons for offenders perceived to be violent) under the rationale that their round-the-clock isolation without access to in-prison vocational, educational, or early-release programs is warranted protection against the sexual violence and harassment quotidian for such individuals when housed in the general population (Mogul, Ritchie, and Whitlock 2011, 107–8; see also Baus, Hunt, and Williams 2006). Ensuing suggestions that queer and trans inmates should be housed in their very own prisons have come to the fore, a dystopian proposal that theorists identify with the axiom that "if they build it, they will fill it" (Bassichis, Lee, and Spade 2011, 34), arguing instead that the only way to reduce violence against trans populations is to abolish the prison system.

The Prisoner Correspondence Project also responds to prison's structural and spatial constraints, which deny inmates access to cultural production. As a pen pal program, the project frequently encounters the structural mechanisms that enforce queer and trans segregation. Although they may receive mail from correspondents on the outside, queer and trans inmates are forbidden to write to one another, as letter writing between inmates is prohibited. Prisoners are also denied use of communication technologies like the Internet upon which many people rely for access to social networks, cultural representation, sexual-health information, queer validation, and community. Some Canadian prisons, such as the Ste-Anne-des-Plaines prison in Quebec, forbid all prisoners to receive any "photocopies." Prisoners are denied access to cultural materials whose production could intervene in the spatial harms and alienation they face. Although prison administrations take multifarious measures to keep queer and trans prisoners apart from each other, such networks have both a rich history and vibrant present of producing community networks and cultural representations of their experiences. Films such as Jean Genet's timeless testament to queer prison love, *Un Chant d'Amour* (1950), as well as Catherine Gund and Debra Levine's (1993) ACT UP documentary about the women's prison in Bedford, New York, and its HIV/AIDS peer-support groups, like AIDS Counseling and Education (ACE), contest structures that seek to exclude queer, gender-nonconforming, and HIV-positive bodies from social and cultural participation. Such networks of queer and trans solidarity in prison have also long been fictionalized, as novels like Chester Himes's classic *Cast the First Stone* (1952) address the potential for queer love and friendship to transgress prison's spatially entrenched ostracism. The Prisoner Correspondence Project therefore uses cultural production to draw links between the structural containment of prisoners and the national and mainstream LGBTQ exclusions enacted on racialized queer and trans bodies on the outside.

Connecting queer and trans communities inside and outside prison, cultural production also becomes a means of promoting harm reduction and sexual health. Recognizing that most safer-sex campaigns are centred on condom use and do not address those who are imprisoned, the Prisoner Correspondence Project also produces a pamphlet series titled *Slamming It*[4] that provides information about cultural representation and sexual health to queer and trans populations who have inconsistent or nonexistent access to condoms. Although one obvious goal of these pamphlets is to provide information about HIV transmission, risk-reduction strategies, and prescriptions for monitoring and improving access to sexual health, the pamphlets follow in the tradition of publications like AIDS Project Los Angeles's *Corpus* (2007–08) that place sexual health as an outcome of other complex factors that contribute to self-esteem, sexual self-worth, and access to seemingly unrelated resources, including housing, education, citizenship status, gender self-determination, support systems, emotional safety, autonomy, and healthcare. As a collaborative process between imprisoned queer and trans populations and local organizations on the outside, the pamphlet series also works to bring inside and outside communities together to produce relevant dialogue about sexual health. Forcing a recognition of the homophobia, cissexism, and general inhumanity of carceral systems themselves, the Prisoner Correspondence Project creates cultural productions to reduce the risk of HIV transmission in prisons, while pointing to the larger structural problems that prove enormous barriers to this particular task.

Like the *Slamming It* series, the Prisoner Correspondence Project's (2008-12) quarterly newsletter, *The Word Is Out,* can also be read as a cultural strategy for representing the experiences, genders, sexualities, and identities of those in prison. Recognizing the queer and trans networks, friendships, and activist movements that already exist inside, this publication envisions incarcerated queer and trans people as a readership and as a community to which those on the outside also belong. The newsletter's distribution also reflects how the inbuilt conditions of inmate isolation are compounded by prison mailroom censorship and regulation policies. Each prison has its own seemingly arbitrary set of customized restrictions based on sentencing, security level, and institution type (e.g., regulations differ between short-term provincial jails and long-term federal prisons) that dictate the nature and quantity of materials that can be sent inside. Prisons often return to senders anything containing explicitly sexual content, including publications on safer sex, queer sex, and sexual health. For example, Montreal's *A Queersafe Zine,* a safer-sex resource published collectively in affiliation with grassroots community organizations, including the Ste Emilie Skillshare and Head and Hands, features safer-sex tips and hand-drawn illustrations by local queer and trans artists. This resource can be sent into prisons only when all representations of sexual body parts are covered by post-it notes and then photocopied with said illustrations blocked by dark squares (see Figures 9.1 and 9.2).

Even once censored, this zine is frequently intercepted by mailroom authorities, either for its sexual content or simply because of arbitrary constraints on the number of pages permitted in an envelope. Accompanying this dearth of explicitly queer, erotic, or sexual information is a vast alienation of queer and trans inmates from one another, from queer communities and movements on the outside, and from representations of themselves as valued and valuable sexual beings. The Prisoner Correspondence Project's newsletter, which is sent inside three times per year, aims to address this gap by creating cultural representations that link queer and trans inmates to movements and sexual cultures outside.

This newsletter accordingly locates the sharing of information, art, literature, poetry, popular culture, resources, interviews, and humour as a link between incarcerated and outside queer and trans communities. This publication follows in the tradition of newsletters like *Gaycon,* a queer prison newsletter from the 1990s published out of San Francisco, and the now archival People with AIDS Coalition's publication *Newsline,* which dates back to 1985. *Newsline* featured regular columns like "Voices from the Inside" and a corresponding prisoner pen pal program that located the experiences of incarcerated queers and people with AIDS as central to the community organizing of all HIV/AIDS activists and queers. *The Word Is Out* also circulates alongside a consortium of linked publications by other prisoner-support organizations, including Boston's *Black and Pink* newsletter, which is another publication dedicated to writing by queer and trans inmates, and PASAN's *Cell Count,* which provides HIV/AIDS information and services for incarcerated populations across Canada. Another newsletter produced outside of prison is *The Fire Inside,* by the California Coalition for Women Prisoners, which is published with the aim of sharing the gendered and political struggles of women incarcerated in California. Bent Bars in the United Kingdom is a similar pen pal project for queer prisoners whose newsletter showcases writing, poetry, and artwork of participants, not to mention the various other publications and supports by queer and trans prison-justice groups that collaborate with the Prisoner Correspondence Project, including the Sylvia Rivera Law Project, the Transgender Gender Variant Intersex Justice Project, Hearts on a Wire in Philadelphia, and Write to Win in Chicago.

This brief overview of activist organizations working in tandem on similar issues also raises questions of exclusion versus coalition building between Indigenous people who are queer and trans, or Two-Spirit, and prison activists

Masturbation

If you don't know what you like, it's probably going to be difficult for anyone else to figure it out. When it comes to the enjoyment of sex, you are your own 'expert'. Masturbating is a safe and fun way to find out what you like. Masturbating is a great way to cope with things as well. If you are feeling stressed out or sad, it can help. If you aren't ready to start having sex with other people or don't want to, masturbate. Masturbation is a great way to be sexually active without the risk of STIs. Masturbate! It's for everyone!

Figure 9.1 "Masturbation."
Excerpt from *A Queersafe Zine*

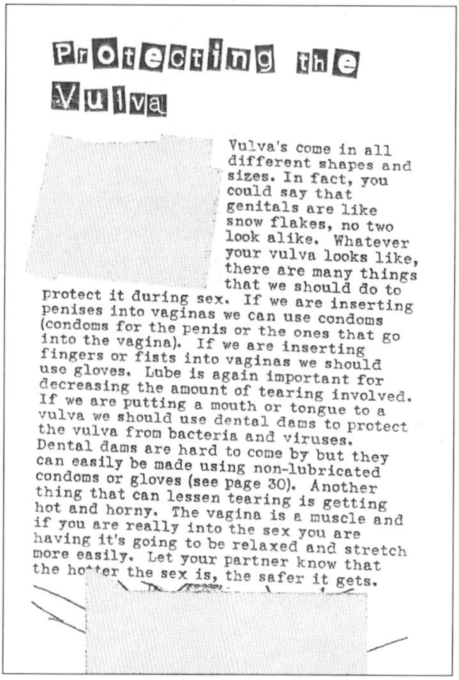

Protecting the Vulva

Vulva's come in all different shapes and sizes. In fact, you could say that genitals are like snow flakes, no two look alike. Whatever your vulva looks like, there are many things that we should do to protect it during sex. If we are inserting penises into vaginas we can use condoms (condoms for the penis or the ones that go into the vagina). If we are inserting fingers or fists into vaginas we should use gloves. Lube is again important for decreasing the amount of tearing involved. If we are putting a mouth or tongue to a vulva we should use dental dams to protect the vulva from bacteria and viruses. Dental dams are hard to come by but they can easily be made using non-lubricated condoms or gloves (see page 30). Another thing that can lessen tearing is getting hot and horny. The vagina is a muscle and if you are really into the sex you are having it's going to be relaxed and stretch more easily. Let your partner know that the hotter the sex is, the safer it gets.

Figure 9.2 "Protecting the Vulva."
Excerpt from *A Queersafe Zine*

who are non-Indigenous and white. Although much of the work that these activist organizations undertake must necessarily address the struggles of incarcerated racialized and Indigenous populations, exclusions of such populations within these groups only further evidences the ways that settler colonialism and racism shape queer and trans movements, even when these movements attempt to adopt radical actions and critiques. The frequent underrepresentation of Indigenous activists in leadership roles within these queer and trans prison movements further reflects the extent to which the colonialist project of incarceration continues to segregate movements led by Indigenous and non-Indigenous peoples in spite of the fact that the issues raised by the Prison Industrial Complex necessarily point to the need to address issues of ongoing colonial violence. These failures in movement unification and in representation show that such violence is not merely top-down and state-sanctioned but also occurs at grassroots and interpersonal levels across queer and trans communities affected by legacies of white settler colonialism that continue to mark national and activist space.

Locating *The Word Is Out* within this complex network of organizations, locations, and publications reveals the importance of linking Canadian decolonization projects to resistance and criminalization issues across seemingly diverse movements transnationally. For instance, *States of Postcoloniality: Palestine-Palestine,* a special edition of Toronto-based *FUSE Magazine,* features an editorial introduction connecting diasporic Palestinian organizing to ongoing decolonization movements and Indigenous activisms within Canada. Editors Gina Badger, Nasrin Himada, and Reena Katz (2013) describe the publication:

> Designed as a critical intervention into the contemporary art discourse in
> southern Canada, where most of our readers are located, the series has not
> addressed colonial realities in our immediate communities but looked else-
> where, hoping to be a part of collectively breaking the public fiction that
> Canada is not a settler state. In the process, we have also had the opportunity
> to articulate solidarity across disparate geographies and histories.

This editorial thus notes the importance of using cultural production to address colonialism within the Canadian state in tandem with a comparative analysis of how colonialism functions transnationally as well. The use of digital technologies and new media to distribute publications like *FUSE* and to build collaborations transnationally can also be traced via the Prisoner Correspondence Project newsletter's distribution patterns and via the Internet. For instance, adapted PDF versions of *The Word Is Out* can reach all outside pen pals with access to computers, pointing to the increasing potential for distribution of new media and for collaboration between queer and trans communities that span a range of locations. Prisoner voices are also beginning to emerge on websites like that of *Original Plumbing,* a publication distributing photographs, personal experiences, interviews, and artistic representations of transmasculine communities and sexualities. *Original Plumbing*'s "Blogging from Jail" (Anonymous 2012) uses new media as a forum for cultural representation and prisoner support (comments from the blog are printed and sent inside by the editors) that draws links between childhood and adolescent cissexism, substance use and survival mechanisms, and criminalization in adulthood. The blog's public comments also reveal frustration with the limited representation of incarcerated people in venues such as *Original Plumbing,* pointing to the growing momentum to include the experiences of inmates within outside trans cultural productions and communities.

The Word Is Out also reflects the possibilities of creating such publications on extremely low budgets, as open-source software provides layout templates for producing the newsletter without overhead costs. However, because those inside can receive only paper copies, *The Word Is Out*'s postage fees are approximately $500 per issue, over one-third of the Prisoner Correspondence Project's total annual budget. This expense is due largely to the great number of pen pals located in the United States at international mailing rates (in contrast to the free distribution of the newsletter online). Such financial obstacles call attention to the multiple ways that national borders act as a gatekeeping force that operates in tandem with prisons via the state's criminalization of the bodies of migrants and undocumented workers who cross it. The movement of the newsletter and of pen pal correspondences across the Canada-US border also calls attention to how border patrol can withhold and censor alliances and divide communities in a fashion that mirrors the operation of prison mailrooms. As an extension of the daily violence of detaining and dispersing families and racialized subjects via the border and the carceral system, the border can also dissolve communications and cultural connections between those it keeps apart. This process of censorship by the Canadian border, for instance, was called to nationwide attention in 1994 by a lawsuit led by the Lesbian Avengers and Vancouver's Little Sisters Bookstore. The civil suit challenged the power of the border to determine whether material that included affirming representations of queer sexuality and safer sex could be withheld during a temporal moment where millions of Canadians were dying of AIDS and looking to this material and to the cultural centres that house it as a means of cultural and physical survival (Busby 2004). The Prisoner Correspondence Project thus envisions the border as a structure established to displace communities by means such as the physical removal and blockage of people from national, social, and economic participation as well as the linked withholding of information, literature, culture, and critical resources on HIV/AIDS prevention and health under the legal and broader narrative practices of equating queerness and gender noncompliance with obscenity.

The Prisoner Correspondence Project's circulation of print culture and information across borders also points to the diasporic and migratory nature of queer and trans cultural production as it moves out of print and into digital forums. The now antiquated mode of epistolary correspondence through which the Prisoner Correspondence Project operates demonstrates a technological access barrier held in place by prisons. In the same way that much cultural material is confiscated by border and mailroom authorities, a great wealth of digital and web-based information is blocked by way of access to the Internet. Responding to this barrier remains a major task of the Prisoner Correspondence Project, as collecting, downloading, and redistributing this material as print culture is among the project's daily tasks. This process further reflects how queer and trans cultural production exists digitally through a transnational constellation of racial identities, contact zones, diasporas, and sites of production that cannot be pinned to a single spatial or temporal point. The Internet makes possible the continual updating, movement, and circulation of such narratives, as sites like Tumblr allow users to update and refresh previous entries, promoting the transience rather than permanence of their own identities, avatars, and URLs (website domain names). Tumblr blogs support an emerging community of queer and trans cultural makers responding to racialization, migration, criminalization, and colonialism, alongside discussions of topics including whiteness, gender, sexuality, fashion, pornography, fatness, and art. Yet, for these resources to enter prisons, they must be moved offline and reformulated in stasis. Barring prisoners from these cultural forums not only prevents their direct participation in queer and trans cultures but also locates their ability to access culture as something rooted in one physical location (as print matter) rather than within the migratory network of digital culture and queer diasporas. Prisoners are thereby also excluded from transnational networks made possible via new media production and self-representation. The message sent by prison censors of both direct information and technological access thus signifies not only a structural exclusion from national culture but also a confinement within the nation's limiting spatial bounds.

It is accordingly through cultural production that queer and trans prisoners can reposition themselves in response to, and as excluded from, these modes of representation. The Prisoner Correspondence Project's newsletter also uses culture to comment on prisoners' double erasure from national belonging and from mainstream queer organizing. How cultural production can become a site of gender and sexual affirmation and prison coalition building can be read within the back covers of issues 2 (spring 2009) and 4 (spring 2012) of *The Word Is Out* (see Figures 9.3 and 9.4). Issue 2's front cover presents a fairly standard layout for a DIY-style newsletter publication, with a hand-drawn title banner at the top, a hand-drawn heading below, text to the left, and the table of contents to the right, and its back cover features a full-page drawing from inside contributor Promethea Persaius H.P. al-Assad (formerly known as Countess Sha'uri). The image depicts a close-up of a bent-over torso clad in a t-shirt cropped well above the midriff. The figure also sports athletic shorts in a 1980s, retro-homo workout fashion that reveal the contour of the model's underpants while guiding the viewer's eye down the curve of a leg and back up along the garment's seam toward the image's (queer) focal point (i.e., the butt).

This sexy and inviting body cannot be marked by gender, although its gender presentation suggests a degree of playfulness that is at once sincerely and campily queer. The figure similarly elides the inclusion of overt racial identifications, as this black and white image does not contain facial features or other essentialist renderings of race. Yet the image's inclusion of queeny workout fashion popularized by 1980s hip-hop and ball cultures suggests the ways that sexual and gender representation interacts with this self-representation and self-fashioning of the queer body in relation to race. "Don't be a stranger now ..." reads the caption positioned at the top of the page. The Prisoner Correspondence Project's mailing address is also printed directly above the image, suggesting that the newsletter is not a distancing tool and that this back matter is not a resolution. This back cover instead functions as an opening or an enticing welcome into communication, feedback, collaboration, and community that positions queer and trans inmates across institutions and national bounds as existing both as valued individuals and as critical and desirable members of queer and trans extended families.

Similarly, issue 4's back cover features another full-page illustration submitted by inside contributor Francisco Martinez (also known as "Paco" from Dallas). This image presents a sexy, muscular, and queerly coded Latino man in black briefs with a hand positioned suggestively below his waistband as his eyes make contact with the reader's. Again the image is layered with the Prisoner Correspondence Project's mailing address and a caption, "keep in touch." The address's position on the page is level not with the man's hand but with his face, thereby urging the viewer to glance alternately between the focal point at the

Figure 9.3 Back cover of *The Word Is Out* featuring art by Promethea Persaius H.P. al-Assad

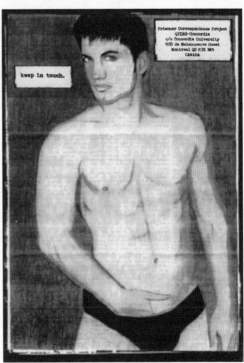

Figure 9.4 Back cover of *The Word Is Out* featuring art by Francisco "Paco" Martinez, Texas Department of Criminal Justice

Marty Fink

end of the arm's arching contour (i.e., the package) and the image's inviting gaze (which thereby returns the desiring look). Eroticizing and linguistically playing with the act of correspondence through a complexly gendered and racialized visual representation, this back cover again aims not to definitively close the newsletter but to reopen communication through the showcased image's direct stare. As Rosemarie Garland-Thomson attests in her analysis of *Staring: How We Look* (2009, 3), the act of staring, even that between an artistic representation and its viewer, can set into motion an impactful "interpersonal relationship." By interfering with the status quo and interrupting the complacency of "visual business-as-usual," staring can alter our sense of who we are through the act of staring at who we think we are not (ibid. 6). This act thus makes space for the inclusion of bodies that are regarded as extraordinary, as surplus, as criminal, or as existing outside of the public sphere. Placing queer and incarcerated bodies into the position of the "staree" can include these bodies and their presence within the rubrics of queer community and national life both inside and outside prison. This broadening of the range of bodies that we might expect to see within the public sphere is a legal, social, and cultural shift resulting from the larger civil rights movement, including the disability rights movement (ibid., 5). This back cover, therefore, not only concludes the newsletter but also places such bodies, identities, and desires back onto a queer political map.[5]

In addition to the literary, poetic, and artistic contributions of inside pen pals, the newsletter also features regular columns like gay horoscopes, gay celebrity gossip, updates on the Prisoner Correspondence Project's programming and activities, updates on queer and trans prisoner struggles, featured resources for inmates (e.g., Toronto's PASAN, the Native Youth Sexual Health Network, Montreal's Open Door Books, Quebec's Trans Health Network, and Vancouver's Letters for the Inside), and up-to-date lists of resources available by request through the Prisoner Correspondence Project's library. *The Word Is Out* plays with the newsletter format and content possibilities to revel in and aesthetically embrace the act of being queer. Queerness and the queer aesthetic, moreover, have become a creative and cultural force behind the Prisoner Correspondence Project's fiscal survival, as in addition to run-of-the-mill fundraising strategies like queer dance parties, grant writing, and gay Christmas card sales, the Prisoner Correspondence Project is about to release its Daddy Program, wherein those who wish to donate large sums of money through the project's PayPal account will be rewarded with a leather-studded cap reading "Daddy," a campy but perhaps effective means of keeping the newsletter in circulation. Jack Halberstam (2005, 187) points to subcultural production and countercultures emerging from within queer and trans communities as a mode of suggesting "alterative histories" necessary to a temporal and spatial restructuring of the future and present. Cultural production hence provides a force through which to imagine a present and future history devoid of the spaces of prison.

With a simultaneous deprioritization by the Harper government of both social services and arts funding, agents in this political moment might be skeptical of the potential for cultural production and social justice rather than biological research and medicalization to address the harms of Indigenous genocide, criminalization, and HIV/AIDS. Yet, at the level of the physical body and of the built environment, cultural production can alter perceptions of those bodies missing from queer and trans community spaces and excluded from activist and national participation. Attaining what José Esteban Muñoz (2009, 32) envisions as a utopic queer future in antithesis to homonationalist and assimilationist politics requires recentring incarcerated queer and trans people both as valued members and as valuable leaders of broader struggles to resist ongoing colonialization and to survive as queer and as trans. Creating art, writing, sexual representation, new media, social media, and public space to link incarcerated queer and trans people to outside communities and to one another might inspire us to "keep in touch" as a way to prevent their disappearance.

Notes

1 Prime Minister Stephen Harper's "tough on crime" agenda represents a $3.6 billion campaign to build new prisons, to enforce mandatory minimum sentencing for nonviolent crimes, and to cut early-release programs, even though extensive research attests that tougher sentencing neither decreases crime rates nor inhibits criminalized activity (see also Piché 2012).
2 See http://www.idlenomore.ca.
3 For a discussion of policing, see Trevenen and DeGagne (this collection).
4 The series was originally titled *Fucking without Fear* (Prisoner Correspondence Project 2009–12), but discussions with inside members led to a title change in order to prevent mailroom censorship. The current title remains provisional and may change yet again based on inside feedback.
5 For a discussion of unsettling normative constructions of desire and the Feminist Porn Awards, see de Szegheo-Lang (this collection).

References

Abunimah, A. 2011. "After Witnessing Palestine's Apartheid, Indigenous and Women of Color Feminists Endorse BDS." 7 December. http://electronicintifada.net/blogs/ali -abunimah/after-witnessing-palestines-apartheid-indigenous-and-women-color -feminists.

ActionAid et al. 2011. "Statement on British 'Aid Cut' Threats to African Countries That Violate LBGTI Rights." *Pambazuka News,* 27 October. http://www.pambazuka.net/ en/category/advocacy/77470.

AIDS Project Los Angeles. 2007–08. *Corpus Magazine: An HIV Prevention Publication.* Vols. 5–7.

Aken'Ova, D., et al. 2007. "Public Statement of Warning." *Monthly Review Zine,* 31 January. http://mrzine.monthlyreview.org/2007/increse310107.html.

Albury, K. 2009. "Reading Porn Reparatively." *Sexualities* 12 (5): 647–53. http://dx.doi. org/10.1177/1363460709340373.

Alexander, M.J. 2006a. "Imperial Desire/Sexual Utopias: White Gay Capital and Transnational Tourism." In *Pedagogies of Crossing: Meditations on Feminism, Sexual Politics, Memory, and the Sacred,* 66–88. Durham, NC: Duke University Press.

–. 2006b. *Pedagogies of Crossing: Meditations on Feminism, Sexual Politics, Memory, and the Sacred.* Durham, NC: Duke University Press.

Alexander, M.J., and C.T. Mohanty, eds. 1997. *Feminist Genealogies, Colonial Legacies, Democratic Futures.* New York: Routledge.

Ali, T. 2003. *The Clash of Fundamentalisms.* London: Verso.

Allen, J.S. 2012. "Black/Queer/Diaspora at the Current Conjuncture." *GLQ: A Journal of Lesbian and Gay Studies* 18 (2–3): 211–48. http://dx.doi.org/10.1215/10642684-1472872.

Althusser, L. 1970. "Ideology and Ideological State Apparatuses." In *"Lenin and Philosophy" and Other Essays,* 127–86. London: New Left Books.

Anonymous. 2012. "Blogging from Jail: Meet Inmate #12004." *Original Plumbing,* 26 January. http://www.originalplumbing.com/index.php/politics-activism/incarceration/ item/201-blogging-from-jail-meet-inmate-.

Anzaldúa, G. 1987. *Borderlands/La Frontera: The New Mestiza*. San Francisco, CA: Aunt Lute Books.

Arat-Koç, S., A. Sundar, and B. Evans. 2007. "Echoes of the 1930's: Today's Hotel Workers Lead the Struggle to 'Upgrade' the Service Economy." *Relay: A Socialist Project Review* 15: 16–17.

Associated Press. 2013. "Russia Passes Anti-Gay-Law." *Guardian* (London), 30 June. http://www.theguardian.com/world/2013/jun/30/russia-passes-anti-gay-law.

Attwood, F. 2007. "No Money Shot? Commerce, Pornography, and New Sex Taste Cultures." *Sexualities* 10 (4): 441–56. http://dx.doi.org/10.1177/1363460707080982.

Ayala, G., C.E. Husted, and A. Spieldenner. 2004. *Holding Open Space: Re-tooling and Re-imagining HIV Prevention for Gay and Bisexual Men of Color*. New York and Los Angeles: Institute for Gay Men's Health.

Bacchetta, P., and J. Haritaworn. 2011. "There Are Many Transatlantics: Homonationalism, Homotransnationalism and Feminist-Queer-Trans of Colour Theories and Practices." In *Transatlantic Conversations: Feminism as Travelling Theory*, ed. K. Davis and M. Evans, 127–44. Surrey, UK, and Burlington, VA: Ashgate.

Backhouse, C. 1999a. "The Ceremony of Marriage." In *Petticoats and Prejudice: Women and Law in Nineteenth-Century Canada*, 9-28. Toronto: CSP and Women's Press.

–. 1999b. *Colour-Coded: A Legal History of Racism in Canada, 1900–1950*. Toronto: University of Toronto Press.

Badger, G., N. Himada, and R. Katz. 2013. "36-2/Editorial." *FUSE Magazine: States of Postcoloniality: Palestine-Palestine* 36 (2). http://fusemagazine.org/2013/03/36-2editorial.

Bailey, M., B. Baines, B. Amani, and A. Kaufman. 2005. "Expanding Recognition of Foreign Polygamous Marriages: Policy Implications for Canada." Queen's University Legal Studies Research Paper No. 07-12. Prepared for Status of Women Canada.

Bakan, A. 2008. "Reconsidering the Underground Railroad: Slavery and Racialization in the Making of the Canadian State." *Social Studies* 4 (1): 3–29.

Baluja, T. 2012. "Tories Unveil Bill to Thwart 'Bogus' Refugees." *Globe and Mail*, 16 February. http://www.theglobeandmail.com/news/politics/tories-unveil-bill-to-thwart-bogus-refugees/article2340521/

Bannerji, H. 1995. *Thinking Through: Essays on Feminism, Marxism, and Anti-Racism*. Toronto: Women's Press.

–. 2000. *The Dark Side of the Nation: Essays on Multiculturalism, Nationalism and Gender*. Toronto: Canadian Scholars' Press.

Bardzell, S. 2010. "Topping from the Viewfinder: The Visual Language of Virtual BDSM Photographs in Second Life." *Journal of Virtual Worlds Research* 2 (4): 1–19.

–. 2011. *Boycott, Divestment, Sanctions: The Global Struggle for Palestinian Rights*. Chicago: Haymarket Books.

Barnard, I. 2008. *Queer Race: Cultural Interventions in the Racial Politics of Queer Theory*. New York: Peter Lang.

Bassichis, M., A. Lee, and D. Spade. 2011. "Building an Abolitionist Trans and Queer Movement with Everything We've Got." In *Captive Genders: Trans Embodiment and the Prison Industrial Complex*, ed. E. Stanley and N. Smith, 15–40. Oakland, CA: AK Press.

Bauer, G.R., R. Hammond, R. Travers, M. Kaay, K.M. Hohenadel, and M. Boyce. 2009. "'I Don't Think This Is Theoretical; This Is Our Lives': How Erasure Impacts Health

Care for Transgender People." *Journal of the Association of Nurses in AIDS Care* 20 (5): 348–61. http://dx.doi.org/10.1016/j.jana.2009.07.004.

Baus, J., D. Hunt, and R. Williams. 2006. *Cruel and Unusual.* Documentary. Outcast Films.

Beaman, L.G. 2014. "Opposing Polygamy: A Matter of Equality or Patriarchy?" In *Of Crime and Religion: Polygamy in Canadian Law,* ed. M.-P. Robert and S. Bernatchez, 131-57. Sherbrooke: Editions Revue de Droit de l'Université de Sherbrooke.

Beeby, D. 2010. "Immigration Minister Pulled Gay Rights from Citizenship Guide, Documents Show." *Globe and Mail,* 2 March. http://www.theglobeandmail.com/news/politics/immigration-minister-pulled-gay-rights-from-citizenship-guide-documents-show/article571718.

Bell, D. 1995. "Pleasure and Danger: The Paradoxical Spaces of Sexual Citizenship." *Political Geography* 14 (2): 139–53. http://dx.doi.org/10.1016/0962-6298(95)91661-M.

Berger, B., and S. Rehaag. 2012. "Stop Vilifying Roma Refugees." *Toronto Star,* 15 September. http://www.thestar.com/opinion/editorialopinion/2012/09/15/stop_vilifying_roma_refugees.html.

Berlant, L. 2011. *Cruel Optimism.* Durham, NC: Duke University Press. http://dx.doi.org/10.1215/9780822394716.

Berlant, L., and M. Warner. 1998. "Sex in Public." *Critical Inquiry* 24 (2): 547–66. http://dx.doi.org/10.1086/448884.

Bernstein Sycamore, M. 2008. "Gay Shame: From Queer Autonomous Public Space to Direct Action Extravaganza." In *That's Revolting: Queer Strategies for Resisting Assimilation,* ed. M. Bernstein Sycamore, 268–95. Brooklyn, NY: Soft Skull.

Bérubé, A. 2001. "How Gay Stays White and What Kind of White It Stays." In *The Making and Unmaking of Whiteness,* ed. B.B. Rasmussen, E. Klinenberg, I.J. Nexica, and M. Wray, 234–65. Durham, NC: Duke University Press. http://dx.doi.org/10.1215/9780822381044-011.

Bilge, S. 2010. "Beyond Subordination vs. Resistance: An Intersectional Approach to the Agency of Veiled Muslim Women." *Journal of Intercultural Studies (Melbourne, Vic.)* 31 (1): 9–28. http://dx.doi.org/10.1080/07256860903477662.

Binnie, J. 2004. *The Globalization of Sexuality.* London: Sage.

Bourgeois, R. 2009. "Deceptive Inclusion: The 2010 Vancouver Olympics and Violence against First Nations People." *Canadian Woman Studies/Les cahiers de la femme* 27 (2–3): 39–44.

Boyd, S.B. 2013. "'Marriage Is More Than Just a Piece of Paper': Feminist Critiques of Same-Sex Marriage." *National Taiwan University Law Review* 8 (2): 263–98.

Boykoff, J. 2011. "Space Matters: The 2010 Winter Olympics and Its Discontents." *Human Geography* 4 (2): 48–60.

Bracke, S. 2012. "From 'Saving Women' to 'Saving Gays': Rescue Narratives and Their Dis/Continuities." *European Journal of Women's Studies* 19 (2): 237–52. http://dx.doi.org/10.1177/1350506811435032.

Brand, D. 1994. *Bread Out of Stone: Reflections on Sex, Recognitions, Dreaming and Politics.* Toronto: Coach House.

Brandzel, A.L. 2011. "Haunted by Citizenship: Whitenormative Citizen-Subjects and the Uses of History in Women's Studies." *Feminist Studies* 37 (3): 503–33.

Brock, D., K. Gillies, C. Oliver, and M. Sutdhibhasilp. 2000. "Migrant Sex Work: A Roundtable Analysis." *Canadian Women's Studies* 20 (2): 84–91.

Burnett, R. 2011. "Violence in Montreal's Gay Village Has Locals up in Arms Over Safety - and Future of Gay Tourism. *Montreal Gazette,* 19 December. http://montrealgazette.com/entertainment/violence-in-montreals-gay-village-has-locals-up-in-arms-over-safety-and-future-of-gay-tourism.

Busby, K. 2004. "The Queer Sensitive Interveners in the *Little Sisters* Case: A Response to Dr. Kendall." In *Eclectic Views on Gay Male Pornography: Pornucopia,* ed. T.G. Morrison, 129–49. Binghampton, NY: Harrington Park.

Butler, J. 1994. "Against Proper Objects: Introduction." *differences: A Journal of Feminist Cultural Studies* 6.2 (3): 1–26.

–. 2008. "Sexual Politics, Torture, and Secular Time." *British Journal of Sociology* 59 (1): 1–23. http://dx.doi.org/10.1111/j.1468-4446.2007.00176.x.

–. 2010. "I Must Distance Myself from This Complicity with Racism." 19 June. http://www.egs.edu/faculty/judith-butler/articles/i-must-distance-myself.

Byrd, J. 2011. *The Transit of Empire: Indigenous Critiques of Colonialism.* Minneapolis: University of Minnesota Press.

Calder, G. 2014. "Conclusion: 'To the Exclusion of All Others' – Polygamy, Monogamy, and the Legal Family in Canada." In *Polygamy's Rights and Wrongs: Perspectives on Harm, Family, and Law,* ed. G. Calder and L.G. Beaman, 215-33. Vancouver: UBC Press.

Califia, P. 1988. *Macho Sluts.* Vancouver: Arsenal Pulp Press.

Campbell, A. 2005. *How Have Policy Approaches to Polygamy Responded to Women's Experiences and Rights? An International, Comparative Analysis.* Ottawa: Status of Women Canada.

–. 2009. "Bountiful Voices." *Osgoode Hall Law Journal* 47 (2): 183–234.

–. 2010. "Bountiful's Plural Marriages." *International Journal of Law in Context* 6 (4): 343–61. http://dx.doi.org/10.1017/S1744552310000297.

Campbell, M. 1973. *Halfbreed.* New York: Saturday Review.

Campbell, M.K. 2001. "Mr. Peay's Horses: The Federal Response to Mormon Polygamy, 1854–1887." *Yale Journal of Law and Feminism* 13 (1): 29–70.

Canadian Broadcasting Corporation (CBC). 2006. "Tories Move to Raise the Age of Consent." *CBC News,* 22 June. http://www.cbc.ca/news/canada/tories-move-to-raise-age-of-consent-1.626307.

–. 2009. "Montreal Gay Pride Festival Funding Denied." *CBC News,* 22 July. http://www.cbc.ca/news/canada/montreal/montreal-gay-pride-festival-funding-denied-1.799790.

–. 2010a. "Refugees Need More Help from Private Groups: Kenney." *CBC News,* 29 June. http://www.cbc.ca/news/canada/refugees-need-more-help-from-private-groups-kenney-1.924322.

–. 2010b. "Toronto Gay Pride Denied Federal Funds." *CBC News,* 7 May. http://www.cbc.ca/news/canada/toronto-gay-pride-denied-federal-funds-1.890428.

–. 2011. "Gay Rights Referenced in New Citizenship Guide." *CBC News,* 14 March. http://www.cbc.ca/news/canada/gay-rights-referenced-in-new-citizenship-guide-1.985389.

Carter, S. 2008. *The Importance of Being Monogamous: Marriage and Nation Building in Western Canada to 1915.* Edmonton: Athabasca University Press.

Chan, M. 2011. "Beyond Bountiful: Toward an Intersectional and Postcolonial Feminist Intervention in the British Columbia Polygamy Reference." *Appeal* 16 (1): 15–30.

Change.org. 2013. "International Olympic Committee (IOC): Strip Sochi of the 2014 Winter Games." 25 July. https://www.change.org/p/international-olympic-committee-ioc-strip-sochi-of-the-2014-winter-games.

Charland, M. 1987. "Constitutive Rhetoric: The Case of the Peuple Québécois." *Quarterly Journal of Speech* 73 (2): 133–50. http://dx.doi.org/10.1080/00335638709383799.

Chow, R. 2002. *The Protestant Ethnic and the Spirit of Capitalism.* New York: Columbia University Press.

Citizenship and Immigration Canada. 2011. *Discover Canada: The Rights and Responsibilities of Citizenship.* http://www.cic.gc.ca/english/pdf/pub/discover.pdf.

Cohen, C. 1997. "Punks, Bulldaggers, and Welfare Queens: The Radical Potential of Queer Politics?" *GLQ: A Journal of Lesbian and Gay Studies* 3 (4): 437–65. http://dx.doi.org/10.1215/10642684-3-4-437.

Cohen, T. 2012. "Controversial Refugee Bill Set to Clear House of Commons Monday." *National Post,* 10 June. http://news.nationalpost.com/2012/06/10/controversial -refugee-bill-set-to-clear-house-of-commons-monday/.

Combahee River Collective. 1977. "The Combahee River Collective Statement." Reprinted in *Home Girls: A Black Feminist Anthology,* ed. B. Smith, 272–82. New York: Kitchen Table, 1983.

Comella, L., and S. Tarrant, eds. 2015. *New Views on Pornography: Sexuality, Politics, and the Law.* Santa Barbara, CA: Praeger.

Cooper, A. 2006. *The Hanging of Angelique: The Untold Story of Canadian Slavery and the Burning of Old Montreal.* Toronto: HarperCollins.

Cossman, B. 2002. "Sexing Citizenship, Privatizing Sex." *Citizenship Studies* 6 (4): 483–506. http://dx.doi.org/10.1080/1362102022000041277.

–. 2007. *Sexual Citizens: The Legal and Cultural Regulation of Sex and Belonging.* Stanford, CA: Stanford University Press.

Cott, N.F. 2000. *Public Vows: A History of Marriage and the Nation.* Cambridge, MA: Harvard University Press.

Crawford, L., and C. Ellison. 2010. "Hate Crimes Demand Fresh Approaches; Harsher Sentences Don't Work." *Edmonton Journal,* 12 May, A15.

Crawford, L., and R. Nichols. 2010. "Rethinking Hate Crimes: The Hard Work of Creating Social Equity." *Fedcan Blog,* 14 May. http://www.ideas-idees.ca/blog/rethinking -hate-crimes-hard-work-creating-social-equity .

Dangerous Bedfellows, ed. 1990. *Policing Public Sex.* Boston: South End.

Dave. 2011. "Inclusiveness Excludes." *Xtra!* 15 August. http://dailyxtra.com/toronto/news/ leather-clad-crowd-marches-village-fair-4890?page=4#comments.

Davis, A. 1983. *Women, Race and Class.* New York: Random House.

–. 2008. "Abolition Democracy and Global Politics." Lecture presented at the Cooper Union, New York, 30 October. http://vimeo.com/4770086.

D'Emilio, J. 1992. *Making Trouble: Essays on Gay History, Politics, and the University.* New York: Routledge.

De Genova, N. 2010. "The Queer Politics of Migration: Reflections on 'Illegality' and Incorrigibility." *Studies in Social Justice* 4 (2): 101–26.

Deleuze, G., and F. Guattari. 2004. *Anti-Oedipus: Capitalism and Schizophrenia.* Minneapolis: University of Minnesota Press.

Denike, M. 2010a. "Homonormative Collusions and the Subject of Rights: Reading Terrorist Assemblages." *Feminist Legal Studies* 18 (1): 85–100. http://dx.doi.org/10.1007/s10691 -010-9148-z.

–. 2010b. "What's Queer about Polygamy?" In *Queer Theory: Law, Culture, Empire,* ed. R. Leckey and K. Brooks, 137–53. London and New York: Routledge.

Derksen, C. 2013. *The Collapse.* Album. Self-produced.

Dias, G., and P. Collins. 2009. *An Inter-sectional Strategy to Address HIV/AIDS and Hepatitis C in Ontario Prisons.* Toronto: Prisoners' HIV/AIDS Support Action Network (PASAN).

Douglas, S., S. Jivraj, and S. Lamble. 2011. "Liabilities of Queer Anti-Racist Critique." *Feminist Legal Studies* 19 (2): 107–18. http://dx.doi.org/10.1007/s10691-011-9181-6.

Driskill, Q.-L. 2010. "Doubleweaving Two-Spirit Critiques: Building Alliances between Native and Queer Studies." *GLQ: A Journal of Lesbian and Gay Studies* 16 (1–2): 69–92. http://dx.doi.org/10.1215/10642684-2009-013.

Drucker, P. 2011. "Toward a Queer Marxism?" *Against the Current* (151). http://www.solidarity-us.org/node/3190.

Drummond, S.G. 2009. "Polygamy's Inscrutable Criminal Mischief." *Osgoode Hall Law Journal* 47 (2): 317–69.

Dua, E., and A. Robertson. 1999. *Scratching the Surface: Canadian Anti-racist Feminist Thought.* Toronto: Women's Press.

Duggan, L. 2002. "The New Homonormativity: The Sexual Politics of Neoliberalism." In *Materializing Democracy: Toward a Revitalized Cultural Politics*, ed. R. Castronova and D. Nelson, 175–94. Durham, NC: Duke University Press. http://dx.doi.org/10.1215/9780822383901-007.

–. 2003. *The Twilight of Equality? Neoliberalism, Cultural Politics, and the Attack on Democracy.* Boston: Beacon.

Dworkin, A., and C.A. MacKinnon. 1988. *Pornography and Civil Rights: A New Day for Women's Equality.* Minneapolis: Organizing against Pornography.

Edelman, L. 1994. *Homographesis: Essays in Gay Literary and Cultural Theory.* New York: Routledge.

Egale Canada. N.d. "About Us." http://egale.ca/category/about-us.

–. 2011a. "A CANADA FOR 'ALL CANADIANS': Statement from Egale Canada on the Results of the 2011 Federal Election." 3 May. http://egale.ca/index.asp?lang=E&menu=1&item=1485.

–. 2011b. "Updated Citizenship Guide Recognizes Gay and Lesbian Equality in Canada Toronto." 14 March. http://egale.ca.

–. 2012. "Egale Issue Brief: Bill C-31 Protecting Canada's Immigration System Act." 24 February. http://egale.ca/index.asp?lang=&menu=1&item=1559.

Ekine, S. 2010. "Two Interviews: African Sexualities and Gay Imperialism – Gay Activism in Germany and Europe." *Blacklooks*, 22 July. http://www.blacklooks.org/2010/07/sokari-ekine-jin-haritaworn-on-sexualities-gay-imperialism-racism-within-the-lgbtiq-community/.

Elliott, L., and L. Payton. 2012. "Refugee Reforms Include Fingerprints, No Appeals for Some." *CBC News*, 15 February. http://www.cbc.ca/news/politics/refugee-reforms-include-fingerprints-no-appeals-for-some-1.1191505.

Eng, D.L. 2010. *The Feeling of Kinship: Queer Liberalism and the Racialization of Intimacy.* Durham, NC: Duke University Press. http://dx.doi.org/10.1215/9780822392828.

–. 2011. "Queering the Black Atlantic, Queering the Brown Atlantic." *GLQ: A Journal of Lesbian and Gay Studies* 17 (1): 193-204.

Engle, K. 2009. *Seeing Ghosts: 9/11 and the Visual Imagination.* Montreal and Kingston: McGill-Queen's University Press.

Engler, Y. 2010. *Canada and Israel: Building Apartheid.* Halifax: Fernwood.

Erickson, L. 2007. "Revealing Femmegimp: A Sex-Positive Reflection on Sites of Shame as Sites of Resistance for People with Disabilities." *Atlantis: Critical Studies in Gender, Culture and Social Justice* 31 (2): 42–52.

–. 2009. "Out of Line: The Sexy Femmegimp Politics of Flaunting It!" In *Sex Matters: The Sexuality and Society Reader*, 3rd ed., ed. M. Stombler, D.M. Baunach, E.O. Burgess, D.J. Donnelly, W.O. Simonds, and E.J. Windsor, 135–40. Upper Saddle River, NJ: Prentice Hall.

Ertman, M. 2010. "Race Treason: The Untold Story of America's Ban on Polygamy." *Columbia Journal of Gender and Law* 19 (2): 287–366.

Eskridge, W.N. 1996. *The Case for Same-Sex Marriage: From Sexual Liberty to Civilized Commitment.* New York: Free Press.

Evans, D.T. 1993. *Sexual Citizenship: The Material Construction of Sexualities.* London and New York: Routledge. http://dx.doi.org/10.4324/9780203412398.

faerie-dust-up. 2011. "Fetish Fair Protest." *Xtra!* 26 July. http://dailyxtra.com/toronto/news/fetish-fair-drops-the-fetish-and-courts-ages-4965.

Fanon, F. 1967. *Black Skin, White Masks.* New York: Grove.

Farber, B.M. 2013. "Something for Jews to Celebrate in Pride Parade." *Toronto Star*, 24 June. http://www.thestar.com/opinion/commentary/2013/06/24/something_for_jews_to_celebrate_in_pride_parade.html.

Farber, B.M., N. Leipciger, and A. Rosensweig. 2012. "Hating the Jew, Hating the 'Gypsy.'" *National Post*, 25 September. http://fullcomment.nationalpost.com/2012/09/25/bernie-m-farber-et-al-hating-the-jew-hating-the-gypsy.

Fisher, W. 1984. "Narration as a Human Communication Paradigm: The Case of Public Moral Argument." *Communication Monographs* 51 (1): 1–22. http://dx.doi.org/10.1080/03637758409390180.

FitzGerald, M., and S. Rayter, eds. 2012. *Queerly Canadian: An Introductory Reader in Sexuality Studies.* Toronto: Canadian Scholars' Press.

Flanagan, T. 2000. *First Nations? Second Thoughts.* Montreal and Quebec: McGill-Queen's University Press.

Floyd, K. 2009. *The Reification of Desire.* Minneapolis: University of Minnesota Press.

Foucault, M. 1990. *The History of Sexuality.* Vol. 1, *An Introduction.* New York: Vintage Books.

–. 2003. *Society Must Be Defended: Lectures at the Collège de France, 1981–1982.* Trans. D. Macey. Ed. M. Bertani and A. Fontana. New York: Picador.

Garland-Thomson, R. 2009. *Staring: How We Look.* Oxford: Oxford University Press.

Genet, J. *Un Chant d'Amour.* Film. 1950.

Gilmore, R.W. 2007. *Golden Gulag: Prisons, Surplus, Crisis and Opposition in Globalizing California.* Berkeley: University of California Press.

Glenwright, D. 2012. "Tory Embrace Just for Show." *Xtra!* 4 October. http://dailyxtra.com/toronto/ideas/tory-embrace-just-show-3544.

GoodForHer.com. N.d. "Feminist Porn Awards." http://www.goodforher.com/feminist_porn_awards.

Gordon, S.B. 2002. *The Mormon Question, Polygamy and Constitutional Conflict in Nineteenth-Century America.* Chapel Hill: University of North Carolina Press.

Government of British Columbia. 2007. *2007 Legislative Session: Third Session, 38th Parliament – Official Report of Debates of the Legislative Assembly (Hansard).* Vol. 15, no. 7, 5 March. http://www.leg.bc.ca/hansard/38th3rd/H70305p.htm.

Government of Canada. 2010. "Message from the Prime Minister." http://www.fin.gov.bc.ca/reports/Canadareport.pdf. Accessed 16 February 2015.

–. 2011. "Discover Canada: The Rights and Responsibilities of Citizenship." http://www.cic.gc.ca/english/resources/publications/discover/.

–. 2013. "Speech from the Throne." 16 October. http://www.speech.gc.ca/eng/full-speech.

Gray, S. 2012. "Tel Aviv 'Best Gay City Destination' of 2011." *PinkNews,* 12 January. http://www.pinknews.co.uk/2012/01/12/tel-aviv-best-gay-destination-of-2011.

Greyson, J. 2011. "Prick." Poster in the series *Poster/Virus.* AAN Toronto.

Grillo, T., and S. Wildman. 1991. "Obscuring the Importance of Race: The Implication of Making Comparisons between Racism and Sexism (or Other -Isms)." *Duke Law Journal* 40 (2): 397–412. http://dx.doi.org/10.2307/1372732.

Guarnieri, M. 2012. "Pinkwashing and Israel, Apartheid, Gay Rights and Military Occupation in the Middle East." *Xtra!* 18 June. http://dailyxtra.com/canada/news/pinkwashing-and-israel-51293.

Guerrero, M.A.J. 1997. "Civil Rights versus Sovereignty: Native American Women in Life and Land Struggles." In *Feminist Genealogies, Colonial Legacies, Democratic Futures,* ed. J.M. Alexander and C.T. Mohanty, 101–21. New York: Routledge.

Gund, C., and D. Levine. 1993. *I'm You, You're Me.* Documentary. AIDS Activist Videotape Collection, New York Public Library.

Gyulai, L. 2009. "Polygamous Union Not out in the Open." *Montreal Gazette,* 23 July. http://www.montrealgazette.com/Polygamous+union+open/1822486/story.html.

Hainsworth, J. 2009. "Gay Athletes Get Pride House for 2010." *Xtra!* 15 May. http://dailyxtra.com/vancouver/news/gay-athletes-get-pride-house-2010-12733.

Halberstam, J. 1997. "Who's Afraid of Queer Theory?" In *Class Issues: Pedagogy, Cultural Studies, and the Public Sphere,* ed. A. Kumar, 256–75. New York: NYU Press.

–. 2005. *In a Queer Time and Place.* New York: NYU Press.

Hall, S. 1990. "Culture Identity and Diaspora." In *Identity: Community, Culture, Difference,* ed. J. Rutherford, 222-37. London: Lawrence & Wishart.

Haque, E. 2012. *Multiculturalism within a Bilingual Framework: Language, Race, and Belonging in Canada.* Toronto: University of Toronto Press.

Haritaworn, J. 2008. "Loyal Repetitions of the Nation: Gay Assimilation and the 'War on Terror.'" *darkmatter,* 2 May. http://www.darkmatter101.org/site/category/journal/issues/3-post-colonial-sexuality.

Haritaworn, J., A. Kuntsman, and S. Posocco, eds. 2014. *Queer Necropolitics.* New York: Routledge.

Haritaworn, J., T. Tauqir, and E. Erdem. 2008. "Gay Imperialism: Gender and Sexuality Discourse in the 'War on Terror.'" In *Out of Place: Interrogating Silences in Queerness/Raciality,* ed. A. Kuntsman and E. Miyake, 71–96. York, UK: Raw Nerve Books.

Hennessy, R. 2000. *Profit and Pleasure: Sexual Identities in Late Capitalism.* New York: Routledge.

Herland, K. 1990–91. *Interviews for CityPulse News.* ACT UP Videotape Collection, 1990–93. Personal collection of Thomas Waugh.

Himes, C. 1952. *Cast the First Stone.* Reprint, New York: New American Library, 1972.

Hoang, N.T. 2004. "The Resurrection of Brandon Lee: The Making of a Gay Asian American Porn Star." In *Porn Studies,* ed. L. Williams, 223–70. Durham, NC: Duke University Press.

Holland, S.P. 2000. *Raising the Dead: Readings of Death and (Black) Subjectivity.* Durham, NC: Duke University Press. http://dx.doi.org/10.1215/9780822380382.

Hong, G.K. 2006. *The Ruptures of American Capital: Women of Color Feminism and the Culture of Immigrant Labor.* Minneapolis: University of Minnesota Press.

hooks, b. 1992. "Eating the Other." In *Black Looks: Race and Representation,* 21–40. Boston: South End.

HotMoviesForHer.com. 2010. *Interview with Tristan Taormino*. http://www.youtube.com/watch?v=UREw3VowCOg&feature=youtu.be.

–. 2011a. *Drew Deveaux at the Public Provocative Porn Panel, Feminist Porn Awards 2011*. http://www.youtube.com/watch?v=WXQaNzN4RUc&feature=youtu.be.

–. 2011b. *Tristan Taormino Opening the Public Provocative Porn Panel at Feminist Porn Awards 2011*. http://www.youtube.com/watch?v=IUVL71L3X7Q&feature=youtu.be.

–. 2012. *HotMoviesForHer Interviews Nenna at The Feminist Porn Awards*. http://www.youtube.com/watch?v=o-kvK9K6BiE&feature=youtu.be.

Houston, A. 2011. "Leather-Clad Crowd Marches through Village Fair: 'We're here! We're queer! We're Kinky!'" *Xtra!* 15 August. http://dailyxtra.com/toronto/news/leather-clad-crowd-marches-village-fair-4890.

–. 2012a. "Dispute Panel Says QuAIA Can March in Pride Parade." *Xtra!* 25 June. http://dailyxtra.com/toronto/news/dispute-panel-says-quaia-can-march-in-pride-parade-3827.

–. 2012b. "Jason Kenney Defends Gay Refugee Email." *Xtra!* 2 October. http://dailyxtra.com/canada/news/jason-kenney-defends-gay-refugee-email-51164.

–. 2012c. "A New Battle over Pride Funding: City Executive Committee Wants 'Israeli Apartheid' Banned." *Xtra!* 11 September. http://dailyxtra.com/toronto/news/new-battle-pride-funding-3602.

Hull, G.T., P.B. Scott, and B. Smith, eds. 1982. *All the Women Are White, All the Blacks Are Men, But Some of Us Are Brave: Black Women's Studies*. New York: Feminist Press.

Jiwani, Y. 2002. "The Criminalization of 'Race,' the Racialization of Crime." In *Crimes of Colour: Racialization and the Criminal Justice System in Canada*, ed. W. Chan and K. Mirchandani, 67–86. Toronto: University of Toronto Press.

–. 2007. *Discourses of Denial: Mediations of Race, Gender and Violence*. Vancouver: UBC Press.

–. 2009. "Helpless Maidens and Chivalrous Knights: Afghan Women in the Canadian Press." *University of Toronto Quarterly* 78 (2): 728–44. http://dx.doi.org/10.3138/utq.78.2.728.

Johnny Ransom. 2011. "BIA Shoves Triangle Pegs into Square Holes." *Xtra!* 15 August. http://dailyxtra.com/toronto/news/leather-clad-crowd-marches-village-fair-4890?page=3#comments.

Johnson, E.P. 2005. "'Quare' Studies, or (Almost) Everything I Know about Queer Studies I Learned from My Grandmother." In *Black Queer Studies: A Critical Anthology*, ed. E.P. Johnson and M. Henderson, 124-58. Durham, NC: Duke University Press.

Jones, C. 2012. *A Cruel Arithmetic: Inside the Case against Polygamy*. Toronto: Irwin Law.

Judd, A. 2014. "Polygamy Charges Approved against 4 People Connected to Bountiful, B.C." 14 August 14. http://globalnews.ca/news/1506655/polygamy-charges-approved-against-4-people-connected-to-bountiful-b-c/. Accessed 16 February 2015.

Keefer, M. 2010. *Anti-Semitism Real and Imagined: Responses to the Canadian Parliamentary Coalition to Combat Anti-Semitism*. Waterloo, ON: Canadian Charger.

Keeling, K. 2007. *The Witch's Flight: The Cinematic, the Black Femme, and the Image of Common Sense*. Durham, NC: Duke University Press. http://dx.doi.org/10.1215/9780822390145.

Keller, J. 2012. "RCMP Renews Polygamy Investigation into Bountiful." *Globe and Mail*, 30 March. http://www.theglobeandmail.com/news/british-columbia/rcmp-renews-polygamy-investigation-into-bountiful/article4097160.

Kempadoo, K. 2003. "Globalizing Sex Workers' Rights." *Canadian Women's Studies* 22 (3–4): 143–50.

Kendall, R., K.F. Tuffin, and K.E. Frewin. 2005. "Reading Hansard: The Struggle for Identity in Aotearoa." *Critical Psychology* (16): 122–45.

Kenney, J. 2011. "Dialogue with the Courts: Judicial Actions and Integrity of Canada's Immigration and Refugee System." 11 February. http://www.cic.gc.ca/english/department/media/speeches/2011/2011-02-11.asp. Accessed 21 July 2012.

–. 2012. "Kenney Responds to Immigration Story." *Xtra!* 27 January. http://dailyxtra.com/kenney-responds-immigration-story-78068.

Kinsman, G. 1996. *The Regulation of Desire: Homo and Hetero Sexualities.* Montreal: Black Rose.

–. 1997. "Managing AIDS Organizing: 'Consultation,' 'Partnership,' and 'Responsibility' as Strategies of Regulation." In *Organizing Dissent: Contemporary Social Movements in Theory and Practice,* ed. W. Carroll, 213–39. Toronto: Garamond.

–. 2001. "Challenging Canadian and Queer Nationalisms." In *A Queer Country: Gay and Lesbian Studies in the Canadian Context,* ed. T. Goldie, 209–34. Vancouver: Arsenal Pulp.

–. 2012. "Gary Kinsman: The Eco-Terrorism Threat." Video interview with Steve Paiken. *Agenda,* 20 December. http://theagenda.tvo.org/blog/agenda-blogs/eco-terrorist-threat-canada.

Kinsman, G., and P. Gentile. 2010. *The Canadian War on Queers: National Security as Sexual Regulation.* Vancouver: UBC Press.

Knegt, P. 2011. *About Canada: Queer Rights.* Halifax: Fernwood.

Konsmo, E. 2013. "Knowing Our Cultures, Knowing Our Bodies: Indigenous Youth Reclaiming Health, Rights, and Justice." Native Youth Sexual Health Network. http://www.cfsh.ca/HeartYourParts/HPBlog/Erin_Konsmo_NYSHN.aspx.

Kuntsman, A. 2008. "Genealogies of Hate, Metonymies of Violence: Immigration, Homophobia, Homopatriotism." In *Out of Place: Interrogating Silences in Queerness/Raciality,* ed. A. Kuntsman and E. Miyake, 103–24. York, UK: Raw Nerve Books.

Kuntsman, A., and E. Miyake, eds. 2008. *Out of Place: Interrogating Silences in Queerness/Raciality.* York, UK: Raw Nerve Books.

LaDuke, W. 1994. "An Indigenous Perspective on Feminism, Militarism and the Environment." *Race, Poverty and the Environment* 4–5 (4 and 1): 7.

Landolt, C.G. 2004a. "Canadians Deceived on Same-Sex Marriage Issue." REAL Women of Canada, 14 December. http://www.realwomenofcanada.ca/publications/analysis-reports/canadians-deceived-on-same-sex-marriage-issue.

–. 2004b. "Same-Sex Unions Are Not Marriages." REAL Women of Canada, 18 May. http://www.realwomenofcanada.ca/publications/analysis-reports/same-sex-unions-are-not-marriages.

Langdridge, D. 2006. "Voices from the Margins: Sadomasochism and Sexual Citizenship." *Citizenship Studies* 10 (4): 373–89. http://dx.doi.org/10.1080/13621020600857940.

Larcher, A.A. 2012. "Canada's Gay Rights Defence Is All Hot Air." *Xtra!* 3 February. http://dailyxtra.com/canada/ideas/canadas-gay-rights-defence-hot-air-51507?qt-event_listing_pages=2.

LaViolette, N. 2007. "Gender-Related Refugee Claims: Expanding the Scope of the Canadian Guidelines." *International Journal of Refugee Law* 19 (2): 169–214. http://dx.doi.org/10.1093/ijrl/eem008.

–. 2010. "Independent Human Rights Documentation and Sexual Minorities: An Ongoing Challenge for the Canadian Refugee Determination Process." In *Protection of Sexual Minorities since Stonewall: Progress and Stalemate in Developed and Developing Countries,* ed. P.C.W. Chan, 303–42. New York: Routledge.

Lawrence, B. 2004. *"Real" Indians and Others: Mixed-Blood Urban Native Peoples and Indigenous Nationhood.* Vancouver: UBC Press.

Lawrence, B., and E. Dua. 2005. "Decolonizing Anti-Racism." *Social Justice (San Francisco, Calif.)* 32 (4): 120–43.

Leckey, R., and K. Brooks. 2010. "Introduction." In *Queer Theory: Law, Culture, Empire,* ed. R. Leckey and K. Brooks, 1–18. New York: Routledge.

Leger, T. 2012. "Dean Spade Speaks on Cece McDonald Trial." *PrettyQueer,* 2 May. http://prettyqueer.com/2012/05/02/dean-spade-speaks-on-cece-mcdonald-trial/.

Lenon, S. 2005. "Marrying Citizens! Raced Subjects? Re-thinking the Terrain of Equal Marriage Discourse." *Canadian Journal of Women and the Law* 17 (2): 405–21.

Letson, R. 2011. "Coming out against Apartheid: A Roundtable about Queer Solidarity and Palestine with Richard Fung, Natalie Kouri-Towe, Tim McCaskell, and Corvin Russell." *Upping the Anti* (13): 137–51.

Lorde, A. 1982. *Zami: A New Spelling of My Name.* Freedom, CA: Crossing.

–. 1984. *Sister Outsider: Essays and Speeches.* New York: Crossing.

Lugones, M. 2007. "Heterosexualism and the Colonial/Modern Gender System." *Hypatia* 22 (1): 186–209.

Luibhéid, E. 2002. *Entry Denied: Controlling Sexuality at the Border.* Minneapolis: University of Minnesota Press.

–. 2005. "Heteronormativity, Responsibility, and Neo-liberal Governance in U.S. Immigration Control." In *Passing Lines: Sexuality and Immigration,* ed. B. Epps, K. Valens, and B.J. González, 69–101. Cambridge, MA: Harvard University Press.

Luongo, M. 2012. "Pinkwashing's Complicated Context." *Gay City News,* 4 January. http://gaycitynews.nyc/pinkwashings-complicated-context/.

Mandlis, L. 2011. "'Formal Equality Can Actually Be Seen to Function as a Barrier to Substantive Equality': An Interview with Lane Mandlis." In *Sex Change, Social Change: Reflections on Identity, Institutions and Imperialism,* 2nd ed., ed. V. Namaste, 169–79. Toronto: Women's Press.

Maracle, L. 1988. *I Am Woman.* Vancouver: Write-On Press.

Massad, J. 2002. "Re-orienting Desire: The Gay International and the Arab World." *Public Culture* 14 (2): 361–86. http://dx.doi.org/10.1215/08992363-14-2-361.

–. 2007. *Desiring Arabs.* Chicago: University of Chicago Press. http://dx.doi.org/10.7208/chicago/9780226509600.001.0001.

McCann, M. 2013. "Panel Dismisses QuAIA Complaints, but City Hall Still a Wildcard." *Xtra!* 10 June. http://dailyxtra.com/toronto/news/panel-dismisses-quaia-complaints-city-hall-still-wildcard-61639.

McCaskell, T. 2010. "Queers against Apartheid: From South Africa to Israel." *Canadian Dimension* 44 (4): 14–18.

McGee, M. 1975. "In Search of 'The People': A Rhetorical Alternative." *Quarterly Journal of Speech* 61 (3): 235–49. http://dx.doi.org/10.1080/00335637509383289.

McGregor, J. 2012. "Same-Sex Divorce Options Explored by Harper Government." *CBC News,* 12 January. http://www.cbc.ca/news/politics/same-sex-divorce-options-explored-by-harper-government-1.1194363.

McKiernan, M. 2011. "Reforms Introduce New Challenges for Gay Refugees." *Law Times*, 4 July. http://www.lawtimesnews.com/index.php?option=com_k2&Itemid=170&id=1891&lang=en&view=item..

McKittrick, K. 2007. "Freedom Is a Secret: The Future Usability of the Underground." In *Black Geographies and the Politics of Place*, ed. K. McKittrick and C. Woods, 97–111. Cambridge, MA: South End.

McRuer, R. 2006. *Crip Theory: Cultural Signs of Queerness and Disability*. New York: NYU Press.

Miles, T. 2005. *Ties That Bind: The Story of an Afro-Cherokee Family in Slavery and Freedom*. Berkeley: University of California Press.

Miles, T., and S.P. Holland, eds. 2006. *Crossing Waters, Crossing Worlds: The African Diaspora in Indian Country*. Durham, NC: Duke University Press.

Milke, M. 2006. "Conservative Back-Flip on Race-Based Fisheries." Canadian Taxpayers Federation, 20 November. http://www.taxpayer.com/commentaries/conservative-back-flip-on-race-based-fisheries.

Millbank, J. 2002. "Imagining Otherness: Refugee Claims on the Basis of Sexuality in Canada and Australia." *Melbourne University Law Review* 26 (1): 144–77.

Miller, A.M. 2005. "Gay Enough: Some Tensions in Seeking the Grant of Asylum and Protecting Global Sexual Diversity." In *Passing Lines: Sexuality and Immigration*, ed. B. Epps, K. Valens, and B.J. González, 137–87. Cambridge, MA: Harvard University Press.

Miller-Young, Mireille. 2014. *A Taste for Brown Sugar: Black Women in Pornography*. Durham, NC: Duke University Press.

Miranda, D.A. 2010. "Extermination of the Joyas: Gendercide in Spanish California." *GLQ: A Journal of Lesbian and Gay Studies* 16 (1–2): 253–84. http://dx.doi.org/10.1215/10642684-2009-022.

Mogul, J.L., A.J. Ritchie, and K. Whitlock. 2011. *Queer (In)Justice: The Criminalization of LGBT People in the United States*. Boston: Beacon.

Monkman, K. 2011. "The Creator Is Watching You Harper!" Poster in the series *Poster/Virus*. AAN Toronto.

Monture-Angus, P. 1995. *Thunder in My Soul: A Mohawk Woman Speaks*. Halifax: Fernwood.

Moraga, C., and G. Anzaldúa, eds. 1981. *This Bridge Called My Back: Writings by Radical Women of Color*. New York: Kitchen Table/Women of Color.

Morgensen, S.L. 2010. "Settler Homonationalism: Theorizing Settler Colonialism within Queer Modernities." *GLQ: A Journal of Lesbian and Gay Studies* 16 (1–2): 105–31. http://dx.doi.org/10.1215/10642684-2009-015.

–. 2011a. "The Biopolitics of Settler Colonialism: Right Here, Right Now." *Settler Colonial Studies* 1 (1): 52–76. http://dx.doi.org/10.1080/2201473X.2011.10648801.

–. 2011b. *Spaces between Us: Queer Settler Colonialism and Indigenous Decolonization*. Minneapolis: University of Minnesota Press.

–. 2013. "Settler Colonialism and Alliance: Comparative Challenges to Pinkwashing and Homonationalism." *Jadaliyya*, 3 April. http://www.jadaliyya.com/pages/index/11016/settler-colonialism-and-alliance_comparative-chall.

Morrison, T. 1992. *Playing in the Dark: Whiteness and the Literary Imagination*. Cambridge, MA: Harvard University Press.

Muñoz, J.E. 1999. *Disidentifications: Queers of Color and the Performance of Politics*. Minneapolis: University of Minnesota Press.

–. 2009. *Cruising Utopia: The Then and There of Queer Futurity*. New York: NYU Press.

Murphy, K.P., J. Ruiz, and D. Serlins, eds. 2008. "Queer Futures." *Radical History Review* (100).

Nadeau, C. 2011. *Rogue in Power: Why Stephen Harper Is Remaking Canada by Stealth.* Trans. B. Chodos, E. Hamovitch, and S. Joanis. Toronto: James Lorimer.

Nadine. 2011. "Bend over, Little Bitch!" *Xtra!* 26 July. http://dailyxtra.com/toronto/news/fetish-fair-drops-the-fetish-and-courts-ages-4965.

Nelson, C. 2004. "Slavery, Portraiture and the Colonial Limits of Canadian Art." *Canadian Woman Studies/Les cahier de la femme* 23 (2): 22–9.

Nerenberg, K. 2012. "Right-Wing Hate, the Roma People and Jason Kenney's Trip to Hungary." *Rabble.ca,* 11 October. http://rabble.ca/blogs/bloggers/karl-nerenberg/2012/10/right-wing-hate-roma-people-and-jason-kenneys-trip-hungary.

Newmahr, S. 2010. "Rethinking Kink: Sadomasochism as Serious Leisure." *Qualitative Sociology* 33 (3): 313–31. http://dx.doi.org/10.1007/s11133-010-9158-9.

–. 2011. *Playing on the Edge: Sadomasochism, Risk, and Intimacy.* Bloomington: Indiana University Press.

Nichols, R. 2010. "Attack Shows Need for New Approach." *Edmonton Journal,* 27 April, A17.

No Homonationalism. 2010. "Guidelines for Using This Blog." 24 June. http://nohomonationalism.blogspot.ca/2010/06/guidelines-for-using-this-blog.html.

No One Is Illegal–Toronto. 2010. "Refugee Process in Canada." http://toronto.nooneisillegal.org/node/378.

–. 2011. "The Wrongs of the Canadian Immigration System." http://toronto.nooneisillegal.org/node/573.

–. 2012. "Undoing Borders: Queer Discussions on Im/migration and Criminalization." http://toronto.nooneisillegal.org/node/627.

No One Is Illegal–Vancouver. 2011. "Ten Reasons to Stop Harper's Conservatives." https://noii-van.resist.ca/.

O'Bonsawin, C.M. 2010. "'No Olympics on Stolen Native Land': Contesting Olympic Narratives and Asserting Indigenous Rights within the Discourse of the 2010 Vancouver Games." *Sport in Society* 13 (1): 143–56. http://dx.doi.org/10.1080/17430430903377987.

Ong, A. 2006. *Neoliberalism as Exception: Mutations in Citizenship and Sovereignty.* Durham, NC: Duke University Press. http://dx.doi.org/10.1215/9780822387879.

Osterlund, K. 2009. "Love, Freedom and Governance: Same-Sex Marriage in Canada." *Social and Legal Studies* 18 (1): 93–109. http://dx.doi.org/10.1177/0964663908100335.

Ottawa Dyke March Committee. 2011. "Letter to Ottawa Police Services." 31 August. http://dearvern.blogspot.ca/2011/08/ottawa-dyke-march-2011.html.

Parliament of Canada. 2011. *C-279: An Act to Amend the Canadian Human Rights Act and the Criminal Code (Gender Identity).* 21 September. http://www.parl.gc.ca/LegisInfo/BillDetails.aspx?billId=5122660&Mode=1&Language=E.

Parsons, V. 1995. *Bad Blood: The Tragedy of the Canadian Tainted Blood Scandal.* Toronto: Lester & Orpen Dennys.

Pateman, C. 1988. *The Sexual Contract.* Stanford, CA: Stanford University Press.

Patton, C. 1990. *Inventing AIDS.* New York: Routledge.

Payton, L. 2011. "Harper Speech Fires Up Convention Crowd." *CBC News,* 10 June. http://www.cbc.ca/news/politics/harper-speech-fires-up-convention-crowd-1.976268.

–. 2012. "Canada Considers Immigrant Stream for Entrepreneurs." *CBC News,* 18 April. http://www.cbc.ca/news/politics/canada-considers-immigrant-stream-for-entrepreneurs-1.1142233.

Picard, A. 1995. *Gift of Death: Confronting Canada's Tainted Blood Tragedy*. Toronto: Harper Collins.

Piché, J. 2012. "Accessing the State of Imprisonment in Canada: Information Barriers and Negotiation Strategies." In *Brokering Access: Politics, Power, and Freedom of Information in Canada*, ed. M. Larsen and K. Walby, 234–60. Vancouver: UBC Press.

Pride House. 2009a. "About PRIDE House Vancouver." http://www.pridehouse.ca/ Vancouver/AboutVancouverPRIDEhouse/tabid/70/Default.apx. Accessed 25 November 2012.

–. 2009b. "About PRIDE House Whistler." http://www.pridehouse.ca/Whistler/ AboutWhistlerPRIDEhouse/tabid/67/Default.aspx. Accessed 25 November 2012.

Pride House International. N.d. "PHI Seeks Partners for Pride House Events in Sochi." http://www.pridehouseinternational.org/pride-house-international-seeks -partners-for-pride-house-events-in-sochi.

Prisoner Correspondence Project. 2008-12. *The Word Is Out*. Newsletter.

–. 2009–12. *Fucking without Fear*. Resource series.

Privacy Commissioner of Canada. 2009. "Privacy and Security at the Vancouver 2010 Winter Games." https://www.priv.gc.ca/resource/fs-fi/02_05_d_42_ol_e.asp.

Puar, J.K. 2002a. "Circuits of Queer Mobility: Tourism, Travel, and Globalization." *GLQ: A Journal of Lesbian and Gay Studies* 8 (1–2): 101–37. http://dx.doi.org/10.1215/ 10642684-8-1-2-101.

–. 2002b. "A Transnational Feminist Critique of Queer Tourism." *Antipode* 34 (5): 935– 46. http://dx.doi.org/10.1111/1467-8330.00283.

–. 2005. "On Torture: Abu Ghraib." *Radical History Review* 93: 13–38.

–. 2007. *Terrorist Assemblages: Homonationalism in Queer Times*. Durham, NC: Duke University Press. http://dx.doi.org/10.1215/9780822390442.

–. 2010a. "In the Wake of It Gets Better." *Guardian* (London), 16 November. http://www. theguardian.com/commentisfree/cifamerica/2010/nov/16/wake-it-gets-better -campaign.

–. 2010b. "Israel's Gay Propaganda War." *Guardian* (London), 1 July. http://www.the guardian.com/commentisfree/2010/jul/01/israels-gay-propaganda-war.

–. 2011. "Citation and Censorship: The Politics of Talking about the Sexual Politics of Israel." *Feminist Legal Studies* 19 (2): 133–42. http://dx.doi.org/10.1007/s10691-011 -9176-3.

–. 2012. "The Golden Handcuffs of Gay Rights: How Pinkwashing Distorts Both LGBTIQ and Anti-occupation Activism." *Feminist Wire*, 30 January. http://thefeministwire. com/2012/01/the-golden-handcuffs-of-gay-rights-how-pinkwashing-distorts -both-lgbtiq-and-anti-occupation-activism/.

–. 2013a. *Keynote from the Homonationalism and Pinkwashing Conference*. http://www. youtube.com/watch?v=3S1eEL8ElDo.

–. 2013b. "Rethinking Homonationalism." *International Journal of Middle East Studies* 45 (2): 336–39. http://dx.doi.org/10.1017/S002074381300007X.

Puar, J.K., and M. Mikdashi. 2012. "Pinkwatching and Pinkwashing: Interpenetration and Its Discontents." *Jadaliyya*, 9 August. http://www.jadaliyya.com/pages/index/6774/.

Puar, J.K., and A.S. Rai. 2002. "Monster, Terrorist, Fag: The War on Terrorism and the Production of Docile Patriots." *Social Text* 20 (3, 72): 117–48. http://dx.doi.org/ 10.1215/01642472-20-3_72-117.

QuAIA (Queers against Israeli Apartheid). 2011. "QuAIA to Mayor: Find Another Pretext for Your Anti-Pride Agenda." 15 April. http://queersagainstapartheid.org/2011/04/15/quaia-to-mayor-find-another-pretext-for-your-anti-pride-agenda/.

–. 2012. "Victory for QuAIA! Pride Toronto Dispute Resolution Panel Dismisses B'nai Brith Complaint against QuAIA." 29 June 2012. http://queersagainstapartheid.org/2012/06/29/victory-for-quaia-pride-torontos-dispute-resolution-panel-dismisses-bnai-brith-complaint-against-quaia/.

–. N.d. "Who We Are." http://queersagainstapartheid.org/who.

Queer Ontario. 2012. "Call to Action: Ask Pride Toronto to Dismantle the Dispute Resolution Process." 25 June. http://queerontario.org/pride-call-to-action.

QueerPornTV. 2011. *Tobi Hill-Meyer for QueerPorn.TV!* http://www.youtube.com/watch?v=8Bozk5v80yw&feature=youtu.be.

Rainbow Railroad. N.d. "What We Do." http://www.rainbowrailroad.ca/who-we-help-and-how.

Raw Nerve Books. 2009. "Peter Tatchell – Apology and Correction." September. http://www.petertatchell.net/about/raw-nerve-apology.htm.

Razack, S.H. 1998. *Looking White People in the Eye: Gender, Race, and Culture in Courtrooms and Classrooms.* Toronto: University of Toronto Press.

–. 2000. "'Simple Logic': Race, the Identity Documents Rule and the Story of a Nation Besieged and Betrayed." *Journal of Law and Social Policy* 15: 181–209.

–. 2004a. *Dark Threats and White Knights: The Somalia Affair, Peacekeeping and the New Imperialism.* Toronto: University of Toronto Press.

–. 2004b. "Imperilled Muslim Women, Dangerous Muslim Men and Civilised Europeans: Legal and Social Responses to Forced Marriages." *Feminist Legal Studies* 12 (2): 129-74.

–. 2008. *Casting Out: The Eviction of Muslims from Western Law and Politics.* Toronto: University of Toronto Press.

–. 2011. "The Space of Difference in Law: Inquests into Aboriginal Deaths in Custody." *Somatechnics* 1 (1): 87–123. http://dx.doi.org/10.3366/soma.2011.0008.

REAL Women of Canada. 2011. *Closing Submission of REAL Women of Canada.* Vancouver Registry, No. S-097767.

Rehaag, S. 2008. "Patrolling the Borders of Sexual Orientation: Bisexual Refugee Claims in Canada." *McGill Law Journal/Revue de Droit de McGill* 53 (1): 59–102.

–. 2010. "Bisexuals Need Not Apply: A Comparative Appraisal of Refugee Law and Policy in Canada, the United States, and Australia." In *Protection of Sexual Minorities since Stonewall: Progress and Stalemate in Developed and Developing Countries,* ed. P.C.W. Chan, 281–302. New York: Routledge.

Rich, A. 1986. *On Lies, Secrets, and Silence: Selected Prose, 1966–1978.* New York: Norton.

–. 2003. "Notes towards a Politics of Location." In *Feminist Postcolonial Theory: A Reader,* ed. R. Lewis and S. Mills, 29–42. Edinburgh: Edinburgh University Press.

Rifkin, M. 2011. *When Did Indians Become Straight? Kinship, the History of Sexuality, and Native Sovereignty.* Oxford: Oxford University Press.

Riggs, D. 2006. *Priscilla, (White) Queen of the Desert: Queer Rights/Race Privilege.* New York: Peter Lang.

Robertson, L. 2011. Unpublished speech at Ottawa Dyke March. 27 August.

Rowsome, D. 2010. "Flaming Fetishes." *Fab Magazine,* 4 August. http://connection. ebscohost.com/c/articles/53527411/flaming-fetishes.

Rubin, G. 2011. "Thinking Sex: Notes for a Radical Theory of the Politics of Sexuality." In *Deviations: A Gayle Rubin Reader,* ed. G. Rubin, 137–81. Durham, NC: Duke University Press. http://dx.doi.org/10.1215/9780822394068-006.

Ruddy, J. 2010a. "Attack against Edmonton Lesbian Not Investigated by Police Until Five Days Later." *Xtra!* 23 April. http://dailyxtra.com/canada/news/attack-edmonton -lesbian-investigated-police-five-days-later-52201?qt-event_listing_pages=3.

–. 2010b. "Edmonton Police Service's Queer Liaison Committee Is out of Touch, Say Activists." *Xtra!* 3 May. http://dailyxtra.com/canada/news/edmonton-police-services -queer-liaison-committee-touch-say-activists.

Rusnell, C. 2010a. "Hate-Crime Investigation Delay Probed." *CBC News,* 22 April. http:// www.cbc.ca/news/canada/edmonton/hate-crime-investigation-delay-probed -1.942863.

–. 2010b. "Lesbian Victim of Assault Says It Was Hate Crime." *CBC News,* 21 April. http:// www.cbc.ca/news/canada/edmonton/lesbian-victim-of-assault-says-it-was-hate -crime-1.917267.

Ryan. 2011. "Rebranding Fail." *Xtra!* 15 August. http://dailyxtra.com/toronto/news/leather -clad-crowd-marches-village-fair-4890?page=4#comments.

Safieddine, H. 2011. "A Shifting Sense of Belonging." *Toronto Star,* 31 March. http:// www.thestar.com/sponsored_sections/2011/03/31/a_shifting_sense_of_belonging. html.

Safra Project. 2011. "Safra Project Statement on East End Gay Pride." 13 March. http:// nohomonationalism.blogspot.ca/2011/03/safra-project-statement-on-east-end-gay. html.

Said, E.W. 1979. *Orientalism.* New York: Vintage.

–. 1986. *After the Last Sky: Palestinian Lives.* New York: Pantheon.

Salerno, R. 2013. "Toronto City Council Passes New Anti-discrimination Policy to Target QuAIA, Pride." *Xtra!* 17 July. http://dailyxtra.com/toronto/news/toronto-city-council -passes-new-anti-discrimination-policy-target-quaia-pride-64882.

Sands, A. 2010. "14-Year-Old Charged in Vicious Attack." *Edmonton Journal,* 25 April. https://groups.google.com/forum/#!topic/transgender-news/0uG1mhuFnVM.

Schulman, S. 2011. "Israel and 'Pinkwashing.'" *New York Times,* 22 November. http://www. nytimes.com/glogin?URI=http://www.nytimes.com/2011/11/23/opinion/pinkwashing -and-israels-use-of-gays-as-a-messaging-tool.html?_r=3&.

–. 2012. *The Gentrification of the Mind: Witness to a Lost Imagination.* Berkeley: University of California Press.

Sedgwick, E.K. 1993. *Tendencies.* Durham, NC: Duke University Press.

–. 2003. *Touching Feeling.* Durham, NC: Duke University Press.

Serano, J. 2007. *Whipping Girl: A Transsexual Woman on Sexism and the Scapegoating of Femininity.* Emeryville, CA: Seal.

Sexual Minorities Liaison Committee (SMLC). 2010. "Open Letter to the Community." 30 April. http://www.scribd.com/doc/211223302/Edmonton-Police-Services -Liaison-Letter#scribd.

Sheppard, M. 2012. "Refugee Claims Show Inconsistent Approval Rates." *CBC News,* 12 March. http://www.cbc.ca/news/canada/refugee-claims-show-inconsistent-approval -rates-1.1166533.

Simpson, L. 2013. "Idle No More: Where the Mainstream Media Went Wrong." *The Dominion*, 27 February. http://dominion.mediacoop.ca/story/idle-no-more-and -mainstream-media/16023.

Smith, A. 2005. *Conquest: Sexual Violence and American Indian Genocide*. Cambridge, MA: South End.

–. 2006. "Heteropatriarchy and the Three Pillars of White Supremacy: Rethinking Women of Colour Organizing." In *Color of Violence: The Incite! Anthology*, ed. Incite! Women of Colour against Violence, 66–73. Cambridge, MA: South End.

–. 2011. "Queer Theory and Native Studies: The Heteronormativity of Settler Colonialism." In *Queer Indigenous Studies: Critical Interventions in Theory, Politics, and Literature*, ed. Q.-L. Driskill, C. Finley, B.J. Gilley, and S. Morgensen, 43–65. Tucson: University of Arizona Press.

Smith, B., ed. 1983. *Home Girls: A Black Feminist Anthology*. New York: Kitchen Table.

Smith, D.E. 1999. *Writing the Social*. Toronto: University of Toronto Press.

–. 2005. *Institutional Ethnography: A Sociology for People*. Lanham, MD: Altamaria.

–. 2006. *Institutional Ethnography as Practice*. Lanham, MD: Rowman and Littlefield.

Smith, G. 1982. "In Defence of Privacy: Or Bluntly Put, No More Shit." *Action! Publication of the Right to Privacy Committee* 3 (1): 1-3.

–. 2012. "Tel Aviv Trumps New York to Be Named World's Best Gay City." *Daily Mail* (London), 24 January. http://www.dailymail.co.uk/news/article-2088319/Tel-Aviv -trumps-New-York-named-worlds-best-gay-city.html.

Smith, M. 1999. *Lesbian and Gay Rights in Canada: Social Movements and Equality-Seeking, 1971–1995*. Toronto: University of Toronto Press.

–. 2008. *Political Institutions and Lesbian and Gay Rights in the United States and Canada*. New York: Routledge.

Somerville, S. 1996. "Scientific Racism and the Invention of the Homosexual Body." In *Queer Studies: A Lesbian, Gay, Bisexual, and Transgender Anthology*, ed. B. Beemyn and M. Eliason, 241–61. New York: NYU Press.

–. 2000. *Queering the Color Line: Race and the Invention of Homosexuality in American Culture*. Durham: Duke University Press.

South Asian Legal Clinic of Ontario. n.d. Perpetuating Myths, Denying Justice: "Zero Tolerance for Barbaric Cultural Practices Act." Toronto, ON.

Spade, D. 2009. *Trickle-Up Social Justice*. Video excerpt from the lecture "Trans Politics on a Neoliberal Landscape," presented at Barnard College, Columbia University, 9 February. http://bcrw.barnard.edu/videos/dean-spade-trickle-up-social-justice -excerpt/.

–. 2011. "Trans Politics and Legal Structures." Lecture presented at Elliott Bay Book Company, Seattle, 21 November.

–. 2012. *Normal Life: Administrative Violence, Critical Trans Politics, and the Limits of Law*. Boston: South End.

Stanley, E. 2011. "Introduction: Fugitive Flesh: Gender Self-determination, Queer Abolition, and Trans Resistance." In *Captive Genders: Trans Embodiment and the Prison Industrial Complex*, ed. E. Stanley and N. Smith, 1–11. Oakland, CA: AK Press.

Stoler, A.L., and C. McGranahan. 2007. "Introduction: Refiguring Imperial Terrains." In *Imperial Formations*, ed. A.L. Stoler, C. McGranahan, and P.C. Perdue, 3–42. Santa Fe, NM: School for Advanced Research Press.

Stryker, S. 2008. *Transgender History*. Berkeley, CA: Seal.

Stychin, C. 2001. "Sexual Citizenship in the European Union." *Citizenship Studies* 5 (3): 285–301. http://dx.doi.org/10.1080/13621020120085252.

Sudbury, J. 2005. "Introduction." In *Global Lockdown: Race, Gender, and the Prison Industrial Complex*, ed. J. Sudbury, xi–xxvii. New York: Routledge.

Sullivan, A. 1996. "Here Comes the Groom: A (Conservative) Case for Gay Marriage." In *Beyond Queer: Challenging Gay Left Orthodoxy*, ed. B. Bawer, 252–58. New York: Free Press.

SUSPECT. 2010. "Where Now? From Pride Scandal to Transnational Movement." *Bully Bloggers*, 26 June. https://bullybloggers.wordpress.com/2010/06/26/where-now-from-pride-scandal-to-transnational-movement.

Taormino, T. 2012. "Buck Angel on Sexing the Transman, plus Tobi Hill-Meyer's Erotic Documentary-in-Progress, *Doing It Again*." Episode of the talk radio show *Sex Out Loud*, 20 July. http://www.voiceamerica.com/episode/63122/buck-angel-on-sexing-the-transman-plus-tobi-hill-meyers-erotic-documentary-in-progress-doing-it.

Taormino, T., C. Parreñas Shimizu, C. Penley, and M. Miller-Young, eds. 2013. *The Feminist Porn Book: The Politics of Producing Pleasure*. New York: Feminist Press at CUNY.

Thobani, S. 2002. "The Speech that Shook the Country." *Herizons: Women's News and Feminist Views*. http://www.herizons.ca/node/131.

–. 2007. *Exalted Subjects: Studies in the Making of Race and Nation in Canada*. Toronto: University of Toronto Press.

Thomarat, M. 2010. "Critical Approach to Crime: Being Tough on Crime Does Not Solve the Underlying Problems." *Vue Magazine*, 5 October.

Thompson, D. 2008. "Nation and Miscegenation: Comparing Anti-miscegenation Regulations in North America." Paper presented at the 80th Annual Conference of the Canadian Political Science Association, University of British Columbia, Vancouver, 4-6 June. http://www.cpsa-acsp.ca/papers-2008/Thompson.pdf.

Tom, A. 2009. "Statimc Native Youth Movement at Stolen Labor on Stolen Land." Speech presented at Ryerson University, Toronto, 22 June. http://www.youtube.com/watch?v=FnSuk-e7BJ0.

Troster, A. 2011. "Unlikely Bedfellows: The Harper Government and Homonationalism." Major research paper, University of Ottawa.

US Palestinian Community Network. 2012. "Palestinians in Solidarity with Idle No More and Indigenous Rights." 23 December. http://uspcn.org/2012/12/23/palestinians-in-solidarity-with-idle-no-more-and-indigenous-rights.

van der Meulen, E., J. Yee, and E.M. Durisin. 2010. "Violence against Indigenous Sex Workers: Combating the Effects of Criminalization and Colonialism in Canada." *Research for Sex Work* 12: n.p.

Walcott, R. 2000. ""Who is she and what is she to you?" Mary Ann Shadd Cary and the (Im)possibility of Black/Canadian Studies." In *Rude: Contemporary Black Canadian Cultural Criticism*, ed. R. Walcott, 27–47. Toronto: Insomniac.

–. 2003. *Black Like Who? Writing Black Canada*. Toronto: Insomniac.

Walia, H. 2010. "Black Bloc Tactics – 10 Quick Points!" Speech presented at W2 Media Arts Centre, Vancouver, 20 February. http://rabble.ca/rabbletv/program-guide/2010/03/features/diversity-tactics-diversity-opinions.

Ware, W. 2011. "Rounding Up the Homosexuals: The Impact of the Juvenile Court on Queer and Trans/Gender-Non-Conforming Youth." In *Captive Genders: Trans*

Embodiment and the Prison Industrial Complex, ed. E. Stanley and N. Smith, 77–84. Oakland, CA: AK Press.

Warner, M. 1993. *Fear of a Queer Planet: Queer Politics and Social Theory.* Minneapolis: University of Minnesota Press.

–. 2005. *Publics and Counterpublics.* New York: Zone Books.

Warner, T. 2002. *Never Going Back: A History of Queer Activism in Canada.* Toronto: University of Toronto Press.

Weiss, M. 2011. *Techniques of Pleasure: BDSM and the Circuits of Sexuality.* Durham, NC: Duke University Press. http://dx.doi.org/10.1215/9780822394914.

Wiegman, R. 2002. "Intimate Publics: Race, Property, and Personhood." *American Literature* 74 (4): 859–85. http://dx.doi.org/10.1215/00029831-74-4-859.

–. 2012. *Object Lessons.* Durham, NC: Duke University Press. http://dx.doi.org/10.1215/9780822394945.

Williams, L. 1999. *Hard Core: Power, Pleasure, and the "Frenzy of the Visible."* Berkeley: University of California Press.

Williams, Z. 2012. "The Saturday Interview: Stuart Hall." *Guardian* (London), 11 February. http://www.theguardian.com/theguardian/2012/feb/11/saturday-interview-stuart-hall?fb=native.

Wolfe, P. 2006. "Settler Colonialism and the Elimination of the Native." *Journal of Genocide Research* 8 (4): 387–409. http://dx.doi.org/10.1080/14623520601056240.

–. 2008. "Structure and Event: Settler Colonialism and the Question of Genocide." In *Empire, Colony, Genocide: Conquest, Occupation and Subaltern Resistance in World History,* ed. A.D. Moses, 102–32. Oxford: Berghahn Books.

Wright, M. 2004. *Becoming Black: Creating Identity in the African Diaspora.* Durham, NC: Duke University Press.

Wright, M., and A. Schuhmann, eds. 2007. *Blackness and Sexualities.* Berlin: Lit Verlag.

Contributors

Julian Awwad is a Canadian lawyer and independent scholar based in the Middle East and a former assistant professor in the Department of Communication Studies at Concordia University. He holds a doctorate in communication studies from the Department of Art History and Communication Studies at McGill University and degrees in common and civil law from the Faculty of Law at McGill University, where he received the Nathan Cotler Memorial Prize in Human Rights Law. His research interests broadly include law, culture, and society as well as global media and cultural studies, particularly in Middle Eastern contexts. His work has appeared in the *Journal of Communication and Critical/Cultural Studies* and the *Journal of South Asian and Middle Eastern Studies*.

Alexa DeGagne is an instructor in the Department of Political Science at the University of Alberta. Her dissertation, "Investigating Citizenship, Sexuality and the Same-Sex Marriage Fight in California's Proposition 8," examines why and how same-sex marriage has become a pivot point in debates about larger ideological issues, including the regulation of sexualities, the criteria for political belonging, and the nature of social justice. She has previously published works on American and Canadian LGBTQ activism and political organizing.

Naomi de Szegheo-Lang is a doctoral candidate in Gender, Feminist, and Women's Studies at York University. Her research takes up cultural studies, affect theory, and sexuality studies frameworks and focuses on constructions of intimacy in popular media and queer cultural production. She has played muse to photographers for over a decade and has been involved in award-winning feminist porn projects. Living in Toronto with her beloved canine companion, she is often found in local coffee shops writing and researching.

Sonny Dhoot is a doctoral candidate in the Women and Gender Studies Institute at the University of Toronto. His doctorate research utilizes queer of colour critique to explore the ways that racial desires are interconnected with the nation, citizenship, borders, and whiteness. He is in the process of forming a working group in collaboration with fellow queers of colour to begin exploring and undoing racial desires and internalized racism.

OmiSoore H. Dryden is an assistant professor in the Department of Women's, Gender, and Sexuality Studies at Thorneloe University (at Laurentian). She teaches in the areas of critical race theory, queer diaspora, and introductory and advanced queer and feminist theories. Her research examines the links between race, sexuality, gender, and community through the themes of blood – how it is donated, discursively constructed, and shared. OmiSoore explores how "gay blood," "black/African blood," and queer identifications intersect with (homo)nation making. Her work has appeared in *Atlantis: A Women's Studies Journal* and in *Women and Environments International Magazine.* You can follow her on twitter @OmiSooreDryden.

Marty Fink is currently a Marion L. Brittain Postdoctoral Fellow in the School of Literature, Media, and Communication at Georgia Tech. Fink works to bridge contemporary queer and trans cultures with early activist histories of HIV/AIDS. Fink's academic writing has appeared in journals such as *Science Fiction Studies, Television and New Media,* and the *Journal for Prisoners on Prisons.* Fink also works with the Prisoner Correspondence Project in Montreal.

Patrizia Gentile is co-author with Gary Kinsman of *The Canadian War on Queers: National Security as Sexual Regulation* (2010) and co-editor with Jane Nicholas of *Contesting Bodies and Nation in Canadian History* (2013). She is currently completing a manuscript on beauty contests and settler femininity.

Gary Kinsman is a long-time queer-liberation, anti-poverty, and anti-capitalist activist. He has been involved in many activist groups, including most recently the Sudbury Coalition against Poverty. He is the author of *The Regulation of Desire: Homo and Hetero Sexualities* (1996), co-author with Patrizia Gentile of

The Canadian War on Queers: National Security as Sexual Regulation (2010), co-editor with Dieter K. Buse and Mercedes Steedman of *Whose National Security? Canadian State Surveillance and the Creation of Enemies* (2000), and co-editor with Caelie Frampton, Andrew Thompson, and Kate Tilleczek of *Sociology for Changing the World: Social Movements/Social Research* (2006). He is currently working with the AIDS Activist History Project and on a new book project called *The Making of the Neo-liberal Queer*. He has recently retired from teaching sociology at Laurentian University, located on the territories of the Atikameksheng Anishnawbek Nation. He lives with his partner, Patrick, and their son, Mike. His website Radical Noise is at http://radicalnoise.ca.

Suzanne Lenon is an associate professor in the Department of Women and Gender Studies at the University of Lethbridge, Alberta. Her research interests lie at the intersections of critical race feminisms and law, gender, and sexuality. Her work has appeared in *Social Identities: Journal for the Study of Race, Nation and Culture; Journal of Intercultural Studies; Canadian Journal of Women and the Law; darkmatter;* and *Atlantis: Critical Studies in Gender, Culture and Social Justice*. She is also co-editor with Stacy Douglas of a special issue of the *Canadian Journal of Law and Society* on "Law and Decolonization." You can follow her on twitter @kootenaydreams.

Kathryn Trevenen is an associate professor at the Institute of Feminist and Gender Studies and the School of Political Studies at the University of Ottawa. Her teaching, research, and activism focus on queer cultures and queer theory; the intersections between feminist, trans, and disability studies; and hip-hop studies. Her work has appeared in *Recherches féministes;* the *Annual Review of Critical Psychology;* the *International Journal of Feminist Politics; Political Theory; Urban Affairs Review;* and *Theory and Event*.

Amar Wahab is an assistant professor of Gender and Sexuality in the School of Gender, Sexuality, and Women's Studies at York University. He teaches in the areas of critical sexuality studies, critical studies in masculinity, critical race studies, introductory and advanced sociological theory, and Caribbean cultural studies. His research interests include sexual citizenship in liberal and post-colonial nation-states (mainly related to the Caribbean and Canada), race and queer transnational politics, critiques of queer liberalism, and race, gender, and the politics of representation. His current research project focuses on queer anti-racist critiques of homonationalism in Canada.

Index

Note: "(f)" after a page number indicates a figure; "LGBT" refers to lesbian, gay, bisexual, and transgender.

Canadian Blood Services, 117–22, 125–26, 129–30, 131*n*3, 131*nn*10–11
Canadian Charter of Rights and Freedoms, 11, 83–84, 97*nn*2–3, 131*n*5, 135–36, 138–39
capitalism, vii, 6, 8, 15, 30, 61, 62, 134, 138, 140, 147, 148*n*4, 149*n*11
Carter, Sarah, 89
Chapin, Jessica, 29
Charland, Maurice, 22–23
Charter of Rights and Freedoms. *See* Canadian Charter of Rights and Freedoms
Chow, Rey, 27
cisgendered people, 62, 74, 75
cisnormativity, 75, 81*n*8
cissexism, 75, 81*n*8, 131*n*12, 152, 159, 163
citizenship, ix, 6, 10
 guide (*see Discover Canada: The Rights and Responsibilities of Citizenship*)
 sexual, ix, 4–5, 7, 9, 12, 13, 16*n*2, 20–29, 32–33, 66–81
Collins, Peter, 154–55
colonialism. *See* settler colonialism
Conservative Party of Canada, 10, 114*n*3
 and immigrants and refugees, 26, 105–6, 114*nn*4–5
 and polygamy, 93–94
 and queers, 12, 14, 19–25, 29, 32, 101–6, 136–37
consumerism, 38, 50, 61, 62, 76, 81*n*9, 140
contagion, 85, 91, 92, 95, 96, 121
 See also blood; miscegenation
Cossman, Brenda, 24, 48*n*5
Crawford, Lucas, 111, 115*n*9
Criminal Code of Canada, 19, 114*n*3
 and hate crimes, 18*n*10, 111, 114*n*1
 and polygamy, 82–84, 87, 88, 89, 95–96, 97*nn*1–3, 98*nn*7–9, 98*n*13
counterpublics, 12, 35, 36–48, 48*n*1, 80*n*3

Davis, Angela, 83, 97, 135
decolonization, 4, 80, 130, 136, 154, 162
 See also Indigenous peoples: and activism
Delgado, Richard, 27
desire, ix, 34, 152–53
 and marginalized bodies, 67, 68, 73–75, 77, 167
 non-normative, viii, 13, 39–40, 67, 69, 154

and public and private spaces, 13, 38–39, 41, 48*n*5, 66–67, 69–73, 78, 80*nn*2–3
Deveaux, Drew, 75
diaspora, 9, 15, 118, 143, 152, 162, 164
Discover Canada: The Rights and Responsibilities of Citizenship, 14, 19–20, 101, 102–4, 107, 111, 113
Duggan, Lisa, 6, 23, 71, 102, 149*n*10

East End Gay Pride, 8, 18*n*7
Edelman, Lee, 21–22
Edmonton Community Response Project, 109–13, 115*n*7
Edmonton Sexual Minorities Liaison Committee, 109–11, 115*n*9
Egale Canada, 14, 101, 102–6, 116–21, 131*nn*5–6
Ellison, Carmen, 111
Eng, David, 20, 23–24, 25, 26, 28, 30, 31, 128
Erdem, Esra, 7, 17*n*5, 48*n*10, 49
Erickson, Loree, 74, 75
Evans, Bryan, 60
exceptionalism, 9–10, 36, 37, 40, 44, 45, 48*n*3, 74
 sexual, 3, 11–12, 20–21, 28–29, 31–34, 107–8, 113, 115*n*11, 116

Feminist Porn Awards
 challenge to normative practices, 13, 40, 67, 69, 154
 definition of feminist porn, 67, 72–73
 and sexual space, 13, 38–39, 41, 48*n*5, 66–67, 69–73, 78, 80*nn*2–3
feminists, 9, 17*n*5, 64, 86–87, 88, 100, 136
 of colour, 3, 5, 11, 61, 135, 142
 and fetish, 39–40, 46
 and Islamophobia, 43, 48*n*10, 94, 143
 and porn (*see* Feminist Porn Awards)
Fetish Fair (Toronto), 12, 35–48
First Nations. *See* Indigenous peoples
Foucault, Michel, 91, 92, 122
Fung, Richard, 146

Garland-Thomson, Rosemarie, 167
gay men, 14, 38, 84, 98*n*5, 112, 140, 146, 148*n*1, 148*n*3
 and military service, 4, 11, 16*n*2, 32, 119, 133, 135